How to Repair Musical Instrument Amplifiers

How to Repair Musical Instrument Amplifiers

Byron Wels

With a specially written chapter for the guidance of the English reader by W. Oliver

FOULSHAM-TAB LIMITED
Slough Bucks England

Foulsham-Tab Limited
Yeovil Road Slough Bucks England

How to Repair Musical Instrument Amplifiers

Library of Congress Number 72–81363
Cat. Code No. 610

ISBN 0–7042–0050–3

Introduction Printed and Made in Great Britain by
A. Wheaton & Co., Exeter

Balance printed in U.S.A.

It is essential that the English reader should read this chapter.

The fact that this is a book of American origin will be self-evident and naturally some re-orientation will be needed here and there for readers of this English edition, owing to differences between British and American electronic practice.

The first major difference is indicated on p. 34 where the author writes about an American technician who was in the habit of connecting a variable-voltage transformer to the input AC line and raising the voltage "up from the accepted 117 volts to 135."

117 volts is typical of the mains voltage normally found on American domestic supplies (though in some cases an alternative source of 220 volts is available), whereas in Britain about 240 volts is the normal standard.

Going back to the account of the technician's "cure or kill" system to deal with intermittent faults, "he lets the unit cook until something burns open. . . . It's a short cut, but one to which we do not subscribe."

Even on 117 volts the procedure is a drastic one, and it should certainly never be used on our much higher standard of 240 volts.

While on the subject it is worth noting that valve circuits will usually stand up to a temporary application of excess voltage especially if it lasts only a few seconds. But solid-state circuits are apt to be much less tolerant and transistors can be destroyed literally instantaneously if they are subjected to a voltage or consequent current in excess of the maxima stipulated by the transistor or other semiconductor manufacturer.

Where a valve may react slowly enough to be protected, from overload or excess voltage, by the circuit-breaking action of a fuse, a solid-state device is affected so instantly that it is likely to be destroyed or at least irreparably damaged before the fastest-blowing fuse can burn out and open the circuit so as to cut off the current.

So don't try drastic short cuts in troubleshooting. Stick to the well-tried and reliable system of logical analysis whereby you gradually narrow down the field of search from the whole amplifier to a single stage and from this small section to a single component which can be checked (after disconnecting and removing from the circuit if need be) for faults. Less sensible and more reckless methods can cause damage to pounds' worth of equipment while trying to pinpoint a fault in some minor item which in itself may cost only a few pence to replace bodily.

On p. 40 the American author mentions a technician who considers the schematic to be an expendable item that is easily replaced and easily billable to his customer. This may not apply in Britain; service sheets and other data sheets are not all that easy to obtain quickly when required and it is not usually a good plan to regard them as expendable over here. One cannot memorize all the details of all the circuits one is likely to handle in the course of commercial servicing, and it is exasperating to find that you have obliterated vital details on your one and only immediately-available copy of a wanted diagram just when you are in the midst of a tricky trouble-shooting job. So it is best to take every care of your servicing data so that all the details you need for future reference will be instantly to hand when you need them.

You will of course find some American versions of technical terms and abbreviations in this book. For example, there is "B+" where we should say "HT positive" or the equivalent supply lead in a transistorized circuit. There is "VOM" (volt-ohm-milliammeter) where we might say "multimeter" or "multi-range test meter," and of course there is "tube" where we should say "valve"; which gives us VTVM (vacuum-tube voltmeter).

On p. 53 there is mention of "60-Hz" and this of course refers to the American mains supply which alternates at a frequency of 60 Hertz whereas on our own mains in Britain the frequency is 50 Hz.

A self-contained miniature signal-injector is shown on p. 62. Similar devices are available in this country.

Turning to p. 66 and the remarks about cleaning volume-controls: noisy carbon tracks due to mechanical wear result in one of the commonest faults in radio and audio equipment. Usually the best plan in the long run is to replace the worn control with a new component. But in some cases one can clean the old one successfully.

Over-drastic use of some cleaning fluids cures the noise immediately for the time being, but after a while the trouble tends to return and may be worse than ever. A lot depends on the quality of the resistance-element and on the type of contact-cleaner used.

The present writer has sometimes succeeded in "re-forming" a carbon track by judicious use of a graphite-loaded lubricant. This is a rather unorthodox trick and must not be recommended indiscriminately! But it is sometimes worth trying on a control that is past normal help.

In Chapter 7, headed "Modifications," there is mention of using amplifiers outdoors. Beware of lethal shock risks if you attempt to adapt an amplifier of a mains-powered type for outdoor use. If, for example, exposed metalwork which is *supposed* to be earthed *isn't*, and through a fault condition has become "live" instead, you could have a lethal situation which may not have been revealed at all when the outfit was in use indoors, with the operator standing on a dry carpeted floor instead of damp ground!

Another possible source of danger is in fitting earphones to a mains amplifier. This should be done properly by a competent technician if it is to be done at all. So if any customers who are "do-it-yourselfers" happen to mention that they are thinking of doing this, you will be doing them a kindness if you warn them against any amateur improvisations on these lines.

In conclusion, a word about official regulations. On p. 33 the author discusses the impact of FCC rules on the use of "wireless mikes." The FCC or Federal Communications Commission is the American department responsible for such matters as radio regulations, transmitting licences, frequency allocations and so on, in the States. Here in Britain the Ministry of Posts and Telecommunications is the body that deals with these things, and the address is Waterloo Bridge House, Waterloo Road, London, SE1 8UA. Anyone who is contemplating the use of any device that may come within the category of a transmitter should check on the prevailing regulations, to see whether the instrument is of a type that contravenes the transmitting licence laws.

Operating a transmitter, or a device classed as one, without the appropriate transmitting licence, permit or official approval is an offence carrying, on conviction, a heavy fine and usually confiscation of the apparatus as well.

Successful servicing depends on getting suitable supplies of good spares and replacement parts. Names of a few firms from which various essential items can be obtained may be useful; so here is a brief selection of typical suppliers: their addresses, telephone numbers and catalogue prices may be found in their latest advertisements in the technical journals.

R.S. (Components) Ltd.—a firm known for many years as Radiospares Ltd.—can supply a wide selection of components etc. for servicing replacements. This firm deals *only* with the Trade; anyone outside the radio trade requiring R.S. parts must order them through a local radio dealer or through one of the mail order firms that stock some R.S. components.

L.S.T. (Components) Ltd. also deals nowadays with trade customers only. But an associated firm at the same address, Arrow Electronics, has been formed to continue dealing with the general public. Solid-state devices in great variety are available from these sources, as well as some general electronic spares, etc.

Home Radio (Components) Ltd. is another well-known firm which lists, in a profusely illustrated catalogue, thousands of items (by dozens of different manufacturers) which can be had by post or bought by retail customers calling at the premises.

Another useful retail and mail-order source of supplies is a London firm, G. W. Smith (Radio) Ltd., also stockists of thousands of different components, semiconductors, accessories, etc.

Dozens of different mail-order and retail firms are now stocking transistors, FET's, diodes and other solid-state devices. Integrated-circuit modules are also obtainable from most of the semiconductor suppliers.

Firms advertising valves are of course far less numerous than they used to be, as a result of widespread transistorization, but one or two businesses still listing a good selection of valves at the time of writing are: Colomor (Electronics) Ltd.; R.S.T. Valve Mail Order Co.; and Z. & I. Aero Services Ltd.

Preface

When a trumpet player has trouble with his horn, he takes it to a musical instrument repair shop. It's the same way with saxophonists, drummers, and trombonists. But lately, there seems to be a greater number of electronically amplified instruments than ever before, and musicians are often hard-put to know what to do when they have trouble. If you get a bad amplifier on an electronic piano, for instance, do you take it to a guy who specializes in repairing pianos? Or do you go to a guy who fixes television sets?

More and more electronic technicians are finding that all it takes is that you hang a shingle outside the shop announcing that you are a specialist, and you'll start getting business from musicians and from local music shops that aren't equipped or prepared to do electronic repairs the way you are.

While repairing a musical instrument amplifier isn't a horrendous problem if you have a knowledge of electronics and an innate curiosity coupled with a lot of patience, there are some specialized things that you ought to know about. That's the why of this book.

You'll also find a schematic section which also includes 8 foldout panels. The dozens of schematics are typical of those you'll encounter. Our thanks to the respective manufacturers for their cooperation in supplying the drawings.

Byron G. Wels

DEDICATION

M. LEONARD SINGER

"It's constantly meeting life's little challenges
that makes it all worthwhile."

Contents

The Scope of the Business

1

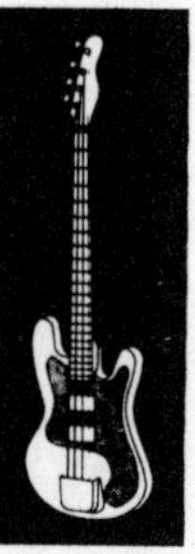

Electronic musical instruments sales are mushrooming, and in all probability will continue to grow at an increasing rate during the years to come. Today's younger set, representing a huge market, is vitally interested in electronically amplified musical instruments, and they're buying them almost as fast as the manufacturers can turn them out. Electric guitars, electric basses, electronic pianos and organs drive huge amplifiers that have, in some medical circles, been accused of damaging hearing ability with their power!

And these instruments do go bad. But that sometimes doesn't stop the kids. One youngster's amplifier developed a noisy transistor that created a horrible buzzing in his speaker every time a string was plucked. Undismayed, he used the instrument anyway. The result? It's called the "fuzz sound" now, and the manufacturers are turning out instruments, amplifiers and accessories with "fuzz" built right in! The big search is on for a new sound, and they jump at anything that's remotely different.

The kids are tough on the instruments themselves. One rock group always ends its concerts by destroying the musical instruments. Some rock singers seem to think that to be successful they've also got to be jugglers, and the things they do to a microphone, swinging it by the cord, dropping it... It's enough to strain your strain relief!

As a direct result of all these shenanigans, there's a tremendous boom in repairing and servicing musical instrument amplifiers and their accessories. The electronics technician who is willing to stretch a point, and who can look beyond just replacing tubes in a TV set, can turn himself a nice buck.

However, there's more than simple electronics involved here. When a client comes in with a malfunctioning instrument, the problem might not be in the amplifier itself, but in

Typical hollow-body electric guitar. Courtesy Lafayette Radio.

the input device or a connecting cord instead. And since it is the amplified sound that provides the symptom of the fault, the unknowing user (and frequently an unknowing technician) can spend much time hassling over an amplifier that is perfectly well and sound, wondering where the real problem is, while the problem just might be in the other equipment, which, of course, the customer doesn't have with him.

By all means, the most common problem you'll encounter will be electric guitar trouble, since there are so many of these available. The amplifiers for these units range from little peanut-whistle transistorized units to tremendous, all-out systems that are suited for the concert hall. Because of the large number of electric guitars, we're concentrating initially on them; therefore, here is a rundown so you'll know what you're dealing with.

THE ELECTRIC GUITAR

The electric guitar comes in two principal types—the solid-body guitar and the hollow-body guitar. The names pretty-well describe the individual instruments. The hollow-body guitar can be played without amplification, for it is an acoustical instrument. But if you try to play a solid-body type without an amplifier, you might eventually introduce such problems as buzzing, for the strings must really be hit in order to make them sound.

A non-electric guitar can be amplified if a suitable pickup or system of pickups is used. The most common of these is the contact microphone which either clips onto the guitar or is forced under the strings at the tail piece.

More elaborate pickup systems consist of one, two or more pickups attached to a plastic pick-guard and mounted under the strings. This type of pickup is made of a series of small coils with magnetic or ferrite cores, arranged with a coil and core combination under each string. As the metal string vibrates over the core, the field density changes and the resultant low-current signal is dispatched to the amplifier. Obviously, a metal string must be used; but in this day of folk and protest singing, gut and nylon strings are finding favor because they are a lot easier on the fingers. However, with a magnetic pickup, such strings just won't work. It's not very likely that a technician would be called in for such a simple

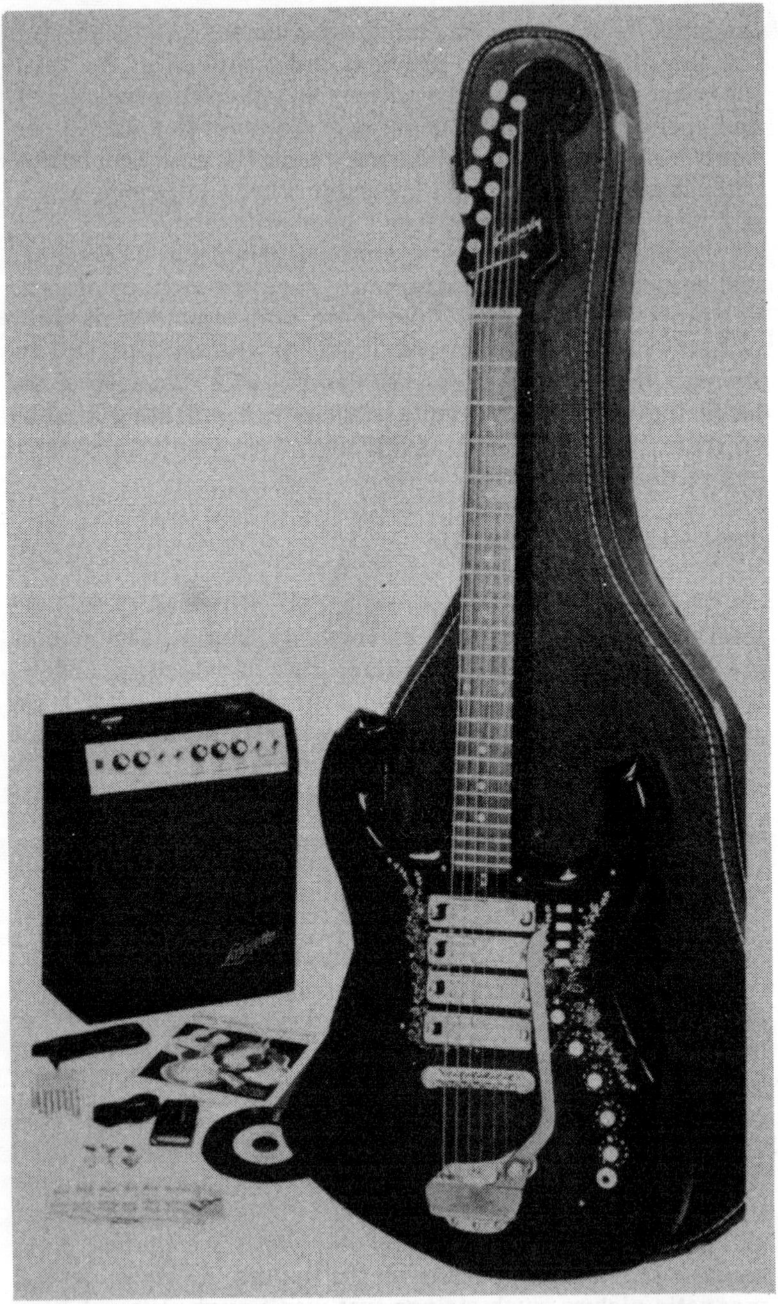

Solid-body electric guitar with four pickups. Courtesy Lafayette Radio.

problem as something mechanical, but once you set yourself up as an all-round expert, you'd better be prepared.

The standard guitar has six strings. The strings are fastened at the body end of the guitar with what is called a tail piece or tail stock. The strings run across the guitar's body and up the neck to the machine head or tuning screws. Across the neck are raised metal pieces—called frets—to mark the various notes. At the body end is a raised device that keeps the strings away from the body, and this is called the bridge. Another raised portion, between the machine head and the neck, is called the nut.

There are other variations as well. The Hawaiian or steel guitar has a raised nut so that the strings cannot be pressed down with the fingers. This instrument is played with a steel bar that is slid along the strings. Modern guitars may be fitted with a tremolo or vibrato lever. This lever raises and lowers the bridge and provides a vibrating effect to the sound. Prior to its invention, a guitarist produced the same effect by vibrating his fingers against the frets.

There are many mechanical things that can go wrong with a guitar to cause problems that are not directly related to the electronics. You should know about these and be able to recognize them when they occur. A guitar that won't play in tune in the higher registers indicates one of two problems. A guitar is tuned with the strings open, or not fingered. If the instrument is tuned in the lower register in this fashion, yet seems out of tune in the higher registers, it might indicate a misplaced bridge. Another common cause of this problem is a warped neck, or one that has pulled loose from the body.

Another frequent complaint that may not be an electronic trouble is buzzing. This can be caused by any of a number of things. The most common is usually a loose section on the machine head. You'll notice a loose tuning knob and, by tightening the small screw on the machine head, you can overcome this problem. Apply a drop of light machine oil to each metal-on-metal surface as well. A fret that is working loose and has risen so that the vibrating strings touch it will also cause a buzz. This can be corrected by replacing the fret entirely, or by regluing and clamping the fret, then dressing it down with a file.

However, the most common cause of buzz beyond these is the lowered bridge action. Many guitarists soon discover that there are small adjusting rings on the guitar's bridge, and by lowering the bridge they need not press so hard to sound the notes. The lowered strings may be easier to play, but the buzzing that results can be a problem. The solution, of course, is to raise the bridge once again, and commiserate with the guy about his calloused fingers! Other causes of buzzing can be loose metal parts, so always be on the lookout for these. A split guitar body can also produce problems of this sort.

If the owner complains that a guitar hasn't got the tone, or sparkle, or life that it once had, take a look at the strings. Guitar strings are usually replaced only when they break, but too often, when a string is out of round, it will lose the ability to resonate. Check the strings carefully, looking for flats or shiny areas where the frets are located. We've seen strings so badly worn that it was a wonder they hadn't broken. Such strings must be replaced.

Talking about strings for a moment, there are several types, as we've already mentioned. Classic, western, flamenco, and folk guitar users seem to favor a gut or nylon string that is plucked with the fingers. This type of playing, called "finger style," is more comfortable with such strings. Other guitars, such as the orchestral and electric types, use steel strings.

The higher-note strings are a finely drawn steel wire where the diameter determines the note. The lower-note strings are of the same steel wires, but are wound with a close-wound spiral of bronze or copper to further lower the tone. The standard winding is a round bronze, but this, when played with an Hawaiian steel, or a contact amplifier pickup, may give some finger sliding noises. To help eliminate this, you can install a flat-wound string, which is wound with a flat or square wire. The result is smoother, easier fingering.

INSTRUMENT ELECTRONICS

Pickups can go bad, as can the controls that operate them. One of the more common problems is the failure of a complete section of pickups in a multi-pickup guitar. Most guitars have switching systems on the instruments as well as separate volume and-or tone controls. By switching combinations of pickups in and out, the instrumentalist can produce varied tonal qualities. Yet, let a wire lead break loose, and the whole thing will go out of whack. Most often, the musician isn't quite sure about how the various switches work; he's only aware that a condition he used to be able to get is no longer available.

Before you get too far into the problem, remember that replacement is usually your best test in isolating the cause of trouble. Determine that the connecting cord and circuit between the guitar and amplifier are sound. Do this by substituting a cord that is known to be good. Many times, intermittent problems are the result of a faulty cord. Then try connecting the guitar into an amplifier known to be good, or connect a good guitar to a suspicious amplifier.

Ampeg Model SVT system amplifier. Output 300 watts RMS (over 700 watts peak music power). The amplifier and speaker systems weigh almost 300 pounds.

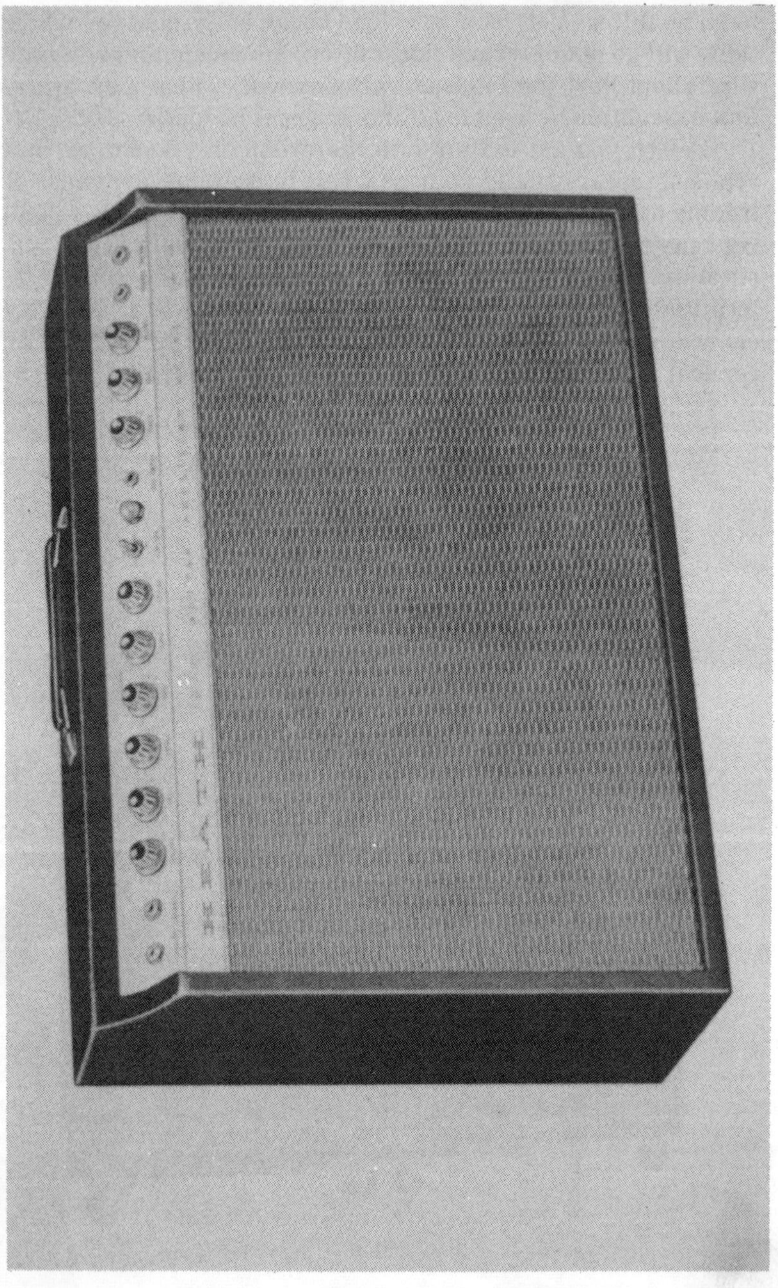

Heathkit Model TA-16 guitar amplifier. Each of the two amplifier channels has two inputs. A special effects channel offers reverb and tremolo.

Control Problems

Control problems most usually reveal themselves in the form of scratchiness as the control is operated. The scratch is picked up and amplified. Of course, the musician doesn't want this kind of action. When you come upon a faulty control, chances are that you can, with one of the commonly available injectors and chemical cleaners, restore the control to proper operation. If this fails, if the control surface is so worn that it can't be fixed by cleaning, the control will have to be replaced.

Connected to many systems, and usually wired right into the guitar, you may find assorted capacitors and dropping resistors. Outside of vibration-caused troubles, there's nothing much else that can go wrong with these, since the operating voltages are really very low. What actually goes wrong inside the guitar from the electrical standpoint is very basic and generally easy to isolate and repair.

ACCESSORIES

Many of today's systems have provision for many accessories—foot controls, foot pads and foot switches to enable the guitarist to add fuzz, electrical tremolo, reverberation, or, especially in the steel guitar, the addition of a sustain feature by a foot-operated level control. These foot controls allow him to add or take out, and without losing a beat.

These external controls are simple enough to check, since they are basic electric devices in which the continuity can be tested with a simple VOM. However, in most instances, the problem is not one of working or not working; it's an intermittent situation. So if you suspect one of these units and the related connecting cords, always flex the cords at the points of entry into switches or plugs to make sure that continuity is good and secure.

MAINTENANCE EDUCATION

Too often, musicians have little or no knowledge of what's required in caring for a relatively sophisticated electronic component. If they get a line cord that came coiled when it was new, by golly, they're going to take good care of it, and re-coil the line cord each time they use the device. We've seen

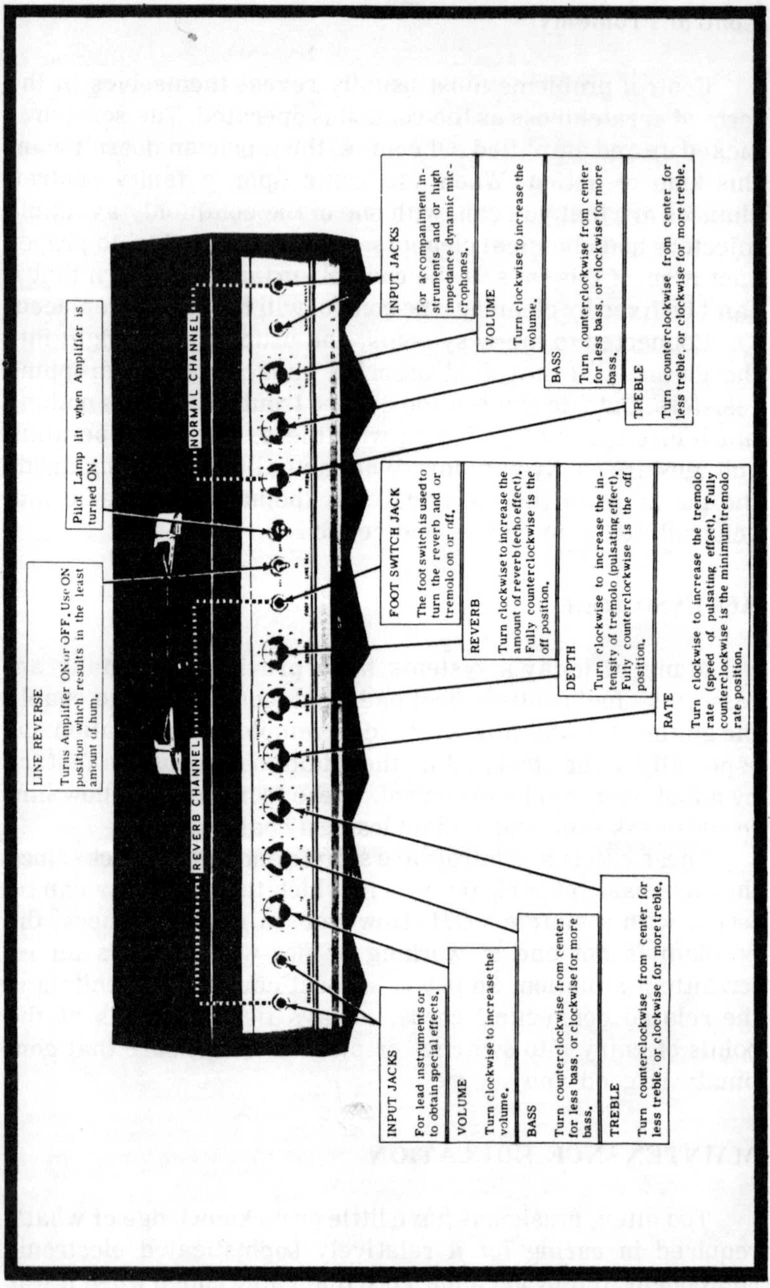

Control layout illustrates the function of each control on the Heathkit Model TA-16 amplifier.

musicians spray detergent liquids all over the outside of a case, and as far inside as they could reach. We ran into one guy who put masking tape over all the ventilation holes to keep the dust out of the insides.

You owe it to your client to inform him of what—and what **not**—to do. Taking out screws is your job and yours alone. Don't encourage the tyro technician to open backs or remove a chassis. He'll only get into trouble doing that, and you'll inherit the trouble.

Caring for an electronic unit, be it amplifier, speaker or control, should involve only cleaning of the outside case. On plastic-finished units, a mild detergent and a soft cloth should be sufficient. Leather-covered units are best cleaned with one of the silicon-base sprays designed for the purpose and wood, such as used in some of the better guitar bodies, is best cared for with a top-grade furniture polish and nothing else. An occasional drop of light machine oil won't hurt the tuning mechanism, and the owner shouldn't hesitate to use it.

In storing a unit for an extended time period, it should first be cleaned and then carefully put away in a proper protective container. Canvas or plastic zipper bags are available for amplifiers and loudspeakers, and suitable heavy chip-board cases should be used to protect instruments. Cords should not be coiled and tightly wrapped; rather, they should be stored by "essing" or zig-zigging and held in place with a rubber band.

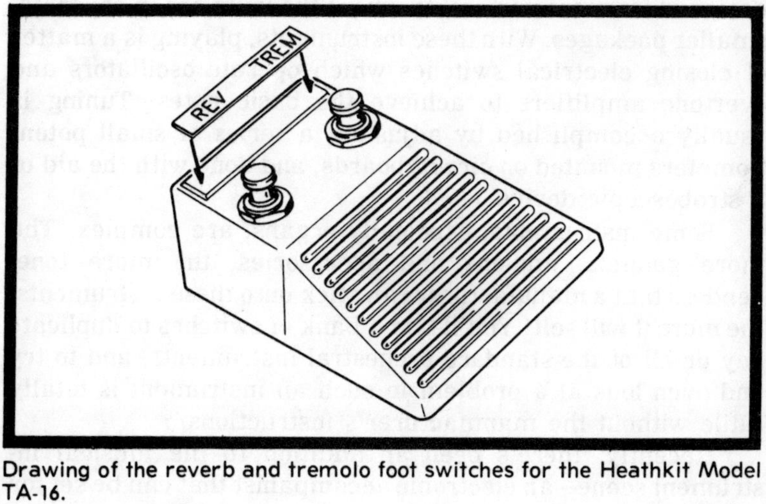

Drawing of the reverb and tremolo foot switches for the Heathkit Model TA-16.

OTHER STRINGED INSTRUMENTS

The electric bass and the bass guitar are other instruments you'll be seeing. The difference is simple. The electric bass is played vertically, just as its ancestor, the acoustic bass, is played. However, it usually has a much thinner body, which is an aid to transporting it. The tone is derived from the strings and pickups. The bass guitar is similar in appearance to an electric guitar, and is held and played in almost the same fashion. However, it has but four strings and these are of fairly large diameter. While the electric bass has no frets, the bass guitar usually does.

Some Hawaiians, or steel guitars, are fitted with a complex system of facilities not found on other guitars. For one thing, this instrument is often available with two separate necks. The steel is usually turned in relation to the neck to form different chords; one neck and set of strings is tuned to a major chord, and the other is tuned to the relative minor, which simplifies playing. Others are fitted with systems of weights and foot pedals so that the individual tuning of a string can be altered by the feet while playing.

KEYBOARD INSTRUMENTS

Instruments such as the electronic organ and electronic piano may be of two types. The integrated instruments have amplifiers and speakers built right in, while others are designed for more portability where the units are in separate, smaller packages. With these instruments, playing is a matter of closing electrical switches which operate oscillators and overtone amplifiers to achieve the basic notes. Tuning is usually accomplished by adjusting a series of small potentiometers mounted on circuit boards, and done with the aid of a stroboscopic device.

Some instruments, especially organs, are complex. The more gadgets, add-ons and accessories, the more tone-benders that a manufacturer can stick onto these instruments, the more it will sell! You'll find a bank of switches to duplicate any or all of the standard orchestral instruments, and to try and even look at a problem in such an instrument is totally futile without the manufacturer's instructions.

Recently, there's been an addition to the musical instrument scene—an electronic accompanist that can be set for

Electric bass guitars; hollow-body on the left and a solid-body type.

any of half a dozen rhythms. It is entirely self-contained with its own loudspeaker and a microphone that picks up the tempo from the musician. It produces such popular rhythms as waltzes, marches, congas, etc. And the sound that comes out is like having your own rhythm section plugged into the nearest wall outlet! Of course, we'll be getting into this later, too.

In the same category, we have to put the electronic metronome, which offers a measured "click" or "beep" at preset intervals to help a student mark time. There are several types, including the little speaker-amplifiers that beep when they are hit with a small voltage, and we've seen some more basic types in which sound is produced by closing relay contacts. In any case, you can depend that the timing is controlled by some sort of a flip-flop circuit, or in the even more basic forms, a resistor-capacitor time constant.

OTHER AMPLIFIED INSTRUMENTS

Over the many preceding years, there have been attempts to amplify the sounds of almost every other kind of instrument made. Highly specialized pickup designs have been tried with the hope that some of the characteristics of the instruments could be amplified with special pickups, and in the final analysis, musicians have found that the best results were achieved by simply playing into a microphone on a floor stand.

Violins have been fitted with small contact pickups, and the results were usually disturbing. The amplification reduced all of the finer qualities of this fine instrument to the point where they were lost, and only the notes themselves could be heard. The sound of a good violin suffered under amplification, and a poor one just sounded worse.

Small pickups that could be fitted to a harmonica have been tried and with mixed success. Similar experiments have been conducted with accordions, but again, both these instruments fare far better with microphones that are totally detached. In the case of the harmonica, especially, musicians feel encumbered by the limits of the connecting cords.

Naturally, you can't talk about electronic musical instruments without mention of the grandaddy of them all, the Theremin. This electronic ancestor of the Moog Synthesizer consists of two antennas, one vertical and one horizontal. One controls pitch, the other the volume. The instrument is sensitive to capacity changes in the antenna circuits and is played—mysteriously to the uninitiated—by waving both hands in the air, near the antennas. The weird sounds produced retain the aura of mystery. The Theremin to this day remains an electronic novelty; we can't recall Bach ever having written a contata for Theremin!

Electronic instruments come and go. Remember the Solovox? This miniature keyboard was attached to many a piano in the '40s, and used along with the piano as an electronic solo instrument.

GETTING STARTED

In this book, we're assuming some electronic knowledge on the part of the reader. We go into generic amplifier types and discuss general repair technology without being specific as to manufacturer's names and model numbers. By applying the information contained in this book, you should be able to handle just about any repair that comes into the shop.

The tools and equipment that you will need are determined by the extent of the work you're going to do. If you plan to restrict yourself to electronic repair and nothing more, the chances are that you already have all the equipment you'll need. If you intend to go into more elaborate work, such as the tuning of electronic organs, you're going to require some specialized equipment and some specialized knowledge to go with it.

Repairing faulty amplifiers is like repairing almost anything else electronic, except for a few small warnings that you should know about. The first of these is that you must never assume anything. Especially don't assume that the musician knows what he's talking about! If he says his amplifier isn't amplifying, it might be caused by anything from an open loudspeaker coil to a disconnected cord socket. Remember that if the musician were a technician, he would not be coming to you. Always start by checking the system, and this means with the instrument plugged in, and, if the speaker is external, with a speaker plugged in.

If you aren't sure of a next step in a repair, always check with the manufacturer's service department. The manufacturer has experts who speak your language, and can save you hours of time in isolating any fault. Remember, too, that it's to the manufacturer's advantage to work with you, because the musician's next recourse is to send the instrument back to him for a repair. Obtain information from the manufacturer in the form of service instructions, schematics and test charts. Most of the manufacturers in the field will be happy to forward all of this to you, and if you like this kind of business and decide to stay in it, the material you collect will soon serve as excellent reference work and stand you in good stead the next time you come upon such a repair.

Electronics is quite a universal pastime these days, and it's entirely possible that a musician who makes electronics his hobby will find enough information in this book to enable him to do his own repairs. At the same time, there are undoubtedly many technicians who play such instruments as pastime, and the book will serve them as well. However, there are certain prerequisites before we get into the subject with both feet, and the casual reader who is passively interested is well-advised to start with some more basic books on electronics servicing, theory and practice. The publisher of this book has several books in these areas that this author highly recommends.

While this book is intended as a guide, it is not intended to relate to specific equipment unless so stated. Manufacturer's designs vary from model to model, and there are no set ground rules regarding design characteristics from one manufacturer to the next. You can't, for example, count transistors and assume that all amplifiers with the same number will be using essentially the same design parameters. The point is that if a unit comes in for repair which has been manufactured by "X" and carries Model number "Y," make sure you posess the pertinent information that applies to "X's" Model "Y" and no other. So with no further ado, let's get right into the subject and see if we can find out what makes these things tick—and stop ticking!

Pickups & Microphones

2

Contact and magnetic pickups are the two basic types in common use today, plus many variations of these types. To decide which is best for a given application you have to have some knowledge of how each operates.

Contact mikes are fitted with a small contact button that picks up the vibrations of the instrument's surface. The resultant signal is fed through a small series-connected control and a plug and cord set to the amplifier. These pickups are mostly employed by folk singers and classic guitarists who use gut or nylon strings. The biggest disadvantage of the contact pickup is that it picks up all sounds that are present in the instrument, including finger noises or drumming sounds from the hands. With a guitar they also pick up and amplify the scraping sound of the fingers over the strings, and, if a pick is used carelessly, the sound of the pick on the pick protector.

There are several types of contact pickups, and this writer, shortly after World War II, found it expedient to use an Air Corps throat microphone as a contact pickup. It worked well, cost little, and ignoring the ugly appearance, was quite suitable. A more-common type is formed of a rubber-like plastic and is attached to a guitar either with a bracket or is slipped under the strings between the bridge and the tail piece.

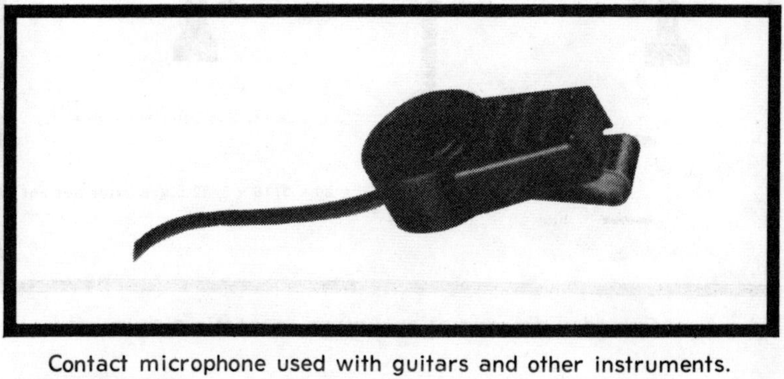

Contact microphone used with guitars and other instruments.

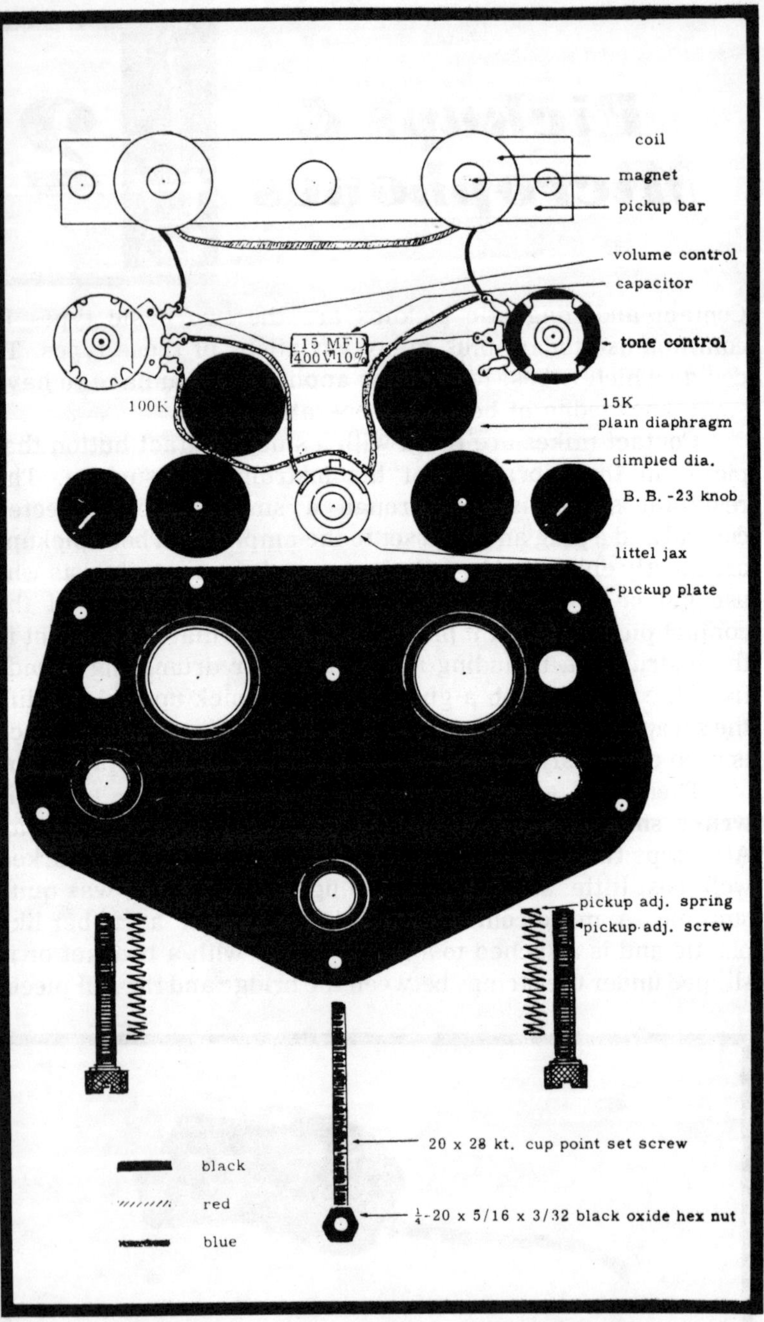

Exploded drawing of an Ampeg magnetic pickup.

More recently, a nicely styled contact pickup has been made available through one of the G-C Electronics subsidiaries. This pickup, manufactured in a highly chromed metal case, is fitted with a jack and cord set, and has a small volume control built in. It comes with a felt-padded metal bracket so it can be attached to a guitar. It is best to mount a pickup of this sort where the guitar provides maximum mechanical resonance. To find this point, hold the pickup in the hand and move it about on the guitar's body while the instrument is being played. Listen for maximum volume. When you find the best position, place the pickup there and attach the bracket to hold the pickup in place. A small projection at the top of the pickup fits into a mating hole in the bracket so there will not be any movement. The adjustable bracket will fit any thickness of guitar body, and can then be tightened into place with a knurled thumbscrew.

If steel strings are used, and these are much favored by professional guitarists who play in combos rather than as soloists, a magnetic pickup can be used. Magnetic pickups consist of six pole pieces, each wound with a small, fine winding. The windings are parallel-connected inside the pickup body and are then brought out to tone and level controls. Each set of six wound pieces is considered a single pickup, and an electric guitar might have as many as five or six such pickups.

On some electric guitars, the pickups are mounted through suitable cutouts in the guitar's wood top. They are placed in such a way that the pole pieces are in close proximity to the strings they are designed to work with. Often, on other types of guitars, the pickups can be added later, and are attached (usually) to a pick-strike protector.

The pickups are obviously placed in a row under the strings. Since the guitar's timbre varies at different points along the length of the strings, the pickup nearest the bottom of the guitar will offer a signal quality different than others further up the line. Frequently, a switching system is provided so the musician can "play" these different sound qualities, using one or two pickups for a "harder" solo sound, and possibly all of them for chording. As the steel string vibrates over its related pole piece, the magnetic field in the coil is altered, thus developing a signal.

There is little or nothing that can be done to repair a pickup economically, but with luck, you might be able to effect a simple repair. It's worth attempting if you look upon it as a cure-or-kill operation. If you care to open one of these units, you might find a simple defect such as a loose or unsoldered wire that you can tack back in place. As long as the unit is to be replaced in any case, nothing can be lost by such an investigation.

When you have to replace a pickup that's actually built into the guitar, you are best advised to use a direct replacement unit available from the manufacturer. On the other hand, if the pickup is an accessory type mounted to the pick protector or is bracket-mounted to the guitar body, you can probably replace the entire unit at much lower cost. Most of the electronic parts catalogs currently list such replacement units and you should unhesitatingly recommend these. They perform quite well, are inexpensive, and easy to install.

Don't forget that steel strings must be used on guitars with magnetic pickups. More than one good musician has heard all kinds of rumors about guitar strings, and when one string breaks, if he's been using steel on his electric he just might experimentally replace it with nylon because he's heard that it is easier on the fingers. His complaint will be that the notes played on the new string aren't as loud. There will be some sound, as the vibrating string sets up similar vibrations in other strings. But the sound will be much reduced. The simple cure is to remove the new nylon or gut string and replace it with the old steel type.

MICROPHONES

Microphones are generally used to amplify singing which is as essential in today's rock and roll combo as it is in modern folk singing. Many of the latter even prefer to use a single microphone to amplify voice and guitar and not use an amplified instrument at all.

To be sure, there is a large number of microphones to select from, and one of the factors that you'll have to consider in helping a musician choose a microphone is its directional pattern. An omni-directional microphone will pick up sound equally from all directions. In other words, it has no directional characteristics at all. The disadvantage with such an instrument is that the performer can get no increased solo effects with such a mike. However, where a group is performing and using only one microphone, this might prove advantageous. At the same time, even the most directional microphone can be used omni-directionally by holding it vertically.

A microphone usually contains a sensitive pickup element mounted at the end of a convenient support, or handle. This, in turn, can be mounted on a stand or hand held. Due to the presence of the handle, a microphone usually has a cardioid or heart-shaped pattern, with a sharp dip occurring at the back, or handle, end.

Most manufacturers enclose a printed pattern showing the pickup characteristics with all new micrphones, but you can determine the pattern of a microphone. Here's an easy way to do it. Start by placing the microphone in a small desk stand and set it horizontally on a phonograph turntable. Make sure that the microphone element is directly over the phonograph spindle. Mark the base of the phonograph with a series of pencil marks at 10-degree increments from zero to 360. Obtain a piece of polar coordinate paper (circular graph paper) and mark the 10-degree increments on it. Connect the microphone to an amplifier and place an AC voltmeter across the loudspeaker terminals, with the speaker disconnected.

Now, set up an audio oscillator, with the frequency at about 800 Hz, well-within the audio range. Place it about ten feet from the turntable and at the zero mark on the base. The microphone should now be facing the oscillator. Turn all of the equipment on, and adjust the amplifier level and the oscillator level until the voltmeter reads 10 volts. Mark the circular lines on the graph paper from 10 volts to zero volts, with 10 as the outermost line.

Now we're ready to test. Do not touch the controls during the following procedure. Rotate the turntable to the first or 10-degree mark. Note the voltage, and, at the same degree increment on the paper, make a pencil dot at the voltage line as read on the meter. Move to the next mark on the turntable and continue until you have returned to the starting position. Connect the dots on the paper and you will have an actual pickup pattern of that particular microphone.

MICROPHONE TROUBLES

The two biggest complaints about microphones are (A) it doesn't work, or (B) sometimes it doesn't work. Again, the treatment that some microphones receive can contribute to the cause of malfunction. Always check a microphone before opening it up. Connect it to an amplifier and try it out. If it works, try flexing the connecting cord at the microphone end and at the plug-in end to see if an intermittent exists and about where. Broken or disconnected wires are fairly commonplace and are easily repaired with a simple soldering job. Sometimes the switches on microphones will malfunction and may require replacing. Also, the element itself will go bad.

If you run into a bad microphone element, do not attempt to repair it. It is a virtually impossible job. Instead, replace the element with a similar one. You'll find a wide assortment of replacement elements at any good electronic supply house. Note the connections, unsolder the old element and solder the new one into place. If it was a bad element, and nothing else was wrong, replacing the element will restore the unit to operation. Reassemble the microphone, and it can be considered repaired.

Shortly after World War II, many ex-GIs went into the music business with some pretty weird ideas about microphones as a result of their military careers. As you probably know, with old carbon mikes there was a tendency for the carbon granules to "pack," causing the microphone to become insensitive. The standard cure for this was to bang the microphone on a hard surface to loosen the granules. This became a standard treatment to make a microphone more sensitive, and it was horrifying to see performers whack their microphones on the edge of a stage. Most of them, at that time, were using crystal mikes, and mechanical shock is about the worst thing you can do with a crystal.

You still see performers who have no knowledge of microphone technology doing some pretty strange things. Is the mike on? They tap it, rap it and blow into it. But you aren't even supposed to talk or sing directly **into** a microphone—you are supposed to talk or sing **across** a microphone! Get too close to a mike and you pick up all sorts of labial noises that you don't want amplified. Need more volume? Don't get closer to the mike; turn the volume up.

Peanuts was a vocalist who sang various small clubs in the New York area shortly after the last big war, and since many of these small night spots had pianos and nothing more, Peanuts had to supply his own electronics. He went down to surplus row and picked up an old and cheap public address amplifier clad in an olive drab metal cabinet. It was originally used for directing troops, and had a separate metal box that was painted a matching color. It worked with a hand-held black carbon mike with a push-to-talk switch. The unit worked all right, and Peanuts carried it to his jobs, clutched the mike in his hand, and sang his heart out. The money he collected for singing weekends was putting him through college. But that mike was the very bane of Peanuts' existence. He hated it with a vengeance. Sure, the system made his voice loud enough to be heard over clinking glassware and various customer arguments, but it totally masked vocal quality.

One day, he had really had enough. He saved his money and went shopping for a real mike. He picked up an Astatic D-104. This fine instrument not only was designed to perform beautifully, but it even looked like a microphone was supposed to look. It was heavily chrome plated, had a mesh-screen front, and was nice and round. Peanuts carried the mike home with loving, tender care. He carefully removed the plug from the carbon mike and tossed it into the nearest trash barrel. He attached the plug to his new mike, and raced off to the next job.

He set up his amplifier, plugged in the new mike, and as the piano player trilled an introduction, Peanuts opened his mouth, sang, and nothing came out. You see, with a carbon microphone a small voltage has to be applied to it in order for it to operate. The new one was a crystal mike, and the worst thing you can do to a crystal is put a voltage through it. Peanuts had blown out his new mike! Naturally, we heard the whole story the next day, when Peanuts brought the mike in for a repair, which consisted of changing the element and selling him a new amplifier to go with the new mike.

REPAIRING A MICROPHONE

Before you can repair a microphone, you have to get to the internal connections and this must be done with great care. If covers and escutcheons are held in place with small screws, you cannot simply bull your way in with a large screwdriver. A set of jeweler's screwdrivers is handy for this purpose. You'll also find that these units are either chromed or painted, and nicks and mars will surely show up, leaving the sign of sloppy workmanship.

On some of the less costly mikes, you'll find drive pins used instead of screws. To remove these, carefully insert a sharp blade under the head of the pin so it lifts slightly away from the base. Then, use end-cutting pliers to carefully lift the pin out, taking care not to clip off the head.

Under the dress cover of the mike, you'll find the microphone element, and probably a packing of absorbent cotton under it to prevent internal vibration. Felt spacers and shims are also commonplace, and these should be removed and placed on the bench in proper sequence so the mike can be reassembled correctly.

The microphone cord usually connects to a switch and then to the microphone element. There are several connecting systems in use, and most of them are relatively easy to understand. A simple SPST switch can be used to interrupt the "hot" line to the mike element, so that with the switch off, the mike is de-sensitized and will not pick up sound.

In tape recorders or communications systems and in some musical amplifiers, the switch circuit is more complex. In addition to cutting off the mike, another segment of the switch is wired back to the plug so that it can control DC to the amplifier, cutting it off as well.

Some method of strain-relief must be provided for the cord; this can be anything from a plastic tension clutch to a simple knot in the cord.

Repair of any microphone of this type simply involves replacement by unsoldering and resoldering. Any work on the switch, of course, will mean that the entire unit must be removed from the microphone housing. You will find that in some cases, access to the switch is provided by a fairly large escutcheon plate that can be removed along with the switch. On other microphones, the switch must be dismounted, the strain-relief system eased, and the cord slid into and through the mike to expose the switch.

After repairs or replacements are made, the unit must be reassembled, and this becomes a problem unless you've got long, thin fingers. As a substitute, there's a handy trick we've learned. Get the switch back in position as near as you can, and insert an awl or scriber into the body clearance hole on one side of the switch. By applying pressure from underneath with a long tool, such as a screwdriver blade, you can jockey the threaded hole in the switch so it is over the scriber. With the one hole lined up like this, it is fairly easy to line up the other hole sufficiently so that one screw can easily be put in and tightened almost completely. Now remove the scriber and insert the other screw. Tighten them both, and the switch is re-installed.

When re-installing escutcheons and covers, you may find that the mounting holes are worn. This is especially true if the microphone has a plastic body. If the mike is metal and has threaded holes, or is plastic with threaded metal inserts, you should have no trouble. However, plastic threads tend to wear, and drivepin holes do also. We have experimented over the years with many systems, including relocating the holes and drilling new pilots for drive pins or self-tapping screws. By far the best method we've come up with from a time and labor standpoint is to align the cover with the old holes, apply a bit of LocTite (thread sealant) to the screws or pins, and then run them in. They hold beautifully, yet are fairly easy to remove the next time you want to get inside. Epoxy cements form a good bond, but don't ever expect to get inside again without performing major surgery on the unit.

GUARANTEEING YOUR WORK

Microphones look like microphones, and if a musician had a set of four, the chances are that they're identical in appearance. If he wants repairs on three mikes, for example, he just might bring in the first one, have you fix it, and then a week later, come in with the second, claiming that it's the first one again and still not working right. Certainly you want to stand behind your work and guarantee that it's sound and proper, but how can you protect yourself against such shenanigans? If the microphone has a serial number, by all means record this on the bill that you make out before you get your money.

If there is no serial number on the mike, you can steal a page from a jeweler's book. For years, jewelers have been making identifying "scratch marks" on the insides of watch cases that they repair. You can do the same thing. Open the cover of the mike and put your initials on the inside someplace, using a scratch awl or a sharp scriber. This will in no way interfere with the operation of the unit, will not mar its outward appearance, and your initials, maybe along with the date, will tell you if and when you saw the unit last.

MICROPHONE ACCESSORIES

You should stock or at least prepare to sell your clients the various accessories that they will need along with their microphones. Microphone extension cords are always in demand, and the new, lightweight coiled cords are extremely popular these days for extending mike cords as well as pickup cords. Microphone stands are fast-moving items, as well as stand appurtenances, such as cord holders, booms, counterweights and the like.

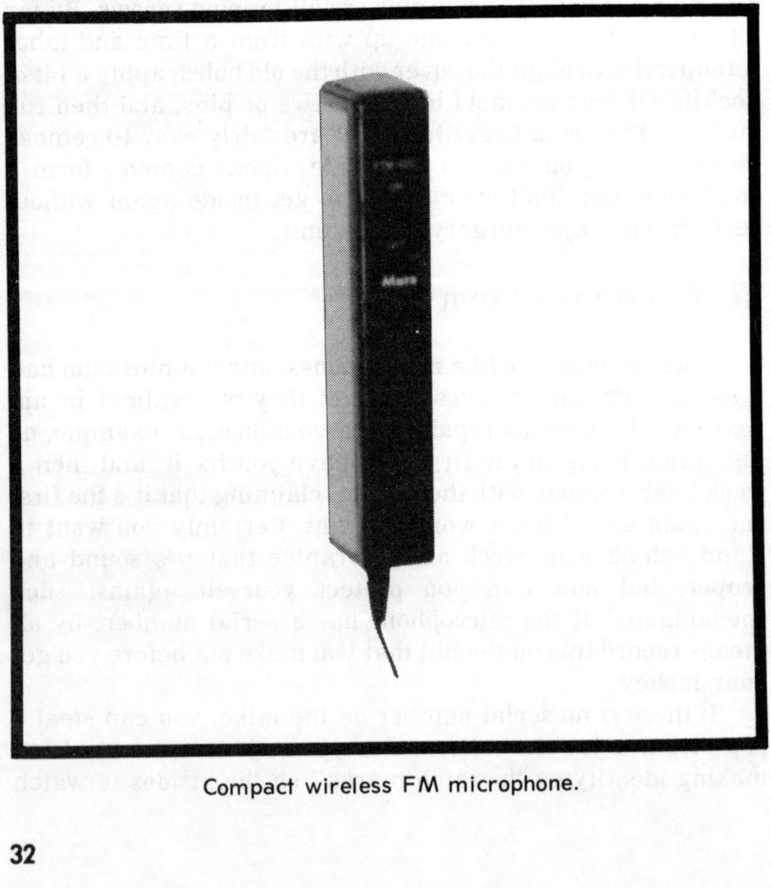

Compact wireless FM microphone.

With more and more groups performing outdoors in rock concerts or in park performances, wind becomes a problem. The wind blowing past a mike can create big problems for a performer, and they are always good customers for those plastic foam jackets that permit sound to enter the mike and still block the wind. Lavalier microphones that go around the neck on a simple braided cord, tie-clip microphones and other hands-free types are also in great demand.

WIRELESS MIKES

About 15 years ago, wireless mikes burst on the scene and they looked for all the world like the answer to thousands of problems. A small FM transmitter was connected to a small microphone and the whole thing was battery operated. It broadcast its signals to a small FM receiver which then connected to the system amplifier. Performers could actually be heard and not be bound by connecting cords. They could even wander into the audience and still be picked up!

Then the FCC cracked down and barred them from use. They were small transmitters and could violate other services. For several years they were totally taboo. But the FCC relented and said as long as they were under 100 milliwatts in power, they could be used.

To use a wireless mike, you tune a small FM receiver to a place on the dial where no regular FM programming is heard. Turn on the microphone, and adjust its tuning to a point where you hear a rushing noise in the FM receiver. This indicates that the small transmitter and receiver are on the same frequency. The receiver couples to the amplifier's input, and you're all set. But there are some problems inherent in these units, and you'd better be prepared for them.

The first of these problems, of course, is drift. Even with the best kind of AFC on the receiver, these little things tend to walk right up the dial. You can adjust the receiver to keep up with them, but only until you come up against a station which overrides the transmitted signal. The better and more expensive units are pretty steady.

3 Approaching Amplifier Repairs

Musical instrument amplifier repairs are very similar to repairs on any other type of electronic equipment. You start with an analysis of the symptoms, follow with a series of diagnoses, some probings to confirm the preliminary diagnosis, and, once confirmation has been achieved, the necessary corrective steps are taken and the job completed. However, as in any electronic equipment, you rarely—if ever—get such a textbook case. More usually, your repair steps go like this:

There is no power coming in. Examination reveals that the fuse is blown. You replace the fuse, and the new one opens as well. A continuity check shows that there's a direct short to ground from B+. You disconnect the circuits from the B+ supply and find that a filter capacitor is shorted. You replace the bad filter, replace the fuse, reconnect the B+ line, and turn the unit on. The fuse blows once again. Disconnecting the B+ line, you find that the new capacitor is still operating, and you detect a short elsewhere in the circuit that might have caused the capacitor to go in the first place. As you can see, it's a complex, involved detective game, and you can only expect the unexpected.

One technician uses a "cure or kill" system to isolate intermittent problems. He connects a variable-voltage transformer to the input AC line and cranks the voltage up from the accepted 117 volts to 135. He lets the unit cook until something burns open, on the theory that the overvoltage will cause an intermittent or weak component to go bad and be more easy to locate. It's a short cut, but one to which we do not subscribe.

In any event, your best ally is the manufacturer and the information that he offers to service technicians. You'll find listings of common malfunctions and how to recognize and cure them. You'll also find troubleshooting and go no-go charts, which include voltage and resistance readings as well as waveform photos. You are best advised to call on the manufacturers to obtain these valuable aids, and if you do get a tough dog in the shop, you would be equally well advised to call the manufacturer's service people for a quick consultation.

Once you have located a faulty component, you're going to have to replace it as a first step to making a repair. For the most part, in all honesty, this will be a simple matter of changing tubes. But where tubes are changed in an amplifier circuit, you might have to make some critical balance adjustments before the job can be called complete. This is especially true with critical pushpull or compound output tubes. Where matched pairs are required, only matched pairs should be used. However, if only one tube is bad, the replacement will have to be matched to the existing tube.

Frequently, a well-meaning technician can do more harm than good. In trying to make a repair, he can do untold damage to an amplifier. Often, he's not even aware that his own best efforts are what caused the problems that he's trying to fix! In a transistorized circuit, for example, be exceedingly careful with ohmmeter continuity tests. Many a perfectly good transistor has succumbed to the voltage applied during a high-range continuity test. Glass or epoxy diodes have gone bad due to some frantic pushing around. Those wire leads are about as fragile as anything can be, and the utmost care is urged. The same goes when you're applying heat around these devices because they are particularly sensitive; therefore, a heat sink should always be used.

The right way to begin troubleshooting is with a planned, carefully organized program of analysis and corrective steps. Let's face it, even the most experienced technician who seems to always be able to lay his finger exactly on the malfunctioning component is still using his "bean" as the best of all possible tools, and all his experience does for him is enable him to go through his analysis so rapidly that it looks almost like an instinct. Let's assume that you turn on an amplifier and nothing appears to be happening. There's no sound, no pilot lamp indications, no nothing. What are your first and immediate reactions? Is the amplifier plugged in? Is the fuse good? Is the pilot lamp burned out? Is the switch operating properly? You see, basic as these thoughts might be, you are still thinking in step-by-step, logical terms! You first eliminate the obvious.

STEP-BY-STEP ANALYSIS

If you get no sound, look at the pilot lamp. If it is lit, check the controls for proper setting, and don't overlook the controls on the instrument itself. Often an amplifier is working all right, but the controls on the instrument can be turned down. If there's a mute switch on the instrument, make sure it is in the operating position.

If there's still no sound, turn the volume all the way up and see if you get a hum. If you do, unplug the connecting cord between the instrument and the amplifier at the instrument. Touch the plug tip with your finger. If you get a loud hum or buzz on contact, it's the instrument's pickup that's at fault. If you don't get the hum, try a new connecting cable.

Now let's go back to where you turned that volume all the way up. If you got no sound then, try disconnecting the speaker and substituting another. If this corrects the problem, you've got speaker troubles. If not, try substituting the speaker connecting cable if there is one, and see if this helps. You can check a speaker by connecting a pair of wires from a 1.5-volt battery to the speaker terminals. If you get a slight "pop" the voice coil is operating. If not, the speaker is probably defective.

After a problem has been isolated and localized to the amplifier itself, the next step is to localize it still further to the specific circuit or circuits that are causing the difficulty. Unfortunately, you rarely get a simple textbook case in which a single component malfunctions and requires only a replacement to get the unit operating again. What generally happens is that a component will malfunction, which starts a chain of events that causes other components to become faulty, and these in turn, affect still other components.

When you get this kind of action, generally, you start at the end and work backward to the beginning. You locate the offending stage, or what appears to be the offending stage, and then locate a bad component in this stage. You replace the bad component with a good one, turn the unit on, and find that the good component is now a bad one. So you continue to look for another bad component that's damaging the good ones that you have been putting in. If you continue in this manner, sooner or later, you will come to the root cause of the problem, but as you can imagine, the process is a lengthy and tedious one.

A better method is a step-by-step isolation process in which you use an amplified probe to detect the presence of signal right up the line from the preamplifier stages. When you reach a stage that is receiving input and not providing output, you have come to a stage that requires some further investigation.

There are two things that can happen to cause this type of symptom. In one case, a chain effect occurs, and you've got to pursue the order of events to a normal, natural conclusion that results in a repair. One of the more common difficulties will lie in a shorted bypass capacitor or in an open coupling device.

In most instances, the manufacturers are pretty careful in producing the product. They don't implement a design until it has been thoroughly tested, and tested for more than the economical viability of the end product. They check very thoroughly before putting a unit into production, and there's very little of the cost-cutting that you might think exists. You can usually tell whether or not a manufacturer has cut costs by simply checking the voltage ratings on components such as capacitors. You'll find that there are usually very few that are marginally rated to save a few cents. For the most part, capacitors and other such components are generally well selected and with good tolerance allowances as well.

Occasionally, however, you run across a design that shouldn't have been allowed off the drawing boards and into production. These units are back in the shop for repairs regularly, and there's not too much that can be done except to send them back to the manufacturer if they are under warranty, and keep your fingers crossed when they aren't.

Sometimes you can save your customer and yourself by not using exact replacement parts. Where you are able, replace units that seem to have marginal voltage ratings with units of a higher voltage rating. Where a resistor seems to be constantly burning out, replace it with one having a higher wattage rating. Manufacturers usually will not release a unit until it has been thoroughly field tested under the very worst operating conditions. They generally offer excellent guarantees and warranties, and as long as the unit they offer is covered, they will honor them.

Once a fault has been isolated to the amplifier itself, you will find that the amplifier is pretty much self analyzing. But there are some basic tests that you can apply simply and easily to help you isolate the problem. If the amplifier is a tube-operated unit, determine first if the filaments heat up when the power is applied. Two of the handier pieces of test equipment you will find include the signal injector and the signal tracer and oscillator. By injecting an audio signal at the input to the various stages, you will soon isolate a faulty stage. The signal injector is also an asset when you are working in conjunction with an oscilloscope. However, there is no replacement tool for the human brain, dutifully applied. Let's face it, you are going to get a good share of "tough dog" problems that just won't respond to any short-cut analysis steps. The way to find the trouble is to methodically check the circuit on a step-by-step basis. In order to properly accomplish this, you will need a schematic diagram, a VOM or a VTVM and a lot of patience.

When you get an amplifier in the shop that isn't responding to a "2-minute cure," the best bet is to set the amplifier on the workbench and open it up. Make a visual check to see if anything obvious is wrong, and then, with a continuity tester, establish that all interconnecting wiring that enters and leaves the amplifier chassis is in good condition. While checking these cables, check for continuity of the separate leads in a cable, and then check to be sure there is no short-circuiting between leads in any given cable. Flex the leads during such checks to expose any intermittents.

We find that one of the best ways to use the schematic diagram is to pin it to a wall above the work table. With the amplifier up-ended on the table you can easily follow the schematic and check the components and internal wiring step by step.

There are certain tools that are needed for such a checkout and others that serve to make the check a lot easier. All of these checks are made with the power off and the line cord disconnected from any power source.

A grounding rod is an essential. The first step in any such procedure is to short all power capacitors to ground, bleeding away any required charge. This can be done with an ordinary insulated clip lead if a grounding rod is not available.

An inorganic prod or probe is also helpful for rooting around in bunched-up wiring bundles. This can be a simple plastic rod, about four to eight inches long, with a chisel shape at one end and a point at the other. With this, you can easily push wiring aside to see what's under it, or you can use this as a pointer to keep an eye on your place in the circuit while you refer to the schematic for a quick reference.

A continuity tester is an essential, because frequently, while checking through a circuit, it's easier to place one probe of the tester on one terminal and place the other probe on the

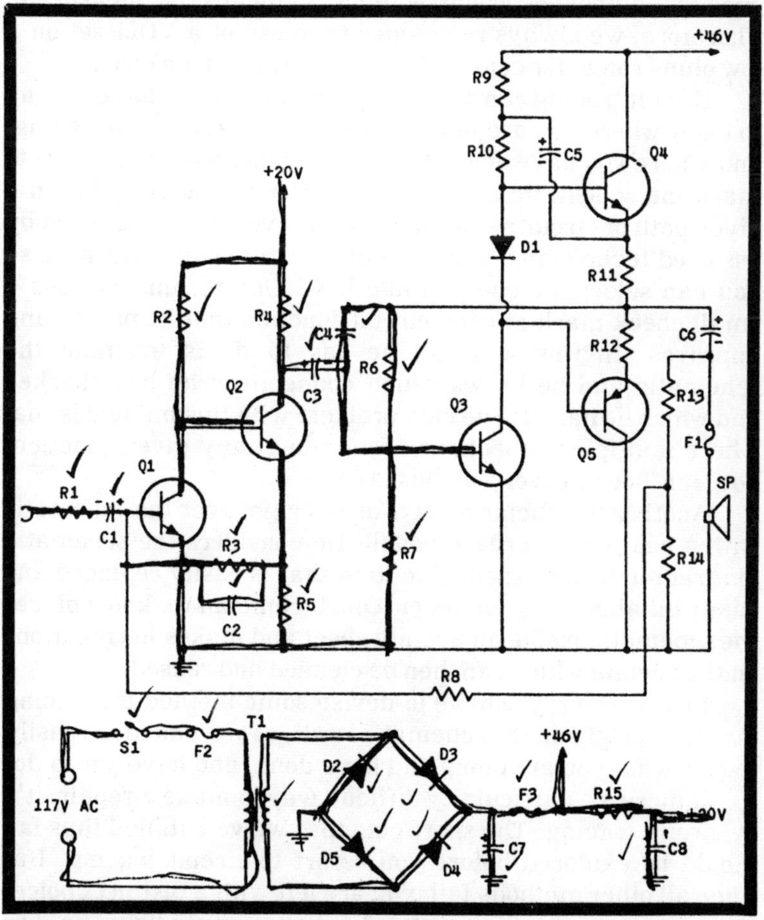

Marking a schematic as you check or build circuits helps you to avoid time waste. Simple pencil marks will keep you from retracing your steps. The check marks indicate components already checked.

terminal to which a given wire is connected, rather than trying to visually follow the wire as it snakes through a maze of circuitry. However, in many instances, you will find places in the schematic where, for example, a resistor is connected to ground. It is much better to be able to check, not just for the **presence** of the resistor and its connection to ground, but at the same time be able to measure the **value** of the resistor while you are checking it. A leaky ground bypass capacitor, for example, might be revealed quickly by measuring resistance to ground through a component. Without such a measurement, you might spend many times the number of hours in hunting such a component down without a means of measuring. Therefore, we always recommend the use of a VOM set on a low ohms range for continuity testing in any given circuit.

Circuit tracing can always be confusing if you have no way to know where you are in the schematic, where you are going, and where you have been. A great convenience is to be able to mark the schematic in some way, after you have followed a given path of circuitry. We have seen several systems used by assorted technicians, and we'll discuss a few of them here so you can select the one you like best. One technician uses a small check mark at each circuit junction that he passes and approves. In this way, all he has to do is examine the schematic and he knows which connections he has checked and which he hasn't. The only problem with this method is that where multiple connections are made at any given junction, you can become very confused.

Another technician always draws right over the schematic with a heavy blue grease pencil. He considers the schematic diagram to be an expendable item that is easily replaced and easily billable to his customer. One technician we know places the schematic inside an acetate sheet and makes his notations on the acetate which can then be cleaned and reused.

In any event, you have to devise some method for tracing the circuit right on the schematic itself, so you can more easily record what you are doing and have done, and have yet to do.

If there's a particularly difficult way to make a repair, it's by circuit tracing. The short cuts that we've outlined thus far should be explored before you resort to circuit tracing. But when all other methods fail, you are left with a distinct choice. You can return the unit to your client and simply "give up," or you can sit yourself down and follow the circuit through until you find something that shouldn't be.

Sure it takes longer to do it this way; it's more expensive, more time consuming, and probably the least efficient way to effect a repair. But when all else fails, it just might reveal something that the other methods didn't show up. We aren't suggesting that this be used as a first step method by any means. We simply advocate it as a last resort, when all else has failed. Experience is probably one of the best allies you can have in doing amplifier repair, for the experienced repairman can usually listen to a symptom and know where (within reason) the trouble lies. But until you gain this level of experience, step-by-step troubleshooting is a good answer. It will help you to gain the experience that will make each succeding job that much easier as well.

With this method, you start with the power supply and go over the schematic component by component. When the power supply has been cleared and checked as operable or at least in agreement with the schematic, go back and start at any of the signal input jacks and trace from each of these to its first termination inside the chassis. Mark each circuit path that you cover.

Where you see an opportunity to check a component for more than simple continuity, measure the value of that component with the meter. If it checks out, mark the component with a check on the schematic diagram. Continue to the next. Where a component does not check out, always pause to unsolder at least one end of it and check the component again. If it's OK, resolder it and attempt to find out why it did not check out. You may find an alternate path to the component's terminal that changes its value in the circuit, and this in itself might lead you to find a circuit fault.

If the component check reveals a defect, by all means replace the component and then make another dry run with power off to establish that the new component checks as it should. If it does, reassemble the amplifier at this point and try applying power. You might well have located the trouble and corrected it.

BASIC AMPLIFIER PROBLEMS

Problems in an electronic amplifier circuit are best diagnosed on the basis of existing symptoms. If there is no output whatever, chances are that a fuse has blown, and in addition to primary or line fuses, B+ fuses must also be checked. Do not try to rely on visual observation alone in checking these fuses; a continuity test is needed to verify an open circuit.

As you may have already guessed, more and more amplifiers are relying on circuitbreakers in place of fuses, and if the circuitbreaker keeps opening, you might be tempted to look elsewhere for the trouble. Usually, this will be correct. However, some circuitbreakers tend to lose their potency after repeated use or aging, and all that really might be required is a new breaker. To determine this, remove the line cord from the power source, reset the circuitbreaker and test for continuity through it. You might well find that the breaker, even though the reset has been pressed, is still open.

As a general rule, you will find that solid-state amplifiers won't be coming in for repair with great regularity. Solid-state devices tend to give trouble—if they're going to—in the first few hours of operation, while a new unit is still covered by guarantees. Once they pass through this initial "burning-in," the troubles they develop are relatively easy to handle. Tube-type amplifiers are something else again.

Tube Problems

If a tube should fail to function entirely, if the filament burns open, for example, the problem is usually an easy one to locate. The tube feels cool when it should be hot. On higher-voltage filament tubes, the filament doesn't light. Making a quick check of all the tubes is a good first step, so you can usually rule out such problems.

Other difficulties that can be traced to tubes include a loud hum in the speaker. This is generally caused by AC leakage from filament to cathode in one of the earlier amplifying stages. Replacing the bad tube will quickly correct this fault. Microphonic tubes are responsible for frequent complaints and this is largely due to the fact that most musical instrument amplifiers are frequently transported, and not always with the very best of care. During such transport, tubes are knocked around, and an internal element can be jarred loose, causing the microphonic. To locate such a problem, turn the unit on and tap the tubes, one after another, until the microphonic tube is located. Of course, such a tube should be replaced and the owner cautioned to use a bit more care. To hold tubes firmly in their sockets, gripping tube shields or spring locks are sometimes used. However, always be sure that the tubes are well-seated in their respective sockets.

Frequently, you run into an intermittent problem, in which an amplifier performs properly for the first 15 minutes or so, and then cuts out. What's usually happening here is that a tube has a heat-sensitive element that opens as it expands under operating heat. Locating such a tube can be a problem indeed, but a fast way to do this is to place an ice cube on the tubes, one at a time, after the unit has quit. When the faulty tube's temperature has been reduced, it will work once again, and you know which tube to suspect. However, avoid using the chilling freon aerosol cans, since the cold they generate is too severe and can thermally shock a tube, cracking the glass envelope.

Tubes can also develop hot spots or gassiness. This condition can be seen if the set is operated in a dimly lit area. A hot spot will appear on the anode of a tube as a cherry-red glow. A gassy tube will exhibit a purplish glow inside the envelope. Such problems can be caused by unbalanced outputs in a pushpull or Williamson circuit.

Transistor Problems

Transistor troubles are similar to those encountered with tubes, except they are a bit more difficult to diagnose, and frequently more of a problem to correct. Solid-state devices are coming into play more and more, especially in low-level areas of musical instrument amplifiers. Where problems are located in such units, the question often arises as to how far one should go in effecting a repair. Are you better advised to remove and replace an entire circuit board? Or is it perhaps a more sensible approach to replace a bad transistor or other such device? Such a decision depends on what you are working with. If you have a plug-in plastic encapsulated board, certainly changing the board is a better idea, and you can generally purchase such replacements as they are needed from the manufacturer.

However, we have run into the situation where a musician desparately needed his amplifier that same night, and there just wasn't time to wait for a replacement. To help the chap out, we tried to make a repair. Fortunately, we had the necessary replacement component, and it was a simple matter to unsolder the bad transistor and replace it with a new one. When the board was put back in the amplifier and wired into place, the guy was in business, and able to work the job that night.

What can go wrong with solid-state devices in an amplifier? The very same things that can go wrong with any solid-state device. And the corrective steps are always essentially the same with neither tricks nor surprises in store for you. To replace transistors that are soldered in, always use caution not to bridge adjacent paths of a circuit board with excess solder during both the removal and re-installation steps. Always use a heat sink on the leads before applying the iron to a new unit. While making tests, be very careful that an ohmmeter, used on a high scale, doesn't burn a transistor open, and always check the schematic first to make sure you aren't applying a reverse-voltage across the unit.

Other Component Troubles

Still speaking in general terms, you will, of course, come upon the usual mix of burned open components, shorted components, and the problems that usually accompany these faults. When a filter capacitor in a power supply short circuits, for example, it applies the entire B+ to the chassis, and, hopefully, will open the fuse. Your job is to locate the bad capacitor and replace it, then take resistance checks with the power off to make sure that something else didn't blow the capacitor. If nothing else is wrong, change the fuse and, with your fingers crossed, try once again.

Happily, you can often get a good indication of what the problem is when the job comes in. If you hear a lurid discussion of smoke, sparking, and horrible odors, apply your own senses to the unit. Take it out of its case, look for signs of smoke damage or charred components, and then apply power while you watch and smell. Frequently this sort of activity can give you an excellent clue as to where you should begin to search.

Frequently, a manufacturer offers more inputs than a musician needs. Yet he will, sooner or later, have occasion to use a second, third, or fourth input. He may find that while the instrument works well on the familiar first input he has used, it will not function on the others. The jacks on the amplifier can easily (and rapidly) become coated with a heavy layer of oxide. To clear this, open the unit up, and using some fine emery paper, remove the oxides. Then apply a liquid contact cleaner and try once again. You can reduce such problems by dropping a few packets of Requa activated charcoal in the Charo Scatter-Pax form inside the amplifier. The charcoal absorbs the oxidants, and prevents a recurrence of this sort of problem.

Loudspeaker Problems

There are many ills that can plague a musical amplifier speaker, and in spite of what you may have heard, most manufacturers recommend that you replace a speaker instead of trying to repair it. A speaker coil can get out of round and hang up or rub on the magnetic pole piece. While such things can be repaired with shims and spiders, it's a very exacting job, best left to the professional speaker repair people. You can remove a faulty speaker from its cabinet, deliver it to a qualified repairman, and have it fixed; then, you re-install it.

In some amplifiers, especially those with transformerless output circuits, the speaker **must** be connected or the amplifier's final stages will be destroyed. In order to insure that this can't happen, some manufacturers who make speakers that detach from the amplifier unit have taken to using electromagnetic loudspeakers with field coils that also function as power chokes in the power supply. Obviously, unless the loudspeaker cable is connected to the amplifier in a set up such as this, no power will get through to the amplifier and no harm can be done. The speaker cord serves as an effective interlock in cases such as this, and the unit is protected.

Of course, speakers with field coils aren't terribly commonplace these days, but if you encounter an open field coil there's a simple way to jury-rig an ordinary permanent magnetic speaker so it will work. Simply mount a filter choke (about 10.5 henrys with sufficient current capacity) inside the speaker box. Connect the output amplifier terminals to the loudspeaker voice coil and the field coil connections to the choke. The unit will prove serviceable until a replacement can be obtained.

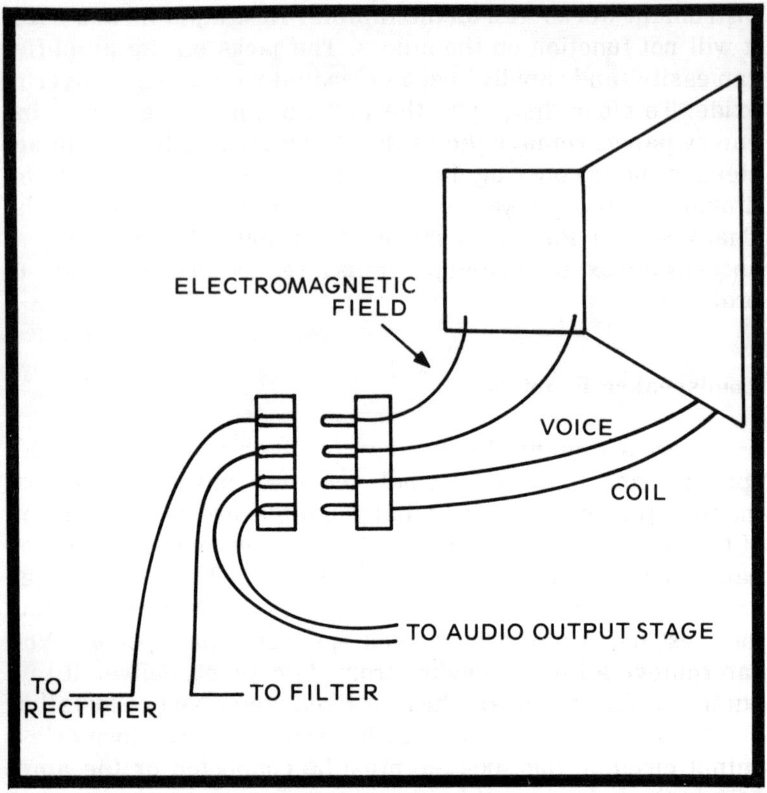

Field-coil speaker connections.

Damage to the speaker cone is also a commonplace. One musician we know had been playing in a pretty tough night club when a bottle was thrown. The grille cloth on his speaker cover gave way, and a small tear appeared in the speaker cone. Since the instrument seemed to be working all right, he ignored the small tear in the cloth. But before long, a rattling and buzzing could be heard that didn't belong.

Opening up the unit revealed the rip in the cone, which had progressed to a sizable tear. Since the guy was something of an electronics hobbyist who always saved the back issues of his magazines, he did some research, and bought a small bottle of speaker cement. Using single layers of toilet tissue and liberal coats of the cement, he built up a nice patch over the tear, covering both sides of the cone. Happy with the money he saved in doing his own repair, he plugged the unit in and hit a chord. The rip opened up, and proceeded to get even worse.

You see, the sound levels involved require that the speaker cone be able to really take it, and this sort of patch, while sufficiently adequate for an AC-DC radio loudspeaker, just couldn't take it. The proper way to solve a problem of this sort is to have the loudspeaker completely reconed, and preferably by the speaker manufacturer, just to play it safe.

Reverb Units

In servicing electronic instrument amplifiers, you're going to find yourself face to face with things you may never have seen before. Typical of these is the reverberation unit, which comes in many forms.

The object of reverberation is to produce a deep, echo effect that heightens the guitar's tone, when used in moderation. In the early days of pre-electronic amplification, a metal disc, perforated with designs, was mounted over the guitar's top and under the strings so that a portion of the sound escaping from the guitar body would be reflected back to the guitar and add the required echo or reverberation. Today, we use some remarkable electronic circuitry to accomplish this, and some that is just plain unbelieveably Rube Goldberg-ian!

Perhaps the most common type that came out, when the need for reverberation was first apparent and technology had not as yet evolved to its present state, was the endless-loop tape. A loop of tape was driven between a capstan and a pinch roller, and a record head took a portion of the signal from the amplifier's early stages, recorded it on the tape, then a playback head picked it up and re-applied it to the amplifier. The distance between heads determined the amount of delay and, therefore, the amount of reverberation.

Reverberation through a delay line was also used. A portion of the signal was applied to one end of a coiled coaxial cable and then re-applied to an input circuit. The longer the line, the longer the delay, and the more reverberation you got.

More recently, we saw the advent of a metal box about 18 inches long. In this device a driver at one end is connected to a coiled spring that runs the length of the box and back, where a receiving pickup is connected. The signal travels to the driver which flexes the spring in a rotary fashion, then the receiving pickup re-translates the mechanical vibrations to an electrical signal that is fed back to the amplifier.

One truly innovative device employs a small neon lamp which is connected to the amplifier and is housed in a light-tight box with a small photo-sensitive resistor. As the light increases and decreases in amplitude with the signal, the resistor changes in value as the light falls on it. The resulting changes are sensed by amplifier circuits and re-played to produce echo or reverberation.

Along with reverberation, some complex circuitry has been developed to control reverberation duration and amplitude, so the musician has his option on how much he wants and how long he wants it sustained. You may find reverb systems incorporated in the amplifier itself, or supplied as outboard add-ons or options.

While reverberators are subject to electronic difficulties, their very nature also makes many of them prone to mechanical failings. In the spring-type reverberators, one very common complaint is that they just don't reverberate. Investigation often reveals that a cord is tied round the spring for transportation so it doesn't rattle around loosely. While most manufacturers of such units always direct the user to loosen this string when the instrument is being played, not all users read all the instructions. Loosening the string so the spring can flex properly will alleviate this condition. Always be sure to check for the possibility of mechanical blocks or stoppages in these units. If they cannot easily be cleared, you are best advised to replace rather than attempt a repair.

Some of the accessories that a musician uses are "add-on" extras that are purchased after he already has his instrument and amplifier. However, many of these units are transistorized and come with a built-in battery supply that is relatively easy for a musician to forget all about. He uses the instrument, and finally, that particular accessory stops working. All that's needed is a battery change, and this should be one of your first checks in dealing with such equipment.

The other most common problem with some of these add-ons is that they are not always directly compatible with the equipment with which they are being used. You should always make sure that the output specifications are in keeping with the amplifier's input requirements. Oftentimes, you get the problem long before the instrument has been put to use.

CONNECTORS

Sam played electric guitar with a small combo and saved his money so he could buy a new guitar. The one he selected had five pickups and more knobs and dials than an amateur radio transmitter. What wasn't covered with knobs was chrome plated. Sam was delighted with his purchase, and couldn't wait to try it out.

That was the trouble. He couldn't try it out. The cord that came with the guitar wouldn't plug into the amplifier, and the old cord wouldn't plug into the guitar. Simple problem? Maybe it is simple to you and me, for we know what to do. Sam didn't. He brought the whole package into the shop, with a woebegone look on his face. "Like man," he said, "You gotta help me, dig?"

We dug. We dug around in the scrap box and found a connector that would fit Sam's amplifier jacks, and right there, under his worried nose, we removed the plug from the connecting cord, replaced it, and our tin ear was treated to Sam's first experimental notes on his new guitar, five pickups and all.

Big deal? Maybe it isn't, but Sam is a typical musician who knows only that "this" is supposed to plug into "that" and when they don't, he's got trouble. That's when he comes to an electronics technician for assistance. The fact of the matter is that most of the problems you're going to be called on to repair are the same sort of big deal as that. What you have to keep in mind is that you are the electronics expert, and your client is going to be, nine times out of ten, a musician with barely enough knowledge of amplifiers to turn them on and off!

The majority of the repairs that come into the shop are routine, small, and require very little in the way of diagnosis or analysis. Most of the intermittents will require only a new connecting cord to straighten out. Most of the completely dead instruments will need only a fuse replacement or a rework of the AC plug. And you're going to find a great number of "silly" problems as well.

PRICING

How much can you charge for a repair? It's a function of how you figure the pricing on any work that you do. It is a matter of similar costs in your own local area, as well.

In general, when a repair comes in, chances are that the musician has recently completed a job and has a couple of days at least before the next one. Maybe it's a job you can do in only ten minutes, but you'd be better advised to ask him to leave the set since you can't get at it immediately. In this way you can, at your leisure, do a thorough analysis of the problems, perhaps find other things wrong, and can do a thorough repair as well. It's a wise move to have a couple of amplifiers in the shop that you can lend to customers while their units are being repaired.

THE DO-IT-YOURSELFER

One certain problem that walks into every repair shop is the guy who tries—unsuccessfully—to roll his own. It's usually the youngsters that bring these home-brew babies into the shop, and before we start digging into how to put them in working order, let's take a look at where they come from.

A group of musicians gets together and decides that they need amplifiers. Amplifiers are expensive, and young musicians aren't particularly known to be rolling in dough before they really make it. So they look for a less expensive way to get the amplifiers, and one of them is sure to suggest that they have a friend who "knows all about electronics" build them one. So they approach the friend with the proposition. He will construct the amplifier, and the group will pay for the parts.

Who's the friend? He's interested in electronics. He always carries an electronic magazine in with his school books. He might even have a ham license. He always gets good grades on his science exams, and always has a chassis full of knobs and switches for the annual Science Fair Experiment. But the truth of the matter is that what he doesn't know about electronics could fill fifty books. When the musicians say that he knows electronics, they're saying that compared to them he knows electronics.

I'm not trying to put down aspiring entrepreneurs. I used to be one, and I'll bet that most readers were as well. And part of being in the friend's position is that you can't resist the flattery in such a request, so you go ahead and agree to build the amplifier.

He might start by trying to design the unit himself. If he did, and it comes into your shop, thank him, but politely turn the job down. There's no way at all to make a profit on a job like this. Of course, if he's a nice kid, and you have the time, start by pushing the amplifier aside, and check over his diagram. If he designed the circuit himself, check it very carefully to find the boo-boo. And I'll bet you can't. Because these kids can justify almost anything, and chances are that the "design" will have been swiped from several existing schematics. Take a look at the components used, too. We've seen sets like these with power transformers swiped from old TV chassis, and assorted hybrid components that were never intended to work with each other.

Your first question should always be, "Did it ever work?" If it did, you're in pretty good shape. Now ask, "For how long?" If it operated for any length of time, you're in even better shape. But try one more question. "How'd it quit?" If it went in a blaze of light or a puff of smoke, take a look under the chassis for a quick clue. If you see something that looks replaceable that gave up the ghost, try replacing it but don't make any guarantees.

There's another factor to consider also. The enterprising friend might be along when your customers bring the amplifier in. For gosh sakes, don't embarass the kid, and don't try to flaunt your own knowledge at his expense. If you suspect that he's along, go out of your way to praise everything from the workmanship to the design. You'll win a friend for life, and you can easily tell which one built the unit when you see the buttons starting to pop.

As we said, don't waste a lot of time on these home-built jobs, but do make them work for you. If you can't find anything immediate to pin the fault on, make the point that it "was a good amplifier, but nothing lasts forever these days—built-in obsolesence. Why don't you guys consider a brand new commercially manufactured amplifier? Probably cost you a lot less than to repair this one. When they start to go, you have to nickel-and-dime them to death anyway, and..." OK. You've got the idea.

A Kit?

Sometimes you'll get a customer who has bought a kit to build the amplifier from. In fact, he may even go so far as to remove any trace of the kit manufacturer's name and substitute his own name in its place. Your problem, in this case, is to figure out which kit it was built from and then get hold of a schematic and troubleshooting manual for it.

With a kit, you've got one big thing going for you. But it may be a problem—a big problem. Ask any kit manufacturer about the repair jobs that come in. You won't believe the stories about the kit builder who was so leery of soldering that he bypassed the whole thing by using a tube of liquid solder. Or the kit builder who misunderstood the step that said "Cement diode to instrument case" and filled his VOM with cement—Portland Cement! So prepare for the worst, hope for the best, and open it up. You just might be lucky and find the problem at once, or it might take you a week or so if you aren't.

If the job is home-cooked, or if you haven't got the schematic, the first sane steps you can take will be hit or miss. Find out how it quit, then try to seek some rationale for the demise. Then sit down with a pencil, paper, and a lot of time, and try to reassemble a schematic out of the chaos.

Give up? That's smart of you. But in case you haven't given up on a tough dog like this one, and have really drawn the schematic, take a very close look at it and see if you can see anything at all that looks as if it has no business being in the circuit. When a do-it-yourselfer works, he first "designs" a circuit and then implements it. He may have made a mistake in the design, or he may have implemented it incorrectly.

Let's be a bit more positive in our approach. Let's assume that the amplifier was put together by a well-qualified and capable technician. The wiring is neatly done, there isn't a cold solder joint in the chassis, the corners are squared, the resistors are all lined up with color bands at the right ends, and are all mounted on component boards. He's gone to great pains to mount all the capacitors with the values pointed up so you can read them, and he even left little ends of each component lead on the boards so you can grasp them with your longnose pliers when you want to remove them. His cabling is so neat that you can trace any wire without having to use a continuity tester.

What do you do with a job like this when it doesn't work? How do you check an amplifier when there is no schematic available? Any chain is only as strong as its weakest link, and in any electronic circuit, that weak link is liable to be a tube. Begin any test by checking the tubes. If it's a solid-state affair, start checking the components most likely to go first. Look for capacitors that have opened or shorted, check fuses, and don't forget resistors that might have changed value with some extended life tests when a musician forgets to shut the equipment down overnight.

Your voltmeter can be pretty revealing as a test instrument also. If you start checking plate voltages on the tubes and come across something a little too low, you might find something suspect right there. Then start looking for some basic symptoms. Does it keep blowing fuses? Look for a dead short upstream of the power transformer. Try a power-off resistance check between B+ and the chassis. You might just turn something up that way, too. But make sure that you bleed the capacitors off first! Discharging power capacitors through your ohmmeter isn't going to do it any good at all!

Did you ever hear the hum that can come through a loudspeaker when you get a 60-Hz source too close to your amplifier? Actually, there are any number of devices that will generate more 60-Hz tone than you'll need to check the low end of any amplifier, and if you feed an audio signal (even 60 Hz) into an input stage, you ought to get something at the speaker.

We've run such tests using a number of devices, including a small demagnetizer for tape recorder heads, but the best yet is a transformer-type soldering gun touched to the input of each of the succeeding stages in the amplifier. It not only tells us where the trouble might be, but it re-melts the solder at those terminals and eliminates any cold solder joints at the same time!

Look for the unexpected in these home-built units, and assume nothing at all. We've seen more than one piece of bus wire (we thought) snaked through a length of cambric insulation. Now who would ever suspect that a simple piece of bus wire, put through an insulating sleeve to minimize shorts, could be open-circuited? Who would ever suspect? Who would take the trouble to put an ohmmeter from one end to another? We did, and we found it was open-circuited. But it turned out not to be bus wire at all; it was a small glass diode that the builder thought so much of that he felt a little insulating spaghetti would help protect it. It also helped keep it from view, and helped keep us from making any profit on the repair job.

Sometimes a commercially-built unit comes in for repair after it has been subjected to an amateur repair job that didn't quite work out. The kids find that their amplifier doesn't amplify so an amateur is called in as a consultant. He tries to figure out what's wrong with the unit. But he doesn't have any test equipment, and what's more, he doesn't have the necessary know-how to make a repair if he could figure out what went wrong. The thing that makes it rough is that these youngsters will make an attempt, based on poor judgment and less information.

They'll see a little wax that's run out of one end of an old paper capacitor and assume that the capacitor has melted. And kids who have seen burned-out light bulbs that have turned black will immediately spot a getter flash on a vacuum tube and decide that the tube has burned out. Sometimes they just think they ought to get a better look at a part and remove it from the circuit. If it passes this visual muster, they might not have time to put it back right away and pull out another part. Before long, they've got a table full of components and no idea at all where they belong.

We've had a chassis come in stripped like that—the parts all in a brown lunch bag—and a very sad and chastened would-be technician asking if we could "find the trouble." The point is that not every amateur repair job starts out as a basic design job that goes wrong. Not by a long shot. Frequently, you will get what looks like a straightforward repair on a standard, commercially-available amplifier. That's what it looks like, but isn't what it really is!

Two youngsters recently brought a Gibson amplifier in for repairs. The amplifier looked clean and typical, the kids had their guitars along, just in case, and we took the time to plug in and try it out while they were there. A quick check with another unit revealed that the guitars and connectors were not at fault, so we asked them to leave the amplifier with us.

When we got to the job, we couldn't get anywhere with a cursory examination, and went at the covers with a screwdriver. Then we pulled the chassis, removed the bottom plate and turned it over. Mr. Gibson never sent out an amplifier looking like that. We harked back to the sad-faced customers and recalled the entire conversation.

"We were playing this gig, and she like quit, man. Nobody was even touching it. Right in the middle of a solo, she pulls a bummer. So we brought it in to be fixed."

The only trouble was that they took it to an amateur first. Now you have to start by unfixing the amateur's work before you can even begin to repair what was wrong before he got it. So dig out the schematic diagram, start the painful process of rebuilding, and then, only then, can you get things straightened out. When the kids come back to pick the unit up, make sure you keep a time record of your work so you can bill it accordingly.

UNUSUAL COMPLAINTS

You will get some pretty strange complaints. Some of them are legitimate, others are the other kind. We've had instrumentalists complain that when they played, they got an electric shock from the steel strings. Of course, we know that the steel strings are completely insulated from any electrical source, and, if anything, the only possible thing they could touch would be the pickup which, unless it is grounded, can't be the cause of shock. When you get this sort of complaint, always check it out, just in case.

Other similar complaints are more worthy of consideration, and can be cured in many different ways. You might find an amplifier with a "hot" chassis, and this isn't any fun for the musician trying to use it. One way, if the amplifier works well other than the live chassis problem, is to insulate everything, so he can't touch bare metal. If you take this route, however, you haven't cured any problem, you've just isolated it. Start by finding the reason for the hot chassis, which could be anything from a shorted capacitor to an AC lead that moved.

Don't try to side-step this kind of problem with a hurry-up cure. Take the time and trouble to rectify the problem so it won't happen again. But what are you supposed to do when the guy comes in just before closing and tells you he needs the unit for a job that night? That money is no object, and can't you hurry it up a bit? Lend him a spare and have him leave his amplifier and a deposit, with the understanding that he brings it back the next night. That gives you all the next day to work on his unit at your leisure.

TEST EQUIPMENT

Maybe you envision an amplifier test setup with at least all of the bench equipment that you used in electronics school.

You may expect to need such equipment as a signal generator with complete coverage of the audio range, a good, broadband oscilloscope, a good VTVM, a circuit tracer, and assorted other test equipment. Since there are components in any amplifier you're going to be working on, you may feel that some well-calibrated component-testing instruments are needed, such as something better than a decade box to check resistors against or a laboratory analyzer to test capacitors to make sure they are of the proper and correct value. And how about those tubes and transistors? Can you test a tube simply with a drug-store type tube checker? Don't you need one of those big, impressive mutual conductance types?

Actually, you don't need any expensive equipment. It's a matter of practicality. Let's take a capacitor, for instance, one that you suspect is bad. Do you really have to know if there's a reason why it went bad? Do you have to know how it went bad? Absolutely not. All you have to know is that it is bad, and replace it. Capacitors aren't that expensive, and the "pull-out-and-replace" method of repair is time-honored. You don't need the fancy equipment, and if you insist on stocking it for your own peace of mind, rest assured that you won't be using it. Repairing musical instrument amplifiers is very like repairing anything else you will ever turn your hand to. It is a dollars and sense operation if you're going to work profitably. Your customer couldn't care less if you tune the amplifier so it exceeds manufacturers specifications. He couldn't be less concerned about the increased frequency response. Chase these gremlins, and you're wasting time and money.

All your customer knows is that he bought the thing and used it, then it quit. Remember, if it were still under warranty, the manufacturer would be looking at it now, not you. All the customer wants is for you to get the thing working again, and he wants you to do it in the fastest, best, least expensive way, and not necessarily in that order, either.

So far, what equipment has been used in the testing we've done? Really, not very much. We've had an assist from a VOM, and we've used a great deal of common sense. We may have even taken a look at a schematic, too. We have not used an oscilloscope, have not used fancy testers, and quite frankly, have not had much need for a lot of the electronic doo-dads we may have learned about in electronic school. And that's precisely what your customer is paying you for. What is wanted are your skills, your perception, your ingenuity and your intelligence, not the fancy equipment.

Most of the amplifiers you're going to be seeing will be plagued with the same sorts of problems, and you will soon come to recognize these problems by their very symptoms. What's more, you will learn that many of the amplifiers produced by any given manufacturer will have the same essential ailments. While it takes a lot of time to develop, you will, in such time, come to know exactly what to expect by the manufacturer's name and the symptoms you hear. When you get to that point, you can just about get rid of all of your test equipment, because you'll use it only to confirm a preconceived notion anyway! As we said earlier, amplifier repairing is a dollars and sense game. The more you have to invest in test equipment before you start, the more you have to amortize before you can start to make a profit.

As far as the actual labor goes, the more time you spend in the textbook method of locating and isolating a fault, the more time it takes, and, therefore, the less profit you make on a given job. You're far better off to take a chance on replacing a component or two that would be suspect due to the symptoms than to start a willy-nilly procedure of circuit tracing. If you should be lucky enough to nail down the bad component with the first shot, the profit on the job can be enormous—almost enough to pay for the time you lose tracing the next job!

Is it really "luck?" No, it isn't. What it really is, when you get right down to it, is intelligence and skill. And there's a little more, too. There's an inborn, investigative sense that makes the difference between a "technician" and a "good technician."

When you've located the source of a problem, don't fool around any longer. If a half-watt resistor is the suspect component, it really doesn't pay to test the old unit, or to fiddle around with it. Just yank it out and replace it. If it turns out that you were right, you've saved all that testing time, and scored a better profit. If you were wrong, then keep looking.

Some technicians take a different route. When they suspect a component, they unsolder one leg of the component to get it out of the circuit, and then they "tack-solder" a new component into place, leaving the leads the full length and unclipped. If they were wrong, the new component can be easily removed in a relatively undamaged condition and returned to the stock. If they were right, the remains of the old component are clipped out and the new one properly connected with the right lead dress and length. We aren't recommending that repairs be made in a slap-dash fashion, just to get them done. What we are saying, however, is that the more time you spend on any given job, the more it costs you and the less profit you will see on the bottom line.

FINAL CHECKOUT

When you feel that a job is complete and the amplifier is functioning properly, your next step should be an operational test in which the amplifier is allowed to sit and cook under power-on operation. We like such checks to run for at least the amplifier's normal on time operation. During a session, an amplifier can be expected to run as long as four hours without a rest. If you can operate the amplifier for this period of time without any problems, you can assume that you've made an adequate repair.

Trouble-shooting Techniques

4

The circuitry in most amplifier systems is relatively simple in comparison with other electronic equipment. There is no problem with convergence or color balance as there is in a television receiver, and no critical tuned circuits as are found in radio receivers. But don't get the idea that an amplifier is a "piece of cake" either. While it's more or less true that an amplifier consists only of amplifier circuits, there's still a lot you've got to know in order to properly troubleshoot and effect a repair. An amplifier circuit—any amplifier—consists of several sub-circuits. To simply look at an amplifier as the back end of something else—a receiver or hi-fi system—is a distorted view to the amplifier. To start with, the amplifier must have a power supply, and many of the problems in an amplifier can be traced to supply trouble.

POWER SUPPLIES

Some of the larger amplifiers have compound supplies that deliver at least two high-voltage DC outputs. Some units need a 250-300 volt low-voltage supply and a separate high-voltage supply on the order of 600 volts to drive the output stages. If an amplifier has such a supply, remember that the higher high voltage can be present while the low high voltage is not. Filament supplies are also sometimes strung in two branches, each operated by a separate winding of the transformer, or even by a separate filament transformer.

The schematic is essential to repair any of these units, for you've got to know how the circuits are wired. Fusing is not always obvious, but there may be a primary fuse in each leg of the AC line, along with B+ fuses in the grounded center tap of the high-voltage transformers. The high-voltage fuses aren't always easy to see either; sometimes they are the type with pigtail leads that are wired into place under the chassis. We have found that the best way to replace these fuses is with a double-ended clip arrangement that snaps onto the burned-out fuse and offers an accommodation to attach the new fuse with no soldering.

Generally, the better quality amplifiers have overrated power supply components that are not easy to damage. However, under severe short-circuit conditions, even the best will burn out. If there's a weak link in any amplifier supply circuit, it's generally the rectifier system. Rectifiers range from epoxy or glass diodes in a bridge configuration to the same components used in voltage doublers in the smaller units. We've also run across selenium stacks, right on up to full-wave tube-type rectifiers.

In keeping with the combined need to impress in order to sell, coupled with the requirements for preheating the filaments of some of the big jobs, some units have a system of pilot lamps and time-delay relays with circuitry complex enough to befuddle a computer expert! In order to assure sufficient preheating of filaments, turning on the filament switch also starts a delay relay. After it has heated sufficiently, the time-delay relay closes the circuit to the B+ supply, and, incidentally, turns on another pilot lamp, usually colored red.

On some of the newer, super-fancy guitars, amplifier controls and indicators are grouped right on the guitar body. Of course, this makes for a more complex connecting cord. Some even have winking LEDs (light-emitting diodes) to attract the fancy of a musician who wants to perform his own light show.

To isolate power supply problems, you're best advised to take voltage readings (refer to manufacturer's voltage charts first) directly at the power supply test points or connecting terminals. To determine whether a no-voltage condition is caused by a supply component or an amplifier-circuit component, disconnect the amplifier components from the supply. Expect a slightly higher reading than indicated if the amplifier circuits are disconnected. Where compound voltages are used, always disconnect **all** supply connections before applying primary voltage. To allow the high-high voltage to remain connected while removing the low-high voltage might cause damage to the amplifier system, especially to output tube screen supplies.

Transistor power supplies will also be encountered, and these can range from simple batteries to rechargeable batteries and straight AC-operated power supplies. Suffice it to say that there are rarely any surprises in store for you with these systems; the only place where you might have trouble is with a rechargeable battery system using nickel-cadmium batteries. Check to see that the charger is functioning correctly and that there is sufficient electrolyte in the cells. If there is any question of the cell's capacity to accept a charge and function, by all means, replace the cell.

Caution! In dealing with the power supply of an amplifier, hazardous voltages may be present. Always work on these units with the power off, and use a grounding rod several times to insure that capacitors are properly discharged! A suitable grounding rod consists of a conductive metal pole piece, usually formed of No. 8 copper wire flattened at one end and attached to a piece of plastic rod at least a foot long. The conductor is connected by flexible braid to a small alligator clip. In use, attach the clip to the chassis ground. Then, while holding the plastic rod, touch the metal tip to all capacitors and to all B+ voltage terminals to drain off any residual charge before working on a unit. It is wise to be extremely careful about electrical safety. The guy who says he's not afraid of electricity is either a fool or a liar. The ones who really aren't afraid are all dead. Wetting your finger and sticking it into a lamp socket to check for electricity doesn't impress me at all!

PREAMPLIFIER STAGES

Many amplifier problems occur in the preamplifier stages. While it was once common practice to use high-output microphones (such as Air Force throat mikes) as contact pickups, the common procedure these days is to use magnetic or dynamic units which require a good measure of preamplification in order to function.

Naturally, the signal is beefed up by the preamp stages, and then whatever output these stages produce is fed to additional amplifiers. If any hum gets in at this level, you get a 60-Hz roar out of the speakers. In fact, most of the hard-to-pinpoint troubles that occur in an amplifier develop in the lower stages of amplification. Two of the most common ills are

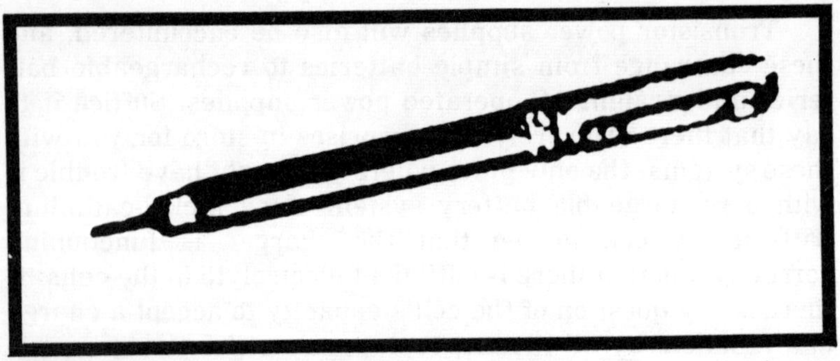

Handy, self-contained "Mosquito" signal injector speeds up troubleshooting.

traceable to this point. A small, relatively minor amount of heater-to-cathode leakage in a preamp stage will provide this kind of hum in sufficient quantity to totally mask the signal you're trying to get through. Another problem is feedback, caused by microphonics. A loose internal element in an early-stage tube will produce howls in the speaker system.

Early-stage problems often manifest themselves at the loudspeaker, and you might be prone to work backwards from the speaker, making it a long, tough row to hoe before you get to the source of the trouble. If a preamplifier stage quits, it will interrupt the passage of signal to the subsequent stages. With the volume raised, you get no signal at all, and a hiss or hum at best, depending on whether the amplifier is a tube or transistor model.

A signal injector can be a handy item at this point, and there are several that are more than adequate, in the form of simple probes with oscillators built right in. Start with maximum level on the injector and work backward from the output stages, applying the injector to the control grid of the tube or the base of a transistor. Continue back through the circuit in this fashion, reducing the injected signal level (which should be in the audio range, incidentally) and reducing the amplifier's volume as you go back; you should be gaining additional amplification at each stage. You'll finally get to the offending stage, and can work further on locating the faulty component.

Another handy device for this sort of circuit tracing is a small oscilloscope. You don't need anything fancy or with sophisticated controls. As long as the scope has a sweep oscillator so you can display a single waveform, you're all set.

Connect the scope to the amplifier's output, and it will tell you what's happening where in the amplifier circuit. Among other things, the scope can be used for operational checks and comparison against the manufacturer's waveform sheets which are usually available to any technician.

One of the critical factors to a musician is that he not just get amplification, but amplification without distortion, unless he elects to introduce controlled distortion himself. A scope will show you if distortion is present; a simple sine wave displayed at the input to a stage should also be a simple sine wave enlarged by amplification at the output of that stage. If it appears at the output with flats, cutoffs, or additional spikes, you've got problems that will appear at the loudspeakers in the form of noise or distortion.

The lower level stages of amplification are also critical when they're being tested. If the charts indicate that a resistance is measured with a 20,000-ohms-per-volt ohmmeter, be sure that you use the same sort of instrument for the test. If you load the circuit down with the wrong type of test equipment, chances are that you will get false readings that have little or no bearing on existing conditions, which can throw you off on the wrong track. Usually, you're going to find that early stage problems are usually traced to the amplifying component itself, tube or transistor. Replacement will generally restore operation in the normal fashion.

However, not all problems in these stages are due to tubes or transistors, and we have seen many instances where capacitors and resistors have opened or shorted. Many technicians make a simple test for open-circuit resistors by simply paralleling a suspect resistor with a resistor that's known to be good, with a value that approximates the value that is supposed to be in the circuit. If a resistor is open, this "bridging" test will suddenly bring the amplifier to life. Naturally, when using a test like this, always replace the faulty resistor with a resistor of exactly the correct value.

Short-circuited capacitors, capacitors that have "punched through," can be isolated only by checking for continuity with an ohmmeter or by the old pull-out-and-replace method. The latter is much to be recommended, unscientific as it seems, for in order to properly check a shorted or leaky capacitor with an ohmmeter, at least one end of it must be removed from the circuit to ensure that the readings you take are not being affected by another portion of the circuit.

CONTROLS

Usually, the balance, tone, and volume controls follow the preamplification stages and precede the intermediate stages. In any decent amplifier circuit, a complex divider network is used with these controls, in which fixed resistors, buffer capacitors and variable resistances are used. Should a control fail to function properly, while everything else seems to be in relatively good order, you might examine the entire divider-buffer network for a component failure.

At the input to the preamplifier stages, there's generally what must be called a "mode" switch which enables the musician to select any of several input jacks so that one or several sources can be played through the amplifier.

Sometimes, a musician gets a bit carried away and forgets that there's a stop on the control. When this happens, and he yanks the control over too hard, you can find either a damaged switch, or, more frequently, a damaged knob. Neither of these problems is terribly difficult to repair by replacement, with a word of caution thrown in.

The various input jacks are always subject to oxidation and corrosion, as we've mentioned before. However, many musicians, especially those that play a fixed stand for months on end, tend to leave their equipment set up from night to night. As a result, many of the jacks can take a "set." The spring contacts of input jacks seem particularly subject to this. While appearing to be making good contact, they may have in reality, lost the ability to flex. If you suspect this sort of problem, which can act like an intermittent, simply apply a probe, such as the eraser-end of a pencil, to the jack's contact spring (with the power off) and press to re-form the spring. If the spring is brittle and snaps off, the entire jack will have to be replaced.

Frequently, we have run into controls on amplifiers that "didn't work right" and found that rotating the control's knob caused the entire control to rotate. This happens when the control mounting nut works loose. In many cases, the owner of the instrument will simply continue to rotate the control until the wires attached to it become taut and twisted, and when the control can rotate no further, the shaft will turn.

When you get a job like this in the shop, don't try to price it until you open up the unit and see what's doing on the inside.

Start by trying to untangle and untwist all the wiring, and dress it in as close a fashion as you think it should go. Then unsolder the connections, remove the control and remount it properly. This may require a large flat washer because an internally-mounted lockwasher acts like a rotary hole saw when it turns and can chew up the inside of the cabinet.

After checking the control to make sure it's still usable, remount it through the washer, placing a 3/8ths lockwasher over the shaft mount first. Run the shaft through the hole, place a flat washer over the mount and then a fine, inside lockwasher over that. Add the nut, tighten it down, and you're all set to rewire the control.

You may find, however, that this sort of operation requires the use of an extra-long threaded mount on the control. You can get such controls from almost any electronics distributor. To use such a control, two separate nuts must be used on the mount, one to act as a stop. In any case, draw the nuts down tight against the lockwashers with a nut-driver, and make sure they're tight.

Frequently, a control needs servicing or replacement. The things that can go wrong with these controls (primarily potentiometers) are exactly the things that you suspected might go wrong. Often, a wirewound pot is set at a level so that in its voltage-dividing function a large portion of the power is allocated to a small portion of the winding. As a result, the potentiometer will burn open.

Your first reaction on seeing this sort of thing might be that it is really a design error. However, this might not always be the case. A musician who wants the biggest and the best might have overpurchased. As a result, if the sound is to be kept within usable limits, he must set controls to a level below that which the unit was primarily designed for. You can usually bring the amplifier back to standard with a direct replacement control, but the problem will only repeat itself. Consultation with the amplifier's owner, however, might reveal that a small parallel fixed resistor across the pot to help absorb some of the load might make for a better type of repair. If you do such a repair, always leave a note inside the case to explain to the next technician what you've done. It's a simple courtesy that isn't practiced often enough these days.

On smaller units, especially, pay close attention to the taper of the potentiometer that you're replacing. While most use an audio taper, we have run across potentiometers with an S taper. The S-taper pot provides a great deal of audio with the beginning of rotation, and then a smaller degree of increase during the remainder of the control range. Many cheaper amplifiers are sold to the unknowing on the basis of "Look at that power, man... You just crack the volume control and it blasts!" If you replace such a pot with one having an audio taper, the user is going to accuse you of everything from stealing his good tubes to downgrading his amplifier "'cause you don't dig rock."

You'll find two types of controls in most amplifiers. There are the wirewound and the deposited carbon types. To a point, servicing these controls is roughly similar. Dirt builds up on both, and if this occurs, you must apply some contact cleaner. There are two types of contact cleaners that are suitable for this sort of operation, and many methods of using them. The large syringe that screws over the control shaft will flood the control with cleaner, and the smaller, hypo-type allows you to place a smaller amount of cleaner where it will do the most good.

Perhaps the most painstaking cleaning we've seen is also the most effective. One technician completely removes a control and unsolders the connections. He then lifts the three small ears from each side, so he can remove the control cover and actually see what's going on inside. If the control is damaged, he can actually see the damage and cleaning is no longer a matter of guesswork. He uses a cotton swab dipped in control cleaner to do this job, and on completion, he easily reassembles the control and installs it once again.

Potentiometers suffer from all sorts of damage. The control that's been used to death (one musician gets his vibrato by jiggling the control) or hasn't been touched at all are subject to wear. Look under the slider to see if the layer of deposited carbon is still intact. If a control is bad, all you can do is either clean it or change it. Many times, after it's been cleaned, you will still have faulty operation. This simply means that the carbon layer is gone and the unit must be replaced.

Switches are another problem area that you will have to deal with, and many of these problems can be caused by the musicians themselves. One do-it-yourself musician thought it would be a good idea to remove the detent ball from a rotary switch so he could effortlessly and smoothly switch from one input to another. It worked out all right until the switch got a little worn and started making up its own mind about which input it liked best. That's when the unit came in for a repair. Now, anybody who has ever tried to remove a detent ball knows they can't just fall out, but by the time a musician gets through explaining "like man, y'know, man, like, dig..." you'll have replaced the ball.

Maybe it's the atmosphere of the places that these chaps play in, or maybe it's just the noxious city air. It isn't our place to comment on ecology, but there's a lot of sulphur dioxide, smoke shade and particulate matter about. As a result, you get switch contacts that are coated with oxidation, and sometimes the best you can hope for is a high-resistance connection. Naturally, you'll clean these contacts and shun the temptation to spray a plastic fixative over them so they stay clean. Actually, this would only insulate the contacts and render them useless. But you **can** take a few simple steps to keep the oxidation from coming back too rapidly. Two materials that will assist tremendously are activated charcoal, which you can obtain under the brand name Requa Charo, and tack inside the amplifier case. This stuff will absorb the gasses before they get to your cherished contacts. Another way out is paradichlorbenzine (mothballs) which have the same effect.

Mounting New Controls

When a control must be replaced, you may find that there are as many as eight wires going to the control. If it's a ganged unit with a switch on the back and more than one wire connected to any of the lugs on the control, the total number of wires can be higher. If you start by desoldering all the wires, and then remove the control, you've got at least a 2-hour job of circuit tracing against the schematic to see which wires are supposed to go where when you install the new control.

You can save yourself a lot of trouble by taking the time to do one of two things. One solution is to draw a pictorial of the control and as you remove a wire from it, note on the pictorial the wire color and where it is connected. Then, after the new control is in place, you have no trouble in reconnecting all of the wires correctly.

A still better way is to draw the pictorial on a piece of paper and assign numbers to each lug. Then, as you remove the wires, you can apply small, self-adhesive wire markers to the wire with matching numbers. It may take a little time, but it sure does pay off when you get to reassembling everything! In our shop, we prefer the latter method, for there's been more than one case where the wires weren't coded in such a way that was meaningful at all. For example, if there are two or three red wires on the control, you may have a problem remembering which red wire goes to which lug. The numbering system may be a little more time-consuming, but it pays off.

Murphy's Law also applies here. If you try to depend on your memory (after all, how long does it take to change a control? I'll **surely** be able to remember what goes where) then you can also depend on the fact that as soon as you disconnect that last wire, the phone will ring, or another customer will come in, or something will happen, and you're going to forget.

Chances are that when you buy a new control, the shaft will be a lot longer than you need. However, the long shaft usually has circular grooves at various points along its length; these are designed so you can cut off the excess part of the shaft. In other cases, the shaft will simply be straight (and too long).

Somebody, who must have worked as a plumber at some point in his life, started passing around the fallacious information that those grooves in the shaft were "snap-offs" and that all you have to do was grip one end of the shaft with pliers and bend it back and forth to break it off. Not so! If you try to do this, the shaft will indeed break, and at its weakest point—right inside the control!

No, to shorten any shaft, you've got to saw it off. And there's a right way to do this, also. Start by clamping the end of the shaft in a vise. Not the control, which will crush in the vise, but the shaft. With the shaft clamped in the vise, measure the length you want to remove and, using a fine-toothed hacksaw, either cut in the proper groove or start cutting the ungrooved shaft at the desired point. Periodically, rotate the shaft to get a new area of cut. When you have completely cut the shaft off, deburr the end with a fine file, and you're ready to install it.

If the shaft on your control is too short, you may be able to use a shaft extension, which can be attached to the short shaft and cut to the length you need, or, if the control is fully recessed, you can use a shaft coupling which will allow you to extend the shaft beyond the panel.

Suppose a control goes bad, and you don't have easy access to a proper and direct replacement? Just how "bendable" are the resistances within which you can work? The fact of the matter is that they are usually **plenty** flexible, and—within reason—any control will work.

This does not mean that you can replace a 1K pot with a 100K pot and make it work satisfactorily. But if you have something that will come close to the required resistance, chances are that it will do the job nicely, and that the customer will never know the difference. What's more, if he wants the unit back in a hurry, and most customers seem to, he'll be a lot happier with the replacement control that you put in than he would be with a long wait while you get an exact replacement.

If a control is designed to cover a full range of resistances in one full rotation, and you have to spread the range with a control of lower value, all it may mean is that the desired setting will appear elsewhere on the control. By the same token, if the higher resistance control is used, this may require that the setting be slightly compressed. The client will never even be aware of the change, if the total resistance is close to that used before. Given a choice in making such replacements, always go for the higher resistance value. We've often had to substitute values in this manner, and have never had a callback because of this.

Occasionally, you will come across a non-standard potentiometer that will defy your ability to identify it. Sometimes a manufacturer manages to save a buck in building his amplifiers by buying up a job lot of controls that aren't provided with any sort of standard marking. Sometimes he simply buys controls made to his own order, and with his own coded identification so you can't tell what it really is.

When this happens, don't feel that you must order the replacement from the manufacturer directly. Of course, if you happen to be in the same town as the manufacturer, it might be worth a phone call to save you some headaches. Otherwise, all need not be lost. What you have to do is measure the resistance so you can approximate the replacement part. If the control is intact, you simply measure the resistance across the two outside terminals.

However, you can depend on the fact that the control will not be intact, or you wouldn't be replacing it in the first place. Place one lead of your ohmmeter at the center terminal or wiper arm and the other lead at one of the end terminals. Start the rotation of the wiper at that end and slowly move the arm, noting the value of resistance when it drops out to infinity at the break. Write this value down, and then place the test leads between the center or wiper contact and the other outside arm. Continue the rotation, and you will see the resistance suddenly reappear as you pass by the break. Rotate to the end, and note that resistance. Now total the two figures, and you will have a resistance value somewhat below the actual value. Select a replacement of the next higher standard value, and you should be all right.

Knob Repairs

Believe it or not, sometimes the musician cranks the gain up a little too high. Lord alone knows why. Perhaps the audience is too noisy, maybe the other guitarist is having problems with his own amplifier, or perhaps the amplifier just doesn't have the output it needs. So he cranks the volume wide open. Then he tries to crank it a little more open and the knob starts spinning free. We've seen cases like this. Believe it or not, a pointed set screw has been known to gouge its own groove in the control shaft and start spinning.

The only quick cure for a thing like this is to remove the knob and reset it with another knob. Use a type with a threaded brass or steel insert and a larger set screw. Tighten it down so it won't turn free again, and caution the customer against any further forcing under penalty of a complete control change. You won't be lying to him about this, for that's truly the next step.

In some cases we have even seen amplifiers with the knobs glued to the control shafts. When this happens, you're going to have your hands full. The best bet is to remove the knob in any way that you can. One of the most efficient ways that we've found is to start by cracking the knob off, and we use a large, old wire cutter for this. If the knob had a metal insert, you'll find this out when the plastic is removed. Getting the insert off once it has been glued in place can also be traumatic, but is not an impossible task.

A tool called a "nut cracker," which is used for removing frozen nuts, will help. Another way is to try heat and lots of it. We like to use a small soldering torch for this, in which case a heat sink must be used between the insert and the control, just to protect the control. And a good heat sink is the panel and nut to which the control is attached. Use plenty of heat and, at the same time, pull on the insert with a pair of pliers. This will usually soften the glue and allow you to remove the insert from the shaft.

Before you can replace the knob, however, you're probably going to have to clean the rest of the glue from the shaft, and this is best accomplished with a small file. The heated and baked glue usually responds well to the file, flaking off rather than having to be filed off. When you get the new knob mounted and return the instrument to the customer, caution him against such actions. When you set the price for the job, remember how hard you had to work at it.

MULTIPLE PREAMPLIFIERS

To add a bit of complexity to the situation, you'll find that several preamplifiers are used in some amplifiers. In order for a combo to function, they need one or two guitars, at least one bass, and a handy assortment of microphones as well. As a general rule, the guitarists will have their own amplifiers, as will the bassist. They also tend to use a microphone input on their own amplifiers for vocals.

However, the trend now is to a pooling of resources, so they can buy one big amplifier that they can all plug into. Since the frequency range of a guitar is different from that of a bass, a microphone, or other instruments, some amplifiers offer the musician a multiplicity of inputs, and each input feeds its own particular preamplifier. The preamp, in turn, drives a single power amplifier section. In some units, the preamplifier is on the same chassis with the power amplifier, or you may find separately mounted preamp units. These can be sold as "add-ons" later, so a guitarist can buy the amplifier, then later on add his friend's bass preamp.

Actually, having these multiple preamplifiers is an excellent aid in diagnosing repair problems in a preamplifier stage. Should the guitar fail to amplify while the bass operates fine, it's a simple process of elimination to isolate the problem. Further isolation can be aided by cross-connecting the two units to determine quite accurately where the trouble lies. It should also be pointed out that separate preamplifier input sections are also available in the form of etched-circuit boards that can easily be plugged in.

REVERBERATION

While not a preamplifier in the strictest sense, reverberation units, which provide "echo chamber" effect, appear on many diagrams as an input system. The reverberation system generally is connected by a plug-in jack to a foot switch. The switch is not a variable control, but an on-off switch circuit.

The reverberation system is a miniature amplifier in itself, with a preamplifier that takes a portion of the signal from the amplifier's preamp circuit, feeds it through the reverb preamplifier to the reverb amplifier, and back into the amplifier's intermediate circuits with a phase delay. If the reverberator is not functioning, make sure the locking cord is free, make sure all connectors are secured, and that the reverberation level control is turned up sufficiently.

ELECTRONIC TREMOLO

Tremolo sounds like the sort of rapid picking one associates with a mandolin. Of course, a skilled guitarist can accomplish tremolo with little difficulty, but now-a-days, an unskilled guitarist can get the same effect by closing a switch.

Typical of the way a tremolo circuit works is this description from the Heath Company: A tremolo oscillator is a phase-shift device which produces a sub-sonic output. This circuit develops a signal that can be varied from about 4 to 14 Hz by a rate control in the phase-shift network. The amplitude of the oscillator signal is varied by the depth control. The signal is then capacitively coupled to the base of the tremolo modulator transistor.

An LDR (light-dependent resistor) is coupled to a lamp. As current is drawn, the lamp glows brighter and dimmer, changing the value of the LDR. This varies from a very low resistance (practically a short circuit) to practically an open circuit. Since the LDR is connected between the reverb channel signal path and ground, its resistance variations modulate the reverb channel signal with the low-frequency tremolo signal.

As you can see, there are many ways to create a tremolo effect by electronic means, which vary from multivibrator circuits to a unique motor-driven chopper in which a variable-speed DC motor is fitted with a disc and aperture located between a light source and photocell.

One of the earlier experiments in this sort of special effect was accomplished on an instrument called the vibraharp, which is like a marimba. The first of this genre of instruments is the xylophone, in which tuned wooden blocks are struck by mallets. An outgrowth of this is a xylophone using tuned metal bars, like those on a door chime. Resonating tubes, added under the bars and also tuned, make the instrument into the marimba, and the addition of motor-driven, rotating discs inside each of the tubes resulted in the vibraharp, with its mellow, pulsating echo that is so haunting.

INTERMEDIATE STAGES

Following the preamplifier, there can be any of a number of driver stages ahead of the output stages. Exactly how many there are and what their function is depends on the type of amplifier you are dealing with, and the amount of drive needed for the finals. Basically, it is the function of the intermediate drivers to build the signal up a bit at a time, so that it will be sufficient to drive the inputs to the final amplifiers. However, in today's more sophisticated units, the driver stages usually perform additional functions as well.

To describe these intermediate stages simply as level increasers is far too simplistic. The output tubes or transistors are fed the signal by a stage called the driver, and the stage preceding this is called the predriver. These stages also control the amount of tonal feed from the preamplifier circuits. Essentially, the intermediate stages are standard circuits, and as such are subject to exactly the same ills as other amplifier stages.

A difficulty in isolating faults in the intermediate stages is that you can't very well use the substitution method to locate a malfunctioning component. This is especially true where more than one problem exists. Frequently, they can be traced to faulty components, more so than in either input stages or final output stages.

Some of the problems you might run into include the following, and you'd just as well prepare for them. In some amplifiers, a portion of the output signal is fed back, generally through a capacitor in a Williamson configuration, to one of the driver stages. Should all else appear in good order, and the level is markedly reduced, you might try replacing this feedback capacitor.

In transistor circuit amplifiers, the intermediate stages are generally direct-coupled, but capacitive and inductive couplings are used as well. Where the signal seems to just disappear in this portion of the circuit, and where a coupling device is used, by all means check the coupling to be sure that the signal is getting through. The handiest way to accomplish this is with an oscilloscope. If you get a signal at the input to the coupling device and nothing at the output, chances are that the coupling device is at fault.

It was once the fashion in musical instrument amplifiers to mount the amplifier chassis inside the loudspeaker enclosure, which was either open or partially open at the back. The chassis was chromium plated, as were the surfaces of all metal parts mounted on the chassis, including tube shields, metal capacitors, and transformer bells. The glare from a reasonably large amplifier could blind you. This fact comes to mind simply because you may still run across an amplifier of this type and find transformer coupling in the intermediate stages. The modern concept is to hide everything electronic except for the control panel, so you need have no qualms about replacing a chromed transformer with an exact duplicate that's simply painted black.

And this brings up another point. What some of the youngsters will do to be a little bit different might give you some intriguing thoughts. Frank is a local New York amplifier specialist, and the rock groups all seem to know that he's the guy to see when they have amplifier troubles. One guitarist came to him with a malfunctioning amplifier, and the problem turned out to be a shorted turn or two in the power transformer.

This musician had a girl friend whose forte was pop art, and she had "done" the amplifier with acrylic paints so it looked like a hash nightmare. But replacing the big transformer with a black one—plain black enamel, mind you—made the violent reds, yellows and greens look sick. The musician was a bit concerned, but Frank solved the problem handily. He removed the screws that held the transformer cover (called bells) in place, and interchanged them so the new transformer looked just like the old one! It's a small detail, but it sure helped. No wonder they keep coming back to him.

One characteristic problem that occurs in the intermediate stages is a reduction in amplification. Should an intermediate stage device, be it tube or transistor, start to go sour, it may not provide sufficient drive to give the final stages a sufficient signal to provide adequate output. Voltage checks and oscilloscope patterns will all seem proper, but there is no amplification and you do get hum. The first thought would naturally be that there is no drive from the microphone or pick-up, yet interchanging or checking will prove that this unit is working adequately. The final amplifier stages are also working well, and it's a problem to isolate the fault.

If the unit is tube-operated, by all means check the tubes. If it is solid state, check everything else first. The proper way to isolate a problem of this type is to work backward through the circuit from the output amplifier(s). Be very suspicious when you lose or find a reduction of signal. One of the problems that can be introduced in the intermediate stages is that the amplifying component, tube or transistor, may be functioning perfectly well itself, yet is hampered in its operation by a faulty circuit component.

A resistor that has changed value can shift the level of bias to a point of almost cutoff. A tube's screen-dropping resistor can have the same effect if it changes value. And, rare as it may seem, a leaky coupling capacitor can create similar problems. We have seen amplifiers that have had insulation abraded from wires because of vibration, and have witnessed cases where capacitive coupling occurred through wires to the extent that a short circuit had developed. The key is that with an amplifier of this type, you've got to start looking for the impossible to happen.

FEEDBACK

When the amplifier volume is turned up high, a howl occurs. Most of the time, you can correct this by changing the location of the speaker in relationship to the pickup. But what if you have this kind of problem where speaker and amplifier are built into one box, and the pickup is a guitar-mounted microphone that can't pick up a sound from the air and feed it back?

Frank, whom we mentioned previously, ran into a strange one like this. There was no question about the problem—it was feedback. When you "cracked" the volume on, the set would oscillate and howl uncontrollably. The volume control had no effect—the noise was at full strength.

Frank turned the unit on and unplugged the mike. It still howled. He removed the final amplifier stage, and the noise stopped completely. That was as it should be. The musician who brought the set in was watching, and he said "Wow! You sure found the trouble fast!" "Not so fast," said Frank, and he replaced the tube. The howling started again. He placed his fingers over the driver tube to pull it out, but before he was able to remove the tube, the howl disappeared and gave way to a soft hum. Frank placed a nearby tube shield over the offending driver, and the amplifier worked properly. But while the problem was solved, it was not cured.

Obviously, the tube was picking up a signal through its glass envelope, but had not been fitted with a shield-type socket. Frank looked at the 7-pin miniature tube, drilled out the two rivets that held the socket in place and added a shield base. He replaced the base and socket with a pair of No. 4 screws, added the proper shield, and the amplifier was repaired and working.

One non-operating amplifier came into a shop with a request for repair. It was a small, 5-tuber, and the bench tech started to pull tubes to see if one of them could be the problem. The first tube out was a 12AX7. It checked OK. The next tube was also a 12AX7. It was good, too. But when the next three tubes all turned out to be the same type, he got a little suspicious, and turned the chassis over to see if he could find a tube diagram. He found one, and the tubes in the chassis in no way agreed with the tubes on the diagram! He looked up at his customer. "You didn't try to fix this yourself, did you?" The customer vehemently denied having touched the set. He checked again, examining tube numbers against the plan. Nope. Somebody had removed **all** the tubes and replaced them with one type!

What had actually happened here was that the customer **knew** how expensive an amplifier repair could be and took it upon himself to try changing tubes. He removed one tube from the chassis, took it to the local electronics store and ordered five like it. He then removed all the old ones, and put in the new ones; lucky that they all had miniature 9-pin bases! Of course, the unit didn't work at all, and having gone as far as he dared, he was ready to bring it to a professional. Now everybody **knows** that if you try to repair your own set, the pro will jack up the prices on you, just to teach you a lesson. So when he brought the set in, he insisted that it had been working and stopped, and that he didn't do a thing to it! Needless to say, the repairman did all right. He put the proper tubes in the proper sockets and the set worked. He collected a service

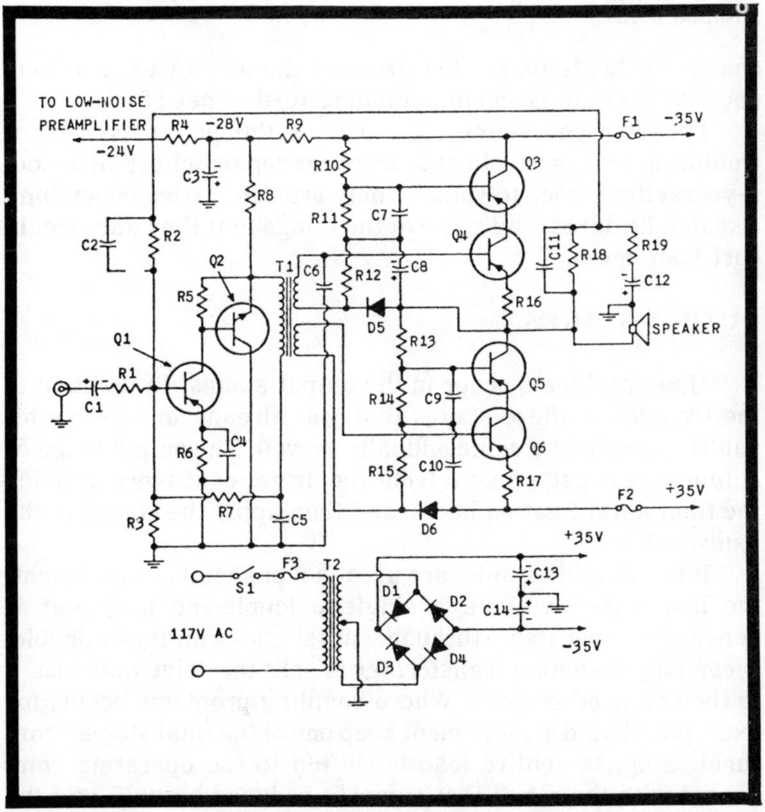

Interstage coupling using a transformer to drive four output transistors. Each half of pushpull stage has two transistors in pushpush.

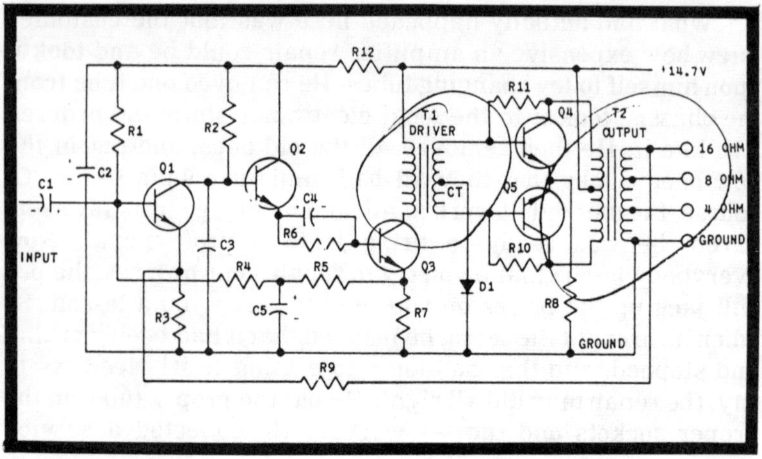

Interstage transformers with a center-tapped secondary used to drive a pushpull output.

charge for his time, the list price on the new tubes, and four new 12AX7s that the customer had no further need for!

The do-it-yourselfers are one of the prime causes of trouble as well as excellent sources for repair jobs. When a do-it-yourselfer comes to you, it's only after he's tried everything else that he dares, and some of the things that they dare would curl your teeth.

OUTPUT STAGES

Many problems occur in the output stages. In addition to the troubles in these stages that you already are aware of, you're going to find some oddballs as well. The output stage or output stages get a signal from the driver or drivers, provide the final amplification boost, and then apply the signal to the loudspeaker.

If two amplifier units are used in a pushpull arrangement, the last driver will be a single-to-double-end unit that is generally operated through a single-primary-to-double-secondary matching transformer to split the drive and pass it to the balanced outputs. Where coupling problems occur, for example, should a component keep one of the final stages from functioning, the entire load is shifted to the operating component with the result that signal is reduced by half, and the operating unit won't continue to operate in this unbalanced mode for very long.

In the normal course of servicing such a unit, you will no doubt locate a faulty amplifier tube or transistor. You replace it, thinking that you have solved the problem. Further investigation may reveal, however, that the amplifier you thought was good is actually not operating, and that this caused the bad one to go bad.

Output Coupling

One constantly occurring problem takes place in transformerless output circuits. These are advertised in the various catalogs as TLO outputs, and if you don't know what TLO means, it sounds like a good thing to have. In some ways it is, and in some ways it isn't. For one thing, the amplifier is a lot lighter and more easily portable. After all, a couple of hefty output transformers added to the circuit can stretch your arm a few inches when you have to carry them. What's more, they add to the cost of the unit. So if they are eliminated from the circuit, you save their cost.

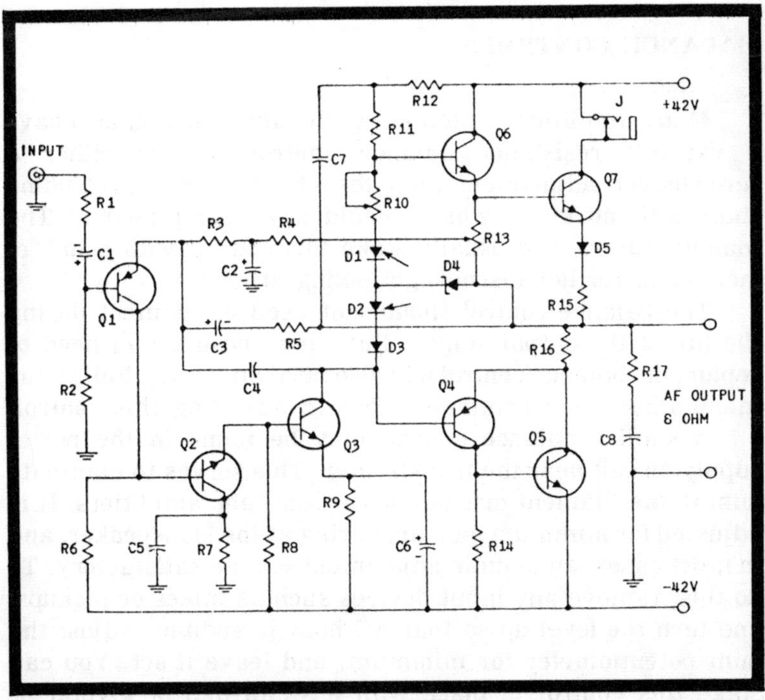

Simple OTL (output transformerless) coupling is designed for direct connection to a loudspeaker.

But a TLO unit has some marked disadvantages as well. You just can't run a circuit without a proper load, or it will run away. The TLO circuit uses the loudspeaker voice coil as its load. There's nothing wrong with this, provided that the loudspeaker is always connected to the amplifier when the amplifier is turned on.

To prevent problems of this nature, many manufacturers use a 4-pin plug at the output. Two pins carry the output, and the other two pins are in series with the AC line inside the chassis. At the speaker end of the plug, the latter two pins are simply shorted. If you try to operate the amplifier with no speaker connected, the AC is disabled.

However, many musicians don't quite understand the nature of this sort of circuitry, and when and if they decide they need or want a larger loudspeaker, they wire a plug themselves. With a little knowledge being the dangerous thing it is, they simply short the shorting pins at the socket in the amplifier, and the first time the instrument is turned on without the speaker, no more amplifier.

BALANCE CONTROLS

Many amplifiers with a pushpull output section also have a variable resistance balance control that is either a screwdriver adjustment atop the chassis, or a protruding shaft with no knob, which should say "don't touch." The manufacturers also usually stake this control with a dab of lacquer to further discourage fooling around.

The balance control should not need adjustment during the life of the output stages. But when these are in need of repair, the balance control will also need adjusting. Follow the manufacturer's recommendations in adjusting this control.

A similar balance control may be found in the power supply circuit near the transformer. This serves to eliminate hum in the filament circuits of vacuum-tube amplifiers. It is adjusted for minimum hum appearing at the loudspeaker, and in most cases, an audible adjustment can be satisfactory. To do this, remove any input devices such as mikes or pickups, and turn the level up so that AC hum is audible. Adjust the hum potentiometer for minimum, and leave it set. You can stake this control in place with a small dab of glyptal or lacquer, applying it between the shaft and housing.

When a tube is manufactured, it is finally evacuated of all air and sealed off. As a final step, the "getter" is flashed. The getter is a small ribbon or strip of highly-volatile metal, and the flashing is accomplished by holding it in proximity to a high-powered, inductively coupled radiation source. The getter ignites and burns rapidly, taking out the remaining oxygen that might be present inside the tube envelope. As a result, a mirrored dark area appears on the inside surface of the tube.

When a tube develops a physical leak in the envelope, a sure sign of such a leak is that the getter flash turns a milky white. If you see any indication of such whitening in the getter flash, the tube should be replaced.

In any tube-type amplifier, checking all of the tubes should be a part of every repair, for very often tubes can still function but not provide the top output if the tube should be weak or marginal. Besides, when a weak tube is found and replaced, it naturally means income on the sale of the tube.

Every repair should also include a thorough clean-up of the entire unit and its component parts. For one thing, by doing this as a first step, it makes the unit more pleasant to work with. Begin with a thorough vacuuming of the top and bottom of the chassis, and use a soft cloth soaked with a mixture of detergent and water to complete the cleaning of what you can easily reach. Tube and transistor bodies and envelopes should also be cleaned to permit proper cooling action and extend the life of the devices.

Now, if you know about cooling fins for transistors, join me in a chuckle as I relate the following story. If you **don't** know about cooling fins, learn from this story:

Some manufacturers use separate cooling fins that slip over a transistor's body to provide added cooling. They're held in place only by friction, and Sam was having all kinds of trouble. Sam didn't know about cooling fins, and the circuit board he was working on was loaded with transistors, all connected through sockets to the board. Each time he tried to lift a transistor out of the socket, the fins came off (of course) leaving the transistor still in the socket. Sam knew what was going on all right. He was **breaking** those transistors! He just didn't know what to do about it!

PRINTED CIRCUIT (PC) BOARDS

To repair damaged circuit boards, start by removing the entire board from the chassis. Write down which connecting wires connect to which terminals, so the board can be replaced without wiring mistakes. If the substrate board is broken or damaged, repair it with epoxy cement first and allow it to set properly. Bridge all damaged foils with wire soldered across the break. Make the broken area the strongest part of the board before you are satisfied that the job is done.

Where the substrate phenolic is intact and the foil itself is damaged, you can often make a suitable repair by using silver or copper conductive paint to bridge the break. However, any subsequent soldering to such a repair will require a careful check of continuity to make sure that it is still intact.

When replacing components on a board, always remove the old component first, and then prepare the board for the replacement by removing the old solder and clearing the holes. This is best done with a tapered aluminum probe and a wire brush. Put the new part into place and carefully resolder it, being careful not to bridge the solder to a nearby foil and create a short circuit. Check carefully to remove all solder splashes before re-installing the board.

Due to the nature of printed-circuit board repairs, many technicians save themselves a lot of time by making good use of jumpers or clip leads to extend the wiring between the board and its connections. By connecting such leads from a given wire to its place on the circuit board, you are able to test a repair prior to making the final installation on the board. If the repair was not the sum total of repairs required, you do not have to go through the problem of reinstallation and removal for each component.

CIRCUIT TRACING AND ANALYSIS

To illustrate practical troubleshooting and circuit tracing, refer to foldout Panel A, which is a typical schematic diagram of the Heath solid-state combo amplifier Model TA-17. Looking at the block diagram you will notice that the amplifier is divided into seven sections separated by dashed lines. These sections are the guitar preamplifier, the bass preamplifier,

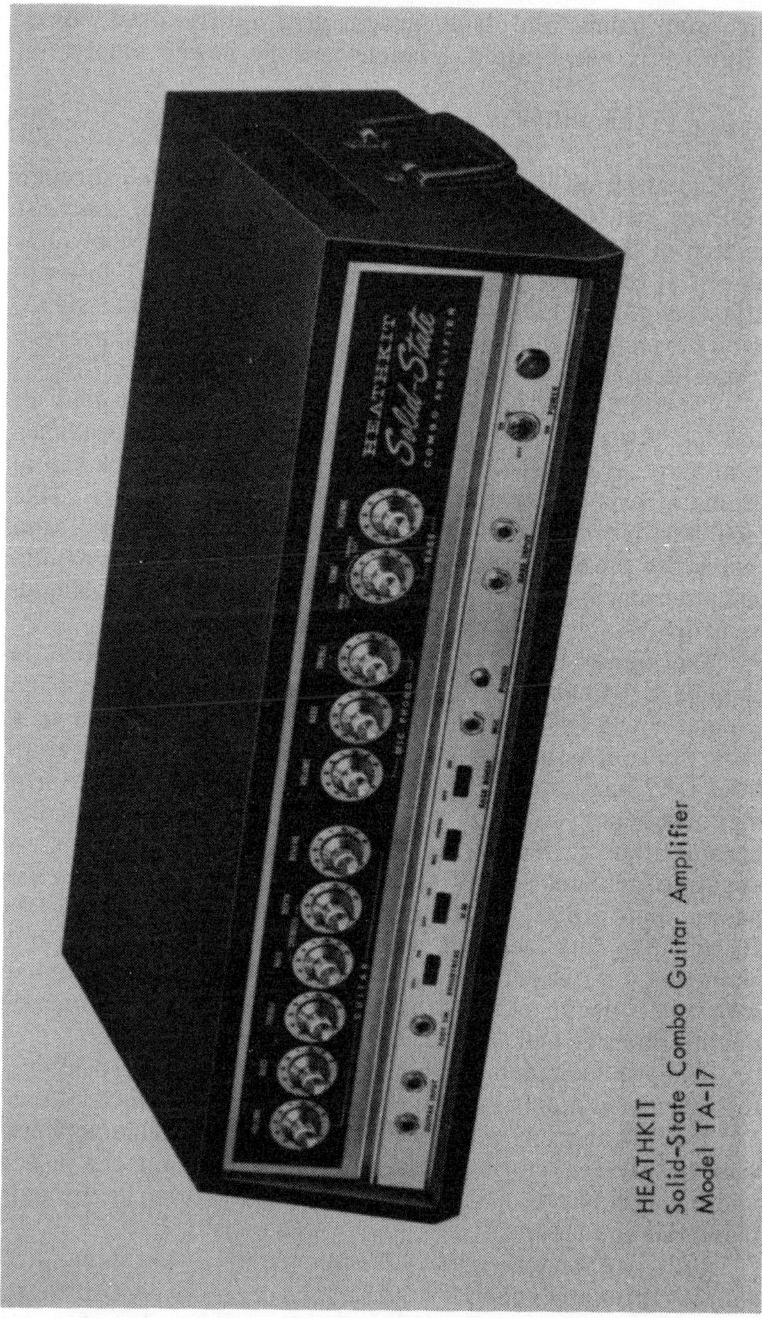

Heathkit Model TA-17 amplifier described in the text.

the microphone and phonograph preamplifier, the power amplifier, reverberation, tremolo and the power supply.

Guitar Preamplifier

Signals from the guitar input jacks are coupled through isolation resistors R1 and R2 to the wiper arm of the first section of dual volume control R601. The volume control is placed at the input jacks to control the signal prior to amplification rather than after amplification. Any strong signal from the instrument that might cause distortion in the preamp stages is thereby eliminated.

Control R603 is the second part of this dual volume control, and as R601 is rotated to maximum, R603 approaches minimum resistance. R603 applies a negative-feedback signal through resistor R602 to the input of transistor Q1. This feedback increases as R603 is rotated toward maximum resistance. The negative-feedback signal reduces that gain and, therefore, the noise level in the preamp at low signal-input levels.

The signal from terminal 1 of volume control R601 is coupled to the base of Q1 (a low-noise input amplifier) through capacitor C1. Q1 amplifies the signal and couples it to Q2's base where it is further amplified and then coupled to amplifier Q3. Capacitors C3 and C5 and resistors R13 and R8 form high-frequency attenuating networks to stabilize the preamplifier at frequencies beyond the audible ranges. A negative feedback signal is coupled from Q3's collector to the base of input amplifier Q1 through voltage divider network R3, R5 and R7. This feedback signal reduces the distortion and stabilizes the gain of the preamplifier. The signal is coupled from the collector of Q3 through C6 and R14 to the harmonic-modification circuit and to the tone control network.

When the harmonic modifier switch is in the on position, the waveform modification network, formed by diodes D1 and D2, R15, C7 and C8, is connected to the circuit. This network modifies the waveform by compressing or clipping the peaks and creating harmonics. Capacitors C7 and C8 charge through diodes D1 and D2 and discharge through resistor R15.

Only the high-frequency components of the signal are coupled through capacitor C601 to lug 3 of treble control R606. Both high- and low-frequency signals are coupled through resistors R17, R604, R605 and R18. The high-frequency signals are bypassed through capacitor C10 to ground from R18, allowing only low-frequency signals to pass through resistor R19 to lug one of the treble control. The high- and low-frequency signals are combined at lug two of the treble control. The amount of each is a function of the bass and treble control settings. The signal is then coupled through resistors R20, R301 and capacitor C301 to the base of transistor Q10, which is the input stage of the power amplifier circuit.

When the brightness switch is in the on position, the tone control network is in parallel with the brightness network consisting of R16 and C9. This boosts the midrange and high-frequency parts of the signal.

Bass Amplifier

Because only a few differences separate the bass preamplifier from the guitar preamplifier, we discuss only the differences. The negative-feedback circuit from the collector of Q6 to the base of input amplifier Q4 has only one resistor, R104 (in the guitar preamp a voltage-divider network is used). You will also notice that the high-frequency attenuator network isn't required either since the bass does not produce high frequencies. The tone control regulates the amount of high and low frequencies that pass through the tone control network. The high end of the signal path is through capacitor C600 then resistors R612, R111 and capacitor C104 to resistor R113. The low-frequency signal path is through capacitor C600 and resistors R610 and R112. Capacitor C602 bypasses the highs to ground. As the tone control is rotated clockwise the high-frequency signal is decreased. Rotation of the tone control in a counterclockwise direction reduces the low-frequency end.

The high- and low-frequency signals are mixed at R113 and go through coupling capacitor C301 to the base of amplifier Q10. When the bass boost switch is in the on position, capacitor C600 is short-circuited to increase the bass.

Microphone and Phonograph Preamplifier

The signal from the microphone jack or phono socket is selected by the mic-phono switch and coupled through C201 to the base of a low-noise input preamplifier, Q7, which feeds the signal to the base of amplifier Q8. A DC negative feedback

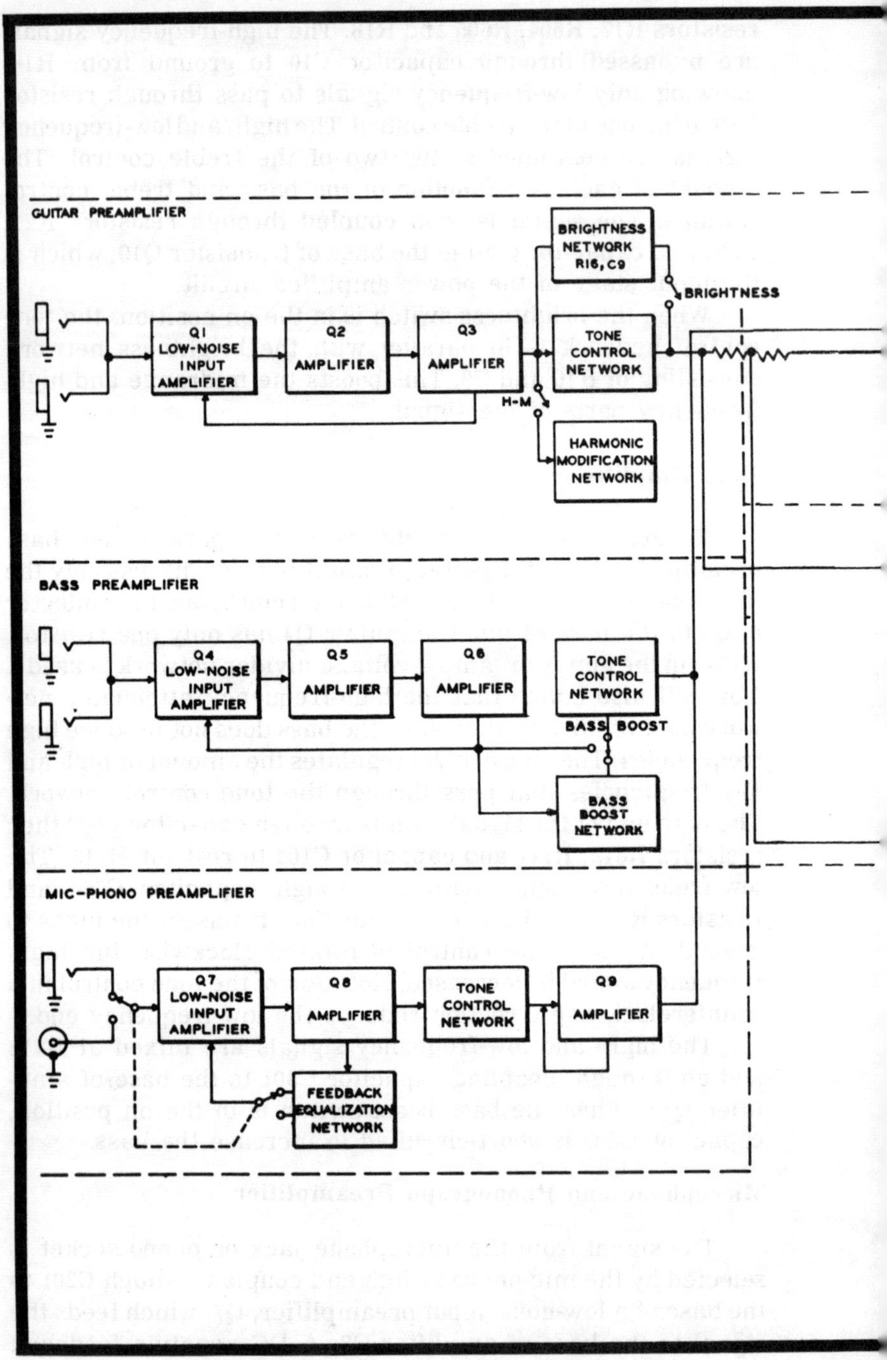

GUITAR PREAMPLIFIER
Q1
LOW-NOISE
INPUT
AMPLIFIER
Q2
AMPLIFIER
Q3
AMPLIFIER
BRIGHTNESS
NETWORK
R16, C9
BRIGHTNESS
TONE
CONTROL
NETWORK
H-M
HARMONIC
MODIFICATION
NETWORK
BASS PREAMPLIFIER
Q4
LOW-NOISE
INPUT
AMPLIFIER
Q5
AMPLIFIER
Q6
AMPLIFIER
TONE
CONTROL
NETWORK
BASS BOOST
BASS
BOOST
NETWORK
MIC-PHONO PREAMPLIFIER
Q7
LOW-NOISE
INPUT
AMPLIFIER
Q8
AMPLIFIER
TONE
CONTROL
NETWORK
Q9
AMPLIFIER
FEEDBACK
EQUALIZATION
NETWORK

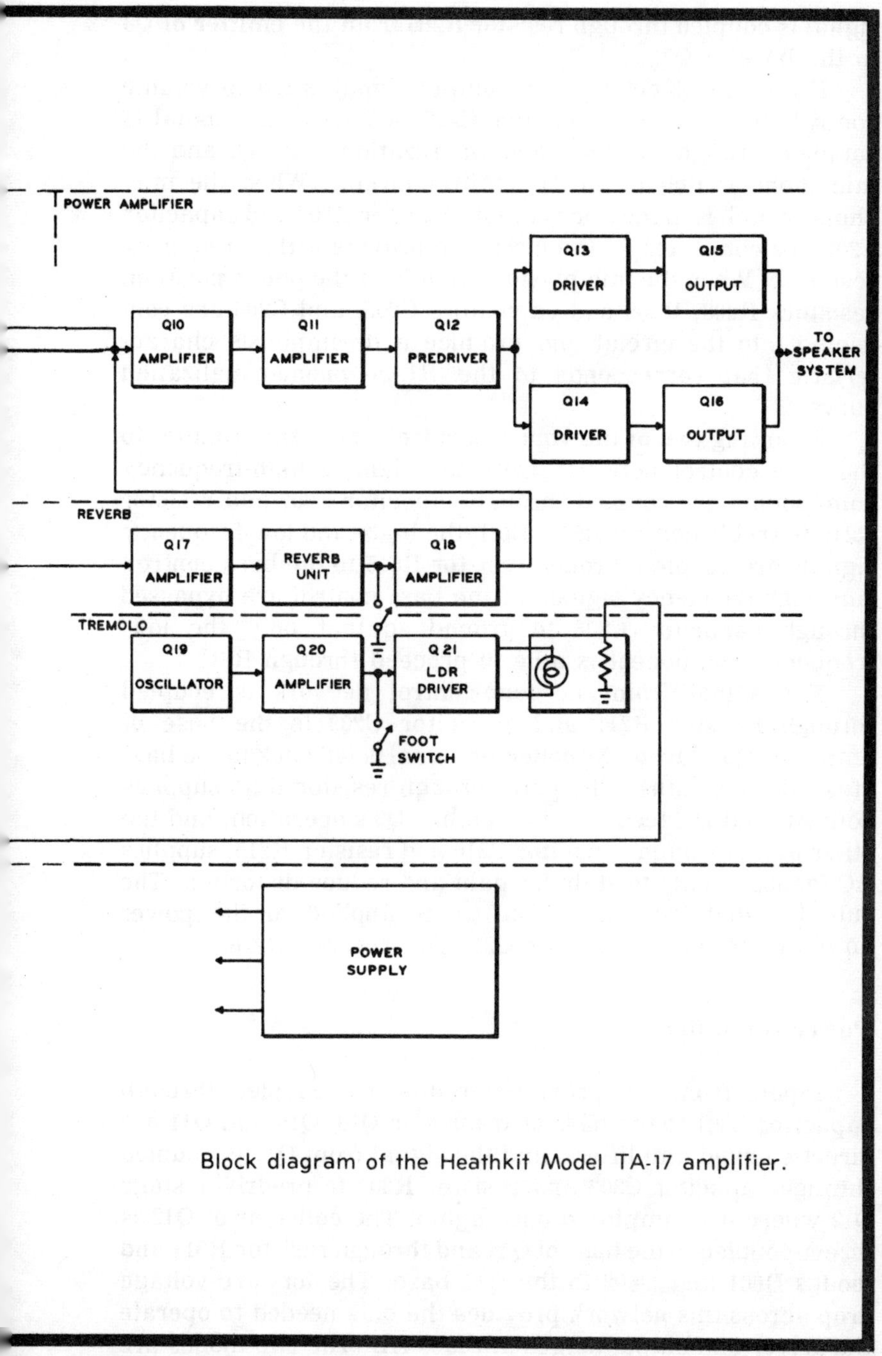

Block diagram of the Heathkit Model TA-17 amplifier.

signal is coupled through resistor R206 from the emitter of Q8 to the base of Q7.

From the Q8 collector the output signal is fed to volume control R614 through capacitor C203. A part of the signal is coupled through the feedback equalization network and the mic-phono switch to the Q7 emitter circuit. When the mic-phono switch is in the mic position, resistor R207 and capacitor C202 are connected in the circuit to provide a flat frequency response. When the mic-phono switch is in the phono position, resistors R208, R209 and capacitors C205, and C206 are connected into the circuit and produce a de-emphasis characteristic that corresponds to the RIAA phono-equalization curve.

From lug two of the volume control, the signal couples to the tone control network. Only the signal's high-frequency components are coupled through capacitor C207 and resistor R210 to treble control R619. Both the high- and low-frequency signals are coupled through resistor R615 to the bass control. Any high-frequency signals at the bass control are bypassed through capacitor C208 to ground so that only the low-frequency component is able to proceed through R618.

The signal from the tone-control network is coupled through resistor R211 and capacitor C209 to the base of amplifier Q9. Part of the collector signal is fed back to the base of Q9 via two paths: The path through resistor R213 supplies both AC and DC feedback to stabilize Q9's operation, and the other path, through capacitor C210 and resistor R215, supplies AC feedback only to stabilize gain and reduce distortion. The output signal from amplifier Q9 is applied to the power amplifier through capacitor C210 and resistor R216.

Power Amplifier

Inputs from the preamp circuits are coupled through capacitor C301 to the base of transistor Q10. Q10 and Q11 are direct-coupled amplifiers, and the signal from Q11 is coupled through capacitor C303 and resistor R307 to predriver stage Q12 where it is amplified once again. The collector of Q12 is direct-coupled to the base of Q14 and through resistor R311 and diodes D601 and D602 to the Q13 base. The forward-voltage drop across this network provides the bias needed to operate the driver and output stages in Class AB. The two diodes are mounted on the output transistor heat sinks to provide thermal stability.

Driver transistors Q13 and Q14 and output transistors Q15 and Q16 form a quasi-complementary output circuit. In this circuit, a positive-going signal applied to Q13's base causes the transistor to conduct. This, in turn, causes Q15 to conduct and charge capacitor C604 through the voice coils of the speakers. When the signal goes negative, Q13 and then Q15 will be cut off. This negative-going signal causes Q14 and Q16 to conduct, discharging capacitor C604 back through the speaker voice coils. The charging and discharging of capacitor C604 through the voice coils causes the speaker cones to move in and out, converting the electrical signal to audible sound. To improve the overall frequency response of the power amplifier, AC feed is provided by capacitor C308 and resistor R318, connected from the output to the base of transistor Q10.

Short-circuit protection is offered by a current-limiting circuit comprising zener diodes D301 and D302, emitter resistors R620 and R621 and capacitor C307. Should a short circuit or a severe overload cause a current greater than 7 amperes to flow through either of the resistors, the zener diodes would conduct and clamp the driver voltage to a level that would prevent further increase in current output. Choke L601, resistor R319 and capacitor C309 stabilize the amplifier for various output loads.

Reverberation Circuits

The treble control in the guitar preamplifier channel provides the input for the reverberation circuit. This signal is coupled through resistor R401 and capacitor C401 to the base of amplifier transistor Q17. From Q17's collector, the signal is coupled through R404 to the reverberation unit consisting of a pair of transducers to convert electrical energy to mechanical energy, and two delay springs. The input transducer accepts the signal, transmits it down the springs of the output transducer, which couples it back into an electrical signal that is applied to the base of Q18. The signal at this point is essentially the same as the input signal, but is somewhat delayed. After amplification by transistor Q18, the signal is coupled through capacitor C405 to lug three of the reverberation control. The setting of this control determines how much of the delayed signal is coupled through resistor R410 and capacitor C301 to the power amplifier.

The base of transistor Q18 is connected through resistors R405 and R406 to a foot switch. When the foot switch is either open or unplugged, Q18 amplifies normally. When the switch cable is inserted in its jack and the switch closed by foot pressure, the base bias of Q18 is shorted to ground, cutting off the transistor and stopping the signal.

Tremolo Circuit

The signal from the guitar preamplifier is applied across the resistance element of the light-dependent resistor (LDR) which is actually the output element of the tremolo circuit. Here's how it operates: Tremolo oscillator transistors Q19 and Q20 are connected in a subsonic, phase-shift oscillator circuit. This develops a signal that can be varied from 3½ to 10 Hz by the rate control in the phase-shift network. The oscillator's amplitude from the emitter of Q20 is varied by the depth control. The signal then couples to the base of LDR driver transistor Q21.

The LDR consists of a low-current lamp and a light-dependent resistance element. The value of this element depends on the brightness of the lamp, with the resistance value inversely proportional to the brightness of the lamp. When the depth control is rotated clockwise from the full counterclockwise position, the oscillator's signal amplitude increases, causing Q21 to conduct on the positive portion of the signal. When Q21 conducts, it draws emitter current through the lamp element in the LDR, causing the lamp to turn on and off with the oscillator signal. Zener diode D401 supplies a regulated 13.5 volts for transistor Q21.

Because the brightness of the lamp varies with the rate and depth of the tremolo signal, the LDR's resistance varies in the same fashion. It goes from a very low resistance (almost a short circuit) to a very high resistance (nearly an open circuit). Since the LDR is connected between the reverb channel signal path and ground, its resistance variations modulate the reverb channel signal with the low-frequency tremolo signal.

The tremolo can be operated by the foot switch which, when it is in the off position, shorts the base of LDR driver Q21 to ground. This circuit is on when the switch is unplugged from the amplifier.

Power Supply

The AC input from the power cord is connected to the line-reversing on-off switch and through the circuitbreaker to the power transformer (T1). In addition to turning the amplifier on and off, the line-reversing switch allows either side of the power line to be connected to the chassis through capacitor C501. This helps reduce stray hum pickup from the instrument itself. The circuitbreaker, a 2.11-ampere unit, protects the amplifier from overloads.

Power transformer T1 has two primary windings that can be connected in parallel for 120-volt input or in series for a 240-volt line. One secondary of this transformer is connected to a full-wave bridge rectifier consisting of diodes D501, D502, D503 and D504. The output of this circuit is filtered by capacitor C503. Eighty volts is provided from this point to the power amplifier circuits. Resistor R501 is a bleeder resistor that discharges capacitor C503 when the amplifier is turned off.

Another T1 secondary goes to a full-wave rectifier formed by diodes D505 and D506. The output of this circuit is filtered by capacitors C504 and C505 and resistor R504. Sixty volts of positive DC goes from here to the preamplifiers. The output of this circuit is further filtered and reduced by capacitors C506 and C507 and resistors R502 and R503. The 25 volts of positive DC from this point goes to the reverb, tremolo and power amplifier circuits. The final secondary winding provides 6.3 volts for the amplifier's pilot lamp.

TROUBLESHOOTING

As you can see, circuit tracing is a valid way to understand what's going on in the amplifier, and while it helps, you needn't go into the detail we've gone through here. It is usually sufficient to follow the circuit through to see if all components called for in the schematic are present and in place. The following charts, prepared by the manufacturer, list many troubles and possible causes.

As a final note of caution, don't believe the markings that you'll find on resistors and capacitors. More than once, we've

TROUBLE CHART

DIFFICULTY	POSSIBLE CAUSE
No sound. POWER light does not light.	1. Circuit breaker tripped. See Circuit Breaker keeps tripping.
Circuit breaker keeps tripping.	1. Speaker wires shorted. 2. Diodes D501, D502, D503, D504, D505, or D506 shorted. 3. Capacitors C503 or C504 shorted. 4. Transistors Q12, Q13, Q14, Q15, or Q16 faulty.
No sound or noise. POWER lamp lights.	1. Speaker wires open or shorted. 2. Diodes D501, D502, D503, D504, D505, or D506 open. 3. Transistors Q10, Q11, Q12, Q13, Q14, Q15, or Q16 faulty.
Noise but no sound on any of the channels. Pilot lamp lights.	1. Transistors Q10 or Q11 faulty. 2. Cable between Amplifier and instrument faulty. 3. Diodes D505 or D506 faulty. 4. Capacitor C504, C505, C506, or C507 faulty. 5. Resistor R502, R503, or R504 faulty.
Distorted or dead Guitar channel. Other two channels OK.	1. Transistors Q1, Q2, or Q3 faulty. 2. Capacitors C1, C4, or C6 faulty. 3. Tone control network incorrectly wired.
Distorted or dead MIC-PHONO channel. Other two channels OK.	1. Transistors Q7, Q8, or Q9 faulty. 2. Excessive input levels. 3. Capacitors C201, C203, C204, or C209 faulty. 4. Switch on microphone in Off position. 5. Cables between record player or microphone and Amplifier faulty.
Distorted or dead BASS channel. Other two channels OK.	1. Transistors Q4, Q5, or Q6 faulty. 2. Capacitors C101 or C103 faulty. 3. Tone control network incorrectly wired.
No tremolo (foot switch not plugged in).	1. Transistors Q19, Q20, or Q21 faulty. 2. Diode D401 faulty. 3. R624 incorrectly wired.

TROUBLE CHART

DIFFICULTY	POSSIBLE CAUSE
No reverb (foot switch not plugged in).	1. Transistors Q17 or Q18 faulty. 2. Cables to reverb unit loose. 3. Coils on reverb unit broken, due to severe jar. 4. Resistor R622 incorrectly wired.
No reverb with foot switch plugged in.	1. Foot switch cable shorted. 2. REV switch on foot switch faulty.
No tremolo with foot switch plugged in.	1. Foot switch cable shorted. 2. TREM switch on foot switch faulty.
Distorted or weak sound on all channels.	1. Transistors Q10, Q11, Q12, Q13, Q14, Q15, or Q16 faulty. 2. Diodes D301 or D302 faulty. 3. Speakers out of phase. See Speakers section, Page 56. 4. Capacitors C503, C504, C505, C506, or C507 faulty.
Excessive hum with musical instrument connected.	1. POWER switch in wrong ON position. 2. Instrument faulty (if hum stops when instrument is unplugged). 3. Hum is being picked up by instrument from other nearby equipment. 4. Instrument cable faulty (open ground connection).
High hum with no inputs connected.	1. Capacitors C503, C506, or C507 faulty. 2. Diodes D501, D502, D503, D504, D505, or D506 faulty.
High hum with REVERB control turned up.	1. Cable to reverb faulty (open ground connection). 2. Capacitor C506 or C507 faulty. 3. Reverb unit not centered in compartment (touching chassis). 4. Hum is being picked up by instrument from other nearby equipment.

located components that were correctly installed and properly marked—that is to say, a 10K resistor that was supposed to be in a given circuit was actually a 10K resistor according to the markings, but it measured nearly 10 megohms! As an amplifier technician, you have to take nothing for granted, must be suspicious of everything, and trust nothing at all.

Repairing Guitars & Other Fretted Instruments

5

If you are going to offer your customer a complete repair service, you must be prepared to cope with problems related to the guitar and other fretted instruments. The following information, provided by the Guitar and Accessory Manufacturers Association, should prove quite helpful.

GUITAR TYPES

The **classic guitar** is a flat-top instrument designed for use with nylon strings only. It has a wide fingerboard with 12 frets clear of the body for classic and folk music. Finger-style playing (without picks) is the accepted form.

The **flamenco** is a variation of the classic guitar. It uses nylon strings and has a special top designed for greater brilliance. Like the classic, it has a wide fingerboard with 12 frets clear of the body. The flamenco is usually played without picks.

The **standard flat-top** guitar is adapted to use metal strings. It has a standard fingerboard with 12 to 14 frets clear of the body. It is used mostly for vocal and rhythm work. Pick-style playing is the accepted form, although finger-style is often used. Flat-top guitars are also available in electric models.

The **arched-top regular non-electric** (hollow body) guitar has a crowned top and back, with F holes on the top. It is designed for use with metal strings only, and has a standard fingerboard with 12 to 14 frets clear of the body. This pick-style guitar is used for solo and rhythm in dance bands and small combos.

The **arched-top electric** is designed for electric pickups; otherwise, it is the same as the non-electric. Some electric guitars have semi-hollow bodies, while others have hollow bodies with flat tops and backs.

The **solid-body electric**, as the name suggests, has a solid wood body without a resonant chamber. It is generally used with electric pickups and metal strings. This pick-style guitar has a standard fingerboard with 14 frets or more clear of the body.

The **Hawaiian electric steel** guitar has a solid wood body designed strictly for electric pickups and metal strings. Tuning and string requirements vary from model to model. Some models have pedal arrangements which change the tuning instantly. The instrument is played with metal finger picks and a steel bar.

The **bass** guitar (electric) is made with both solid and hollow bodies and uses a special scale and strings. The fingerboard has 14 frets clear of the body. The instrument is used for all popular music forms where a lower voicing range is desired. Picks are usually used, but finger-style picking is also acceptable. It is tuned one octave lower than a standard guitar.

Four-string guitars come in flat-top, arched-top and solid bodies. Hollow bodies are made in both acoustic and electric models. The standard 4-string fingerboard has 14 or more frets clear of the body. The most popular scales are tenor (short scale), and plectrum (long scale).

Nylon strings are used on classic and flamenco models. Non-magnetic bronze and steel strings are used on non-electric arched and flat-top instruments requiring metal strings. All electric guitars use regular wound magnetic steel strings or flat-wound strings. There are many variations of the above string classifications based on metal content, alloys, core wire, etc.

GUITAR BRIDGES

Modern guitars use many types of bridges, both mechanical and stationary. Most flat-top guitars come with a stationary glued-on type of bridge, where the action is preset by the manufacturer. However, there are flat-top bridges that do have action adjustments which work in the same fashion as regular arched-top bridges. The player can adjust the height of the strings above the fingerboard by turning the bridge post wheels up or down to the desired level.

Individually adjustable sliding string bridges allow intonation adjustments which enable the player to properly adjust the intonation of each string by sliding the string saddles forward or backward. Each string can be set to fret true over the entire scale. Factory adjustments are usually quite accurate, so the less tampering the better.

A string space bridge allows a player to space the strings to fit his particular style of playing. Each string has a traversing wheel or slot adjustment which makes it possible to set a broad spread of strings for finger-style playing or a narrow spread for pick and chord work.

Rocker bridges are often used with hand vibrato devices so the bridge saddle can move with the movement of the strings when the vibrato device is operated. This facility of both string and bridge movement helps to keep the guitar in tune and reduces friction. Constant use of a hand vibrato device will often cause the bridge base to "walk" out of position. Therefore, it is important to check the bridge at regular intervals and reset it in the proper position when necessary. Players who use these devices often complain that their guitar does not fret true. This means that the bridge base has moved out of line and needs to be reset.

INTONATION CHECKS

There are five things to check for correcting intonation trouble. First, put on a complete set of new strings, then check the instrument in various positions. Many players fail to change strings as often as they should. A worn string does not stretch out evenly, causing it to vibrate irregularly and produce a false tone. Also, all metal strings will rust and corrode in time and will become dead or out of pitch.

Excessively worn frets or a worn fingerboard will cause false tones. Check to see that the neck is perfectly straight. If there is a slight hump or hollow in the fingerboard, it can cause difficulty. To check, "sight" down the neck or place a straightedge on the frets. A truss rod adjustment (if the guitar has one) will usually correct the trouble.

Often the bridge on guitars with movable bridges will be displaced slightly during the installation of new strings. The bridge should be approximately the same distance from the 12th fret as the 12th fret is from the string nut at the top of the fingerboard. In other words, the 12th fret is approximately one-half the distance from the string nut to the treble side of the bridge saddle or one-half the full scale length. The bass side of the bridge saddle is usually slightly closer to the tailpiece end. Most manufacturers lightly scratch guidelines on the guitar top. The bridge should be positioned between the guidelines.

Also check to see that the machine heads are holding properly and that the string is securely locked on the head post. Occasionally, the machine heads will slip and need replacing. If a string is not securely locked on the post, it will slip.

TRUSS ROD ADJUSTMENTS

Most guitars are equipped with a truss rod; some have fixed steel rods which strengthen the neck, while others have an adjustable rod which both strenghtens the neck and facilitates adjustment of a bowed or warped neck. Because all guitar necks are subject to great stress as a result of string tension and other factors, there are times when a neck will become bowed, warped or twisted.

To correct such deformities, loosen the third and fourth strings, but do not remove the strings from the guitar. Pull the loose strings to one side to allow free access to the nut cover. Remove the cover so the neck adjustment nut is exposed. Sight down the neck from the top and observe how much of a set the neck has taken. Hold the neck up at eye level and sight along the edge of the fingerboard on both treble and bass sides. Place the guitar wrench on the adjustment nut and turn clockwise very slowly (a small fraction of a turn at a time). Keep checking the neck as you proceed with each nut turn. Once the neck is straight, give the adjustment nut a very slight added turn to compensate for the tension the third and fourth strings will add when they are replaced and tuned. If the neck should raise or hump up in the center of the fingerboard, the truss rod nut should be loosened until the neck comes down and is perfectly level.

When making these adjustments, it is best to place a straightedge on the frets to assure a perfect adjustment. Be careful not to tighten the nut too much, because it could result in stripping the threads or breaking the truss rod.

On certain models, the truss rod is adjusted at the lower end of the fingerboard. Some require a special wrench, while

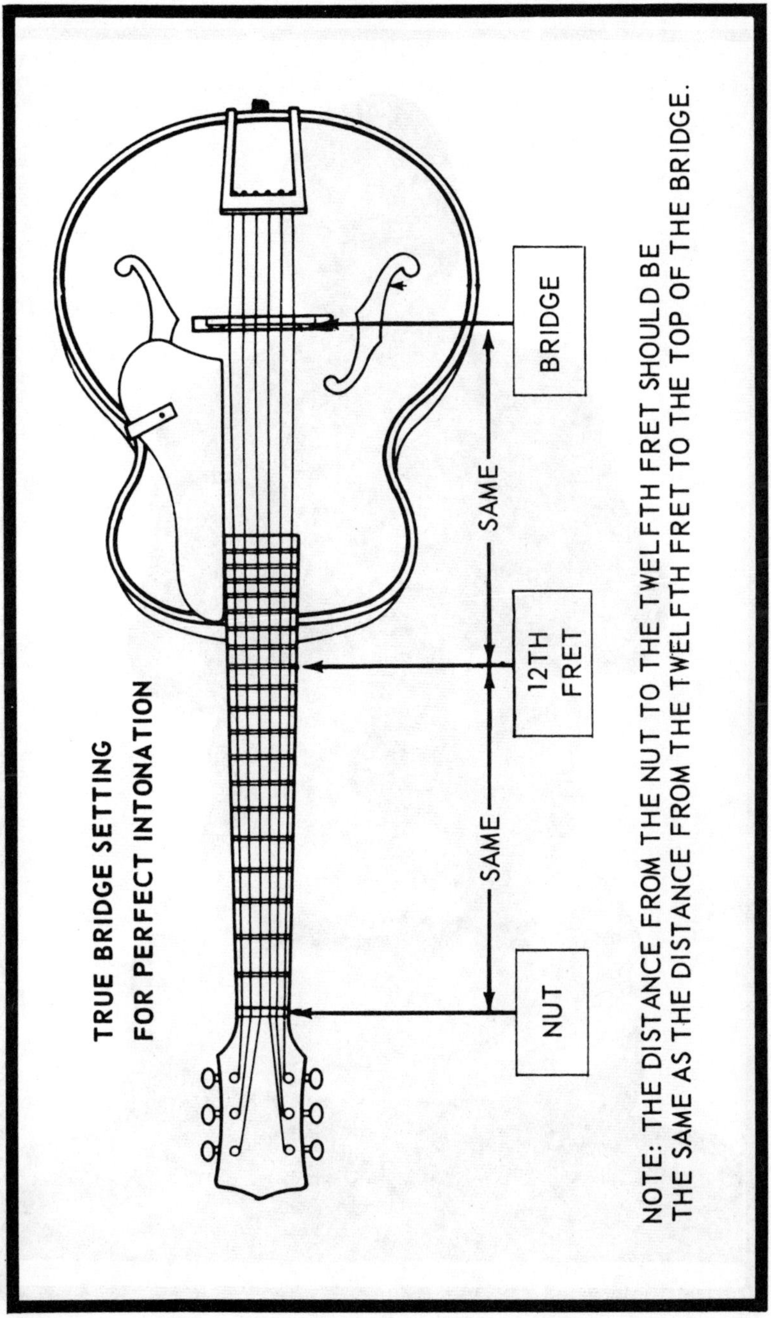

Drawing showing the correct location of the bridge.

Correct position to hold a guitar to ''sight'' the neck.

others are adjusted with a screwdriver or Allen wrench. Be sure to use the proper tool and follow the same pattern just described. There is one exception: Some adjustments work counterclockwise, while others must be turned clockwise. Make certain that you have the proper information from the manufacturer before attempting a neck correction. Do not attempt to change the action of a guitar by adjusting the truss rod!

STRING BUZZING & FALSE TONES

A slight hump in the fingerboard of a fretted instrument can cause string rattle and false tones. The best way to correct this trouble is to straighten the neck as described shortly. Loosening the adjustable truss rod nut slightly should correct the situation.

A high fret will do two things—produce a string buzz or a false tone—when a certain note is played. When this happens the first thing to do is strike the string at the playing position that buzzes or plays falsely—keeping in mind that it's the fret above (closer to the body) that is creating the trouble, not the fret on which you are playing. What has happened is that the fret above has worked out of its slot, thus creating a high fret. When a string is pressed down in the trouble position, the fret above is just high enough to touch the vibrating string, causing it to buzz, or high enough to block out the intended tone altogether, producing instead a tone higher.

To correct this condition, loosen the strings so that you have access to the entire width of the fret. Place a soft cloth over the fret, then gently tap the fret with a tack hammer until it reseats itself in the slot. If the same fret works up again, it's best to remove it entirely, turn it over and notch the edge of the thin fin lightly with the sharp edge of a tack hammer. Apply Elmer's white glue along the thin fin of the back side of the fret, then reseat it firmly in the slot with gentle taps of the tack hammer. A worn low fret will create the same effects as a high fret. If such is the case, remove the old fret and replace it with a new one in the manner described later.

"ACTIONS"

"Action" is described as the distance the string is pressed before it meets the fret. Standard actions are preset by the

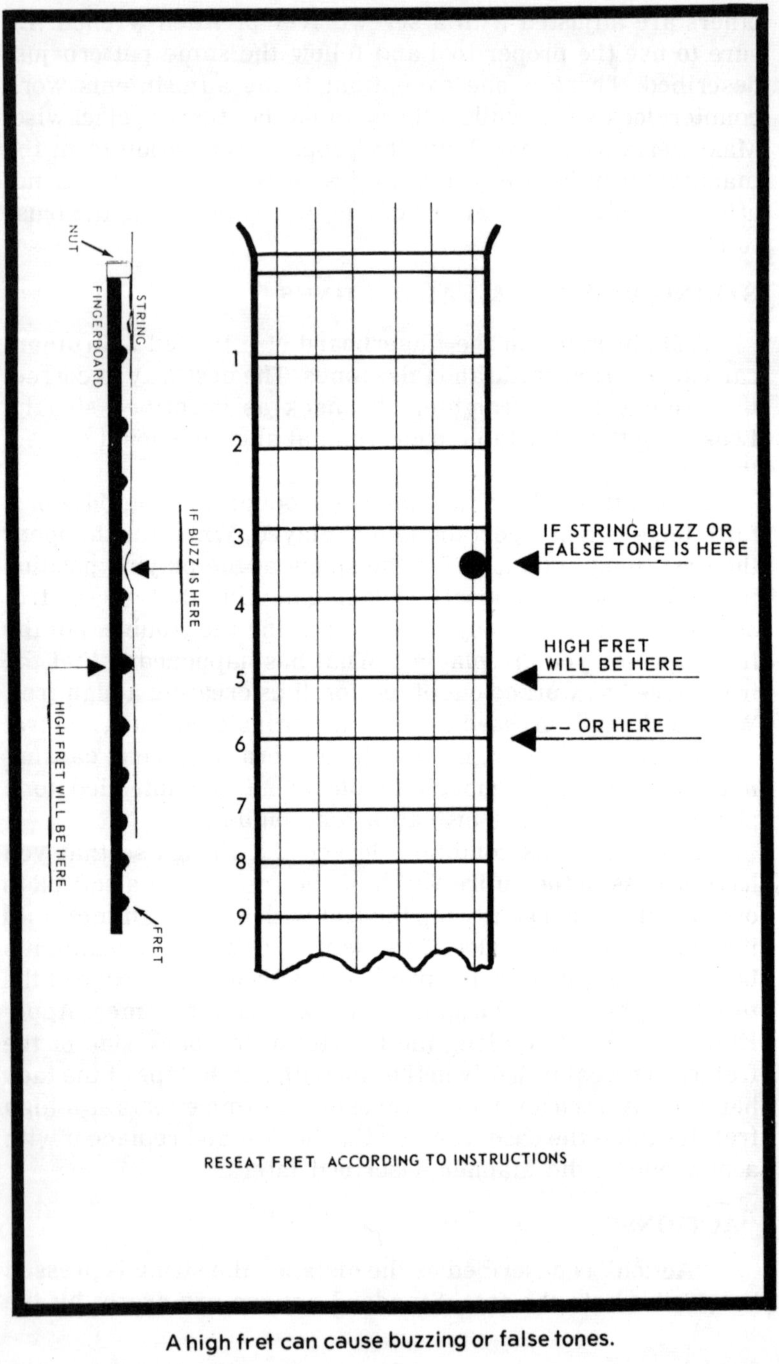

A high fret can cause buzzing or false tones.

manufacturer. However, a certain player may want a higher or lower action to fit his style. Before any such adjustments are made, the owner should realize that settings below standard may induce rattles, caused by the string vibrating against the frets, unless a very light pick stroke is used. Rattles or buzzes caused by an improper setting of the action are not considered a defect because they can be removed by adjustment.

The action can easily be adjusted by raising or lowering the bridge saddle on models with an adjustable bridge, or by cutting down or building up the saddle on non-adjustable models. Certain flat-top acoustic guitars have replaceable saddles in the bridge. These saddles may be glued into the slots or may be press-fit only, but either type can be removed and replaced with a higher or lower saddle.

Extremely low string action may be caused by a warped neck or back bend of the neck (back bend is the result of adjusting the truss rod too tight). If there is a slight bow or dip in the neck, the truss rod needs tightening. When this is done, place the guitar on a table, lower the adjusting screws on the bridge, which in turn will lower the strings until the bass string (looking at it from the bass side) has about one-sixteenth inch clearance from the 12th fret. Do the same with the treble side. The treble side can be slightly lower. Tune the instrument. Then use your first finger, picking each note on the first string going down the fingerboard, starting at the 12th fret, 11th fret, 10th fret, etc., to see if there are buzzes. If there are buzzes, it means that the string is too close to the board. Do the same with all strings. If you find a string that rattles or buzzes, raise the bridge slightly.

True Fretting by Accurate Bridge Adjustment

First, tune the guitar perfectly on open strings. Then lay the guitar on a table face up. On the E first string, pick the harmonic on the 12th fret; this is done by barely touching your finger to the string at the 12th fret and releasing your finger very quickly. Then, place your finger down on the first string at the 12th fret and pick again. The note just picked and the previous harmonic should be exactly the same. If the note you picked is sharper than the harmonic, it means the string length from the 12th fret to the bridge is too short, causing the

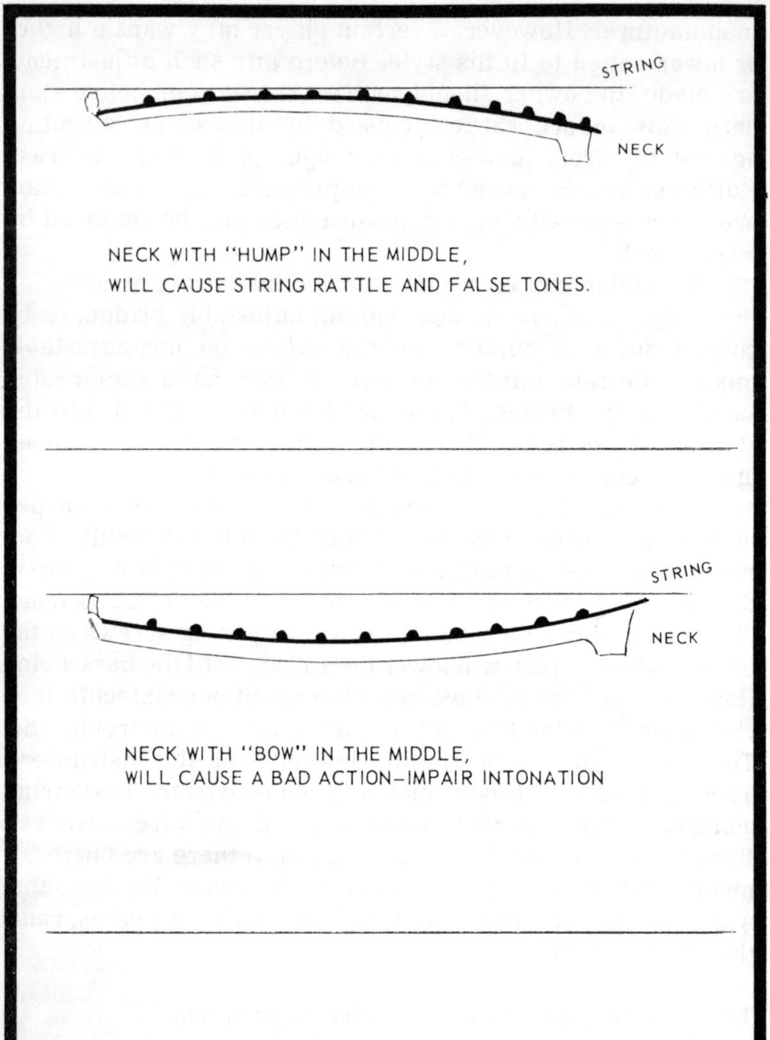

Drawings showing three major neck trouble spots.

12th fret note to be sharp. Move the bridge toward the tailpiece until the harmonic and the picked note are exactly the same. This string will now fret true over the entire fingerboard. Repeat the procedure with the E sixth string. If a wooden bridge is used, the two outside strings will be perfectly in tune and the inside strings will be very close.

For absolutely perfect adjustment, the same thing can be done with an offset sliding saddle bridge. First, set the two outside strings and then, with the adjusting screws, move the offset saddles back and forth until the exact point is reached where the fretted note and the harmonic are exactly the same. Do this with each string. The bridge should then be perfectly set.

String Spacing Adjustment

Looking down the bridge saddle, check to see that the strings are the exact same distance apart. If they are not equally spaced, use a very small file and make a new notch to allow respacing, or replace the bridge saddle.

If you are not getting a clean sound, check to see if the string might be embedded too deeply in the bridge saddle slot. If it is, file down some of the wood, bone or metal saddle until the slot or notch is no longer so deep, and the string is embedded no deeper than its thickness in the slot. This will give more sustain and a cleaner sound.

Dressing a Fingerboard or Redressing Worn Frets

A quick way to dress a fingerboard or redress worn frets is to use No. 180 emery cloth. Remove all the strings, place the instrument on a flat surface. Fold the emery cloth in the palm of your hand and, starting from the nut, rub all the way to the end of the fingerboard. Keep doing this until the grooves in the fret you are trying to dress are completely gone. The fret will then be dressed down along with all the frets on the entire fingerboard. The frets could be replaced, but dressing the fingerboard in this manner makes a beautiful action. The frets will be rounded and polished and feel very professional.

CORRECTING RATTLES AND NOISES

First check and tighten every screw on the instrument, then check these other vital points: One of the most common

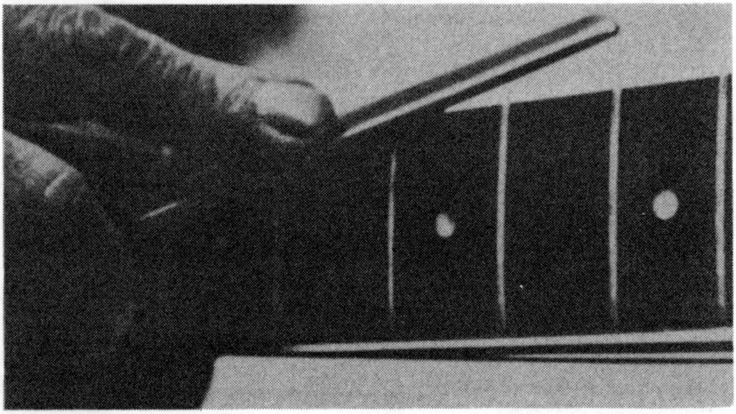
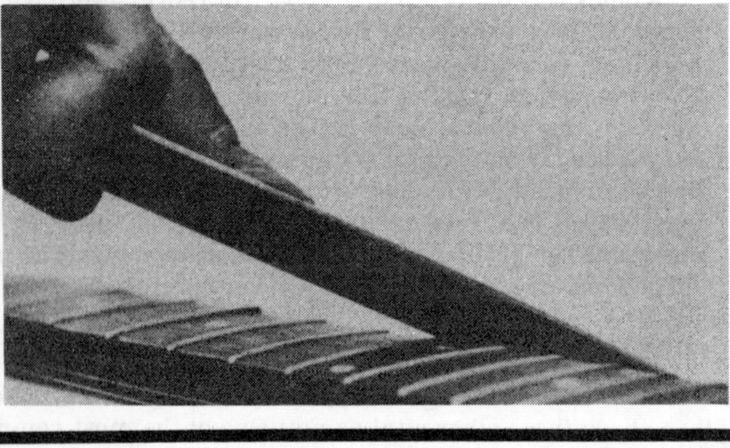

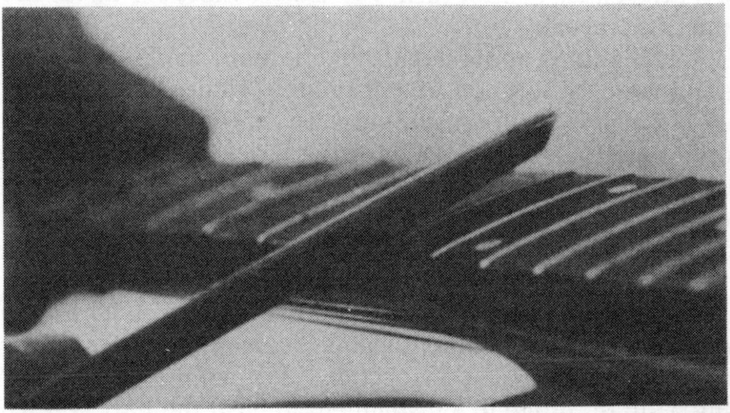

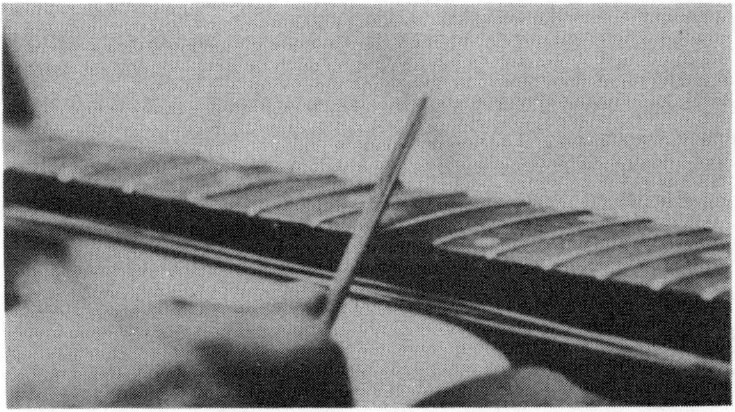

Photos showing how to correct sharp-edged frets.

causes of rattle are loose retaining nuts on the volume and tone controls. If any are loose, remove the control knobs and tighten the nuts. **Caution**: First, turn the control fully counterclockwise, then hold the shaft firmly with your fingers while tightening the nut with an open-end wrench or pliers. If you let the entire control turn, wires or connections inside the guitar may break.

Another rattle or noise that sometimes occurs is caused by the adjusting screws on offset saddle bridges that become worn or loose through constant use. To correct this problem, a drop of liquid glue or nail polish on the screw will bind and stop the rattle. Anytime you have to readjust the offset screw, a screwdriver will break the bond. Be careful not to drop any nail polish on the wood finish!

Another rattle may be caused by an electronic component or wire inside the guitar that has gradually worked its way to the surface of the instrument and is touching the treble bar or the top, thereby causing a vibration. This can be corrected by using a small, probe-like instrument to push the part or wire away from the contact point. Infrequently, a truss rod will work loose and cause what sounds like a fret buzz. This may be corrected by tightening the truss rod slightly. To locate any of the above mentioned rattles, strum the strings with your ear close to the instrument until you locate the general area.

A rattling sound or vibration in a machine head or tuning key will occasionally occur. It is corrected by a very slight tightening motion through the thumb piece. **Note**: Electric guitars by their very nature, due to extra metal parts, controls, wires, etc., build up a slight rattle-type sound when played without amplification. When connected to an amplifier, it disappears. Such rattles occur because the strings are forced to produce a sound when played without amplification, thus the rattle.

SHARP-EDGED FRETS

Sometimes a fingerboard will shrink, due to climatic conditions, leaving the frets jutting out from the edge of the fingerboard. This is most noticeable on fingerboards without edge bindings. To correct the condition, loosen the strings and pull them well away from the fingerboard (see the accompanying illustrations). With a fine flat file, smooth the frets along the edge of the board with easy, firm strokes. Follow this procedure with a slight downward stroke, filing at the corner of the frets to round them off. With No. 4 sandpaper, briskly sand the entire board, including the frets, in up-and-down strokes parallel with the fingerboard for about 30 seconds. The same procedure is followed with No. 6 sand-paper. Then, with No. 400 sandpaper, work back and forth across the board and frets, instead of up and down as before. Use firm strokes to smooth away any rough spots the file and other sandpapers might have left. Apply "3-in-1"(TM) or other light oil to a cloth and rub the face of the fingerboard briskly, then wipe again with a clean cloth.

TUNING MACHINE CARE AND REPAIR

For long reliable service use a drop of oil on bearing units. Be sure the screw and gear assembly is not too loose or too tight. Adjustments can be made with a small screwdriver. It's also a good policy to take up all screws when checking a gear assembly. When a machine becomes stuck, it is best to replace the gear with a new one. Slipping machines may mean that the gear screw should be tightened, but not too tight. One of the main faults may lie in poor stringing and not the machine. Make certain the string is wrapped around the post properly.

REGLUING LOOSE BINDINGS

Occasionally, bindings open up or pull away from a fingerboard or body. To repair the trouble, make sure the area to be reglued is cleaned of old glue and dirt. Cover exposed wood areas around the section to be repaired with masking tape. Then, with a thin strip of wood, work Duco(TM) cement into the binding area. Bind the freshly glued area with masking tape. Let stand for an hour, then remove the tape. If the body binding pulls away, follow the procedure above, except in the curves of the body and cutaways areas use 1-inch upholstery webbing instead of masking tape. Wrap the webbing very tightly around the entire guitar and let stand for 6 hours.

REPAIRING NECK PULL-AWAY

Remove all the strings completely. Stand the guitar upright and very carefully apply small amounts of scalding

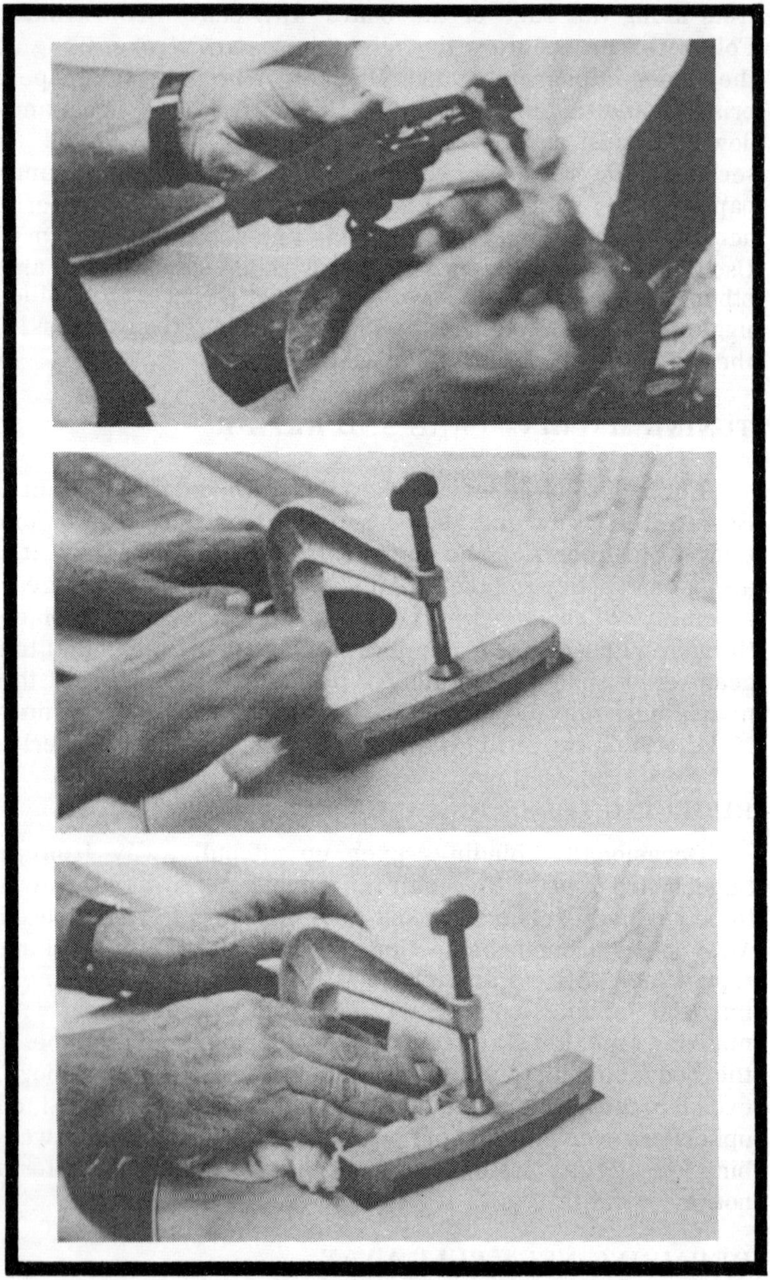

Here are the three steps to regluing a flat-top bridge.

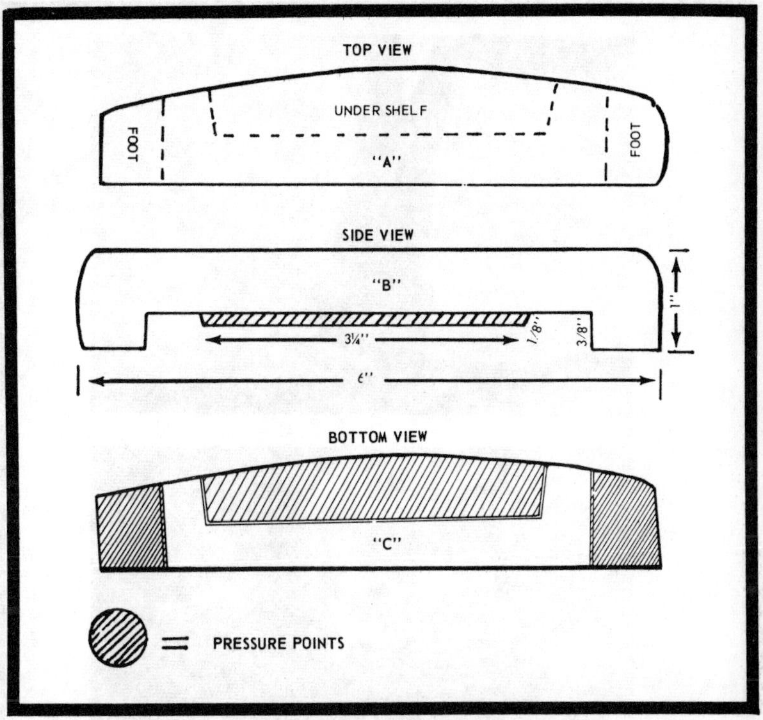

Pressure block for regluing a flat-top bridge. Shown one-half exact size.

water into the pull-away area with a teaspoon. Work the neck back and forth gently until the old glue is softened. The neck should lift out of the slot without too much trouble. If it doesn't, a tap with a rubber hammer on the neck heel will drive it out.

Wipe all areas clean of water and soft glue and allow to dry completely. Clean all glue from the heel area and body slot. Apply hot glue to the body and heel tongue and reseat in place firmly. Let stand for 24 hours before restringing.

REGLUING FLAT-TOP BRIDGES

If a bridge pulls away or comes off completely, remove all strings from the guitar. With fine sandpaper remove the old glue, sanding down to the bare wood, from the bottom of the bridge and the bridge area on the top of the guitar. Place the bridge on top of the guitar in the same spot it stood before and trace lightly around it with a pencil. This will serve as a guide when gluing the bridge in place.

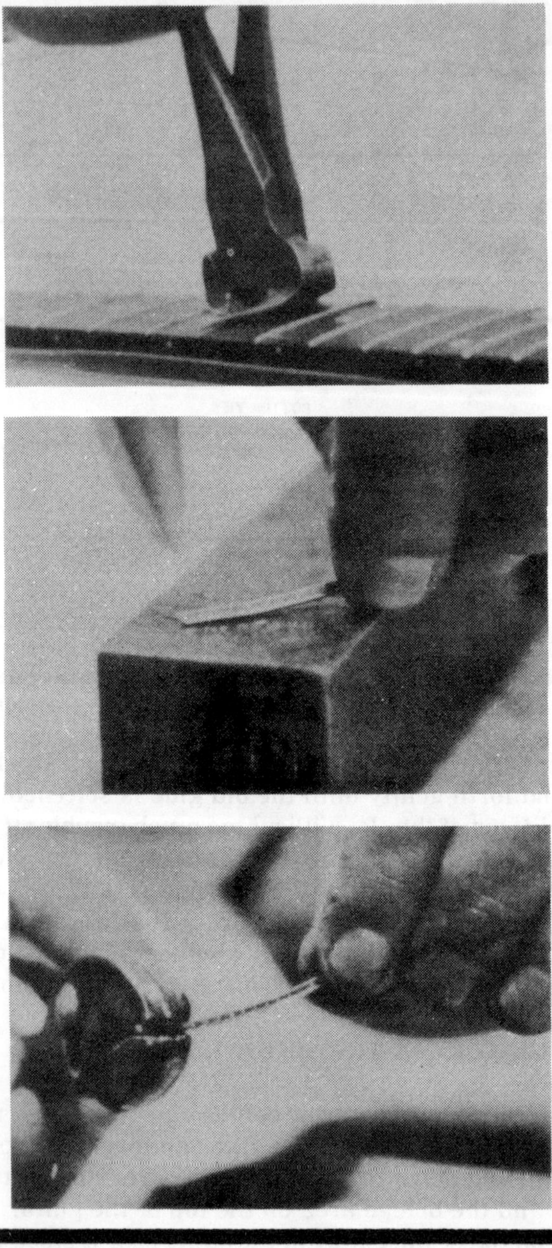

How to remove and replace a fret. (Part 1 of 3 parts.)

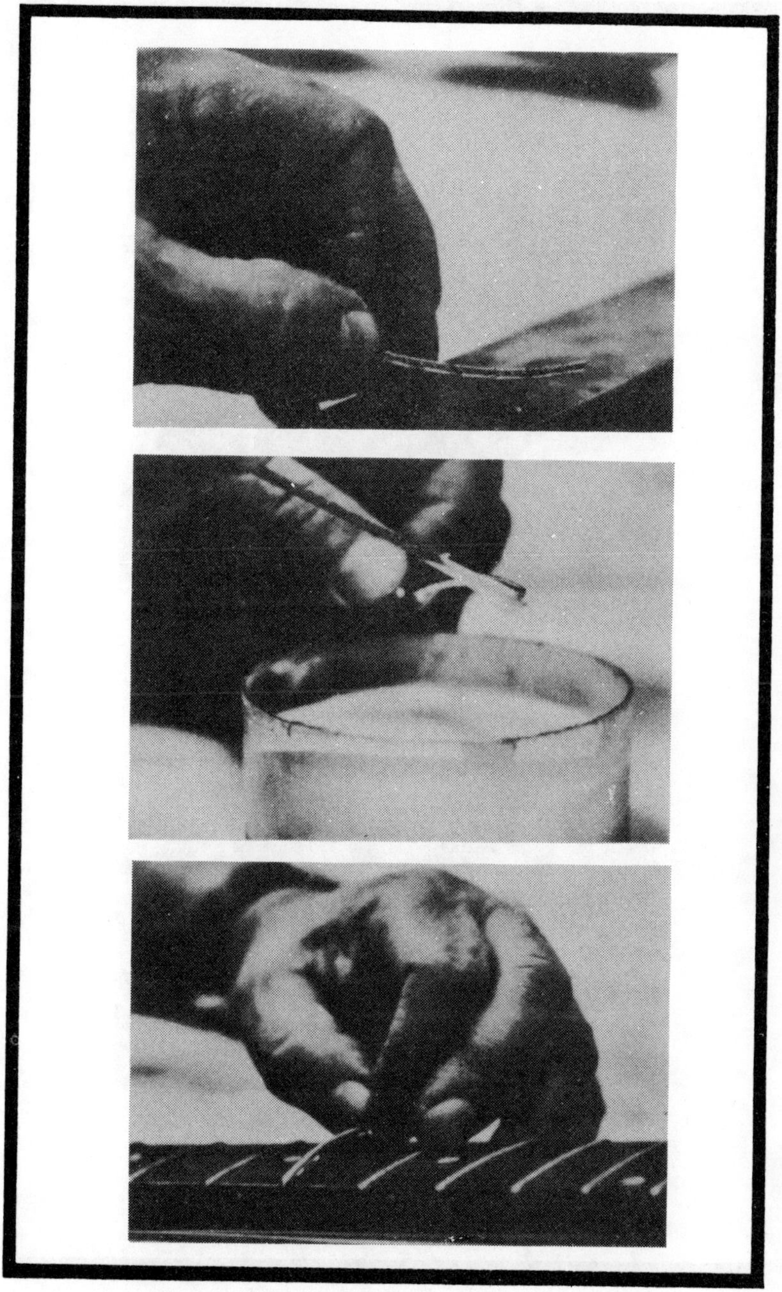

How to remove and replace a fret. (Part 2 of 3 parts.)

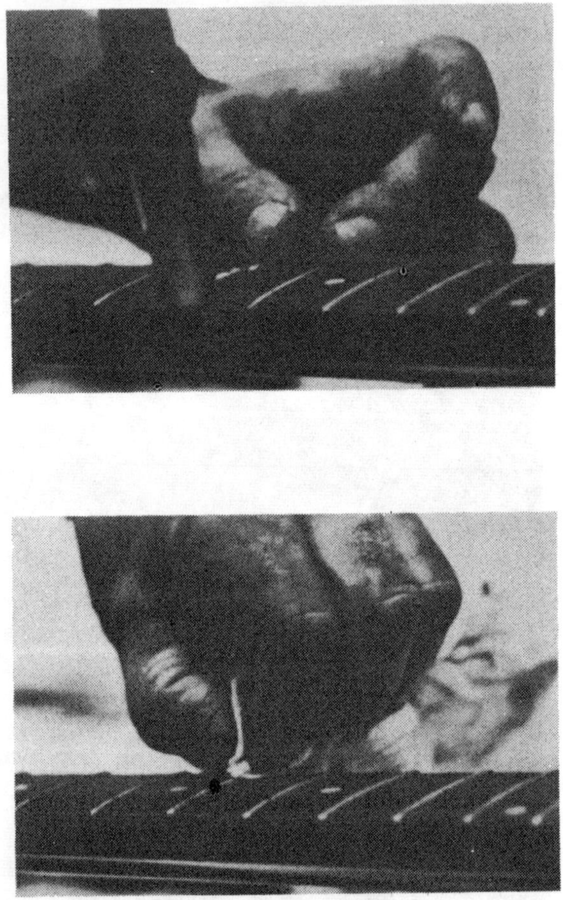

How to remove and replace a fret. (Part 3 of 3 parts.)

Apply glue, either hot or Elmer's, to the bottom of the bridge and to the bridge area on top of the guitar. Place the bridge in the exact position outlined with the pencil. Place a wooden pressure block on top of the bridge, apply a C clamp and tighten it. With a wet cloth wipe off all excess glue, then wipe dry with a clean cloth. Allow to remain in place for 24 hours. A good pressure block is necessary if a good glue job is to result. The accompanying illustrations show the exact construction details.

REPLACING FRETS

With end-cutting pliers, grip the fret firmly and gently, as shown in Step 1 in the illustrations, and pull it out of the slot. Turn the fret over and notch it slightly with the sharp edge of a tack hammer. Bend the fret to the contour of the fingerboard. Apply glue to the underside fin of the fret, then center the fret directly over the slot. Tap the fret into place with a tack hammer, then wipe the fret clean of glue. When installing a new fret, be sure to cut it to the length of the old one before installing it.

6 Repairing Electronic Organs

At one time, an organ consisted of various size pipes which sounded when air was forced into them. It wasn't until the advent of the electronic organ that this versatile instrument became suited for use in a private home. However, so complex are the many functions of these instruments, that numerous books have been published concerning them. While this book is basically involved with amplifiers, the circuitry providing signals to the amplifier of an electronic organ is sufficiently involved and complex that it might be a good idea to trace one completely, just to give an indication of the involvement of such instruments.

We selected the Lowrey Citation Theater Console, simply because it is about as versatile as any electronic organ in the moderate price range. If you can follow this circuit description through, keeping one eye on the schematic diagram, you'll have a good understanding of how electronic organs operate. There is very little in any electronic organ that you'll run across that is not covered. You are urged to take the time to go through this, and to follow the circuits described with the schematic diagram.

The block diagram defines the various circuits discussed, and should be examined at this point so you know which circuits are applied at what points in the overall scheme of things.

VIBRATO (See Schematic 1)

Vibrato oscillator Q1 develops a continual low-frequency, high-impedance sine wave of sufficient amplitude to drive vibrato emitter follower Q2, which converts the high-impedance sine wave from Q1 to a low-impedance alternating current. This alternating current alternately shifts the frequency of the twelve master oscillators represented by Q3.

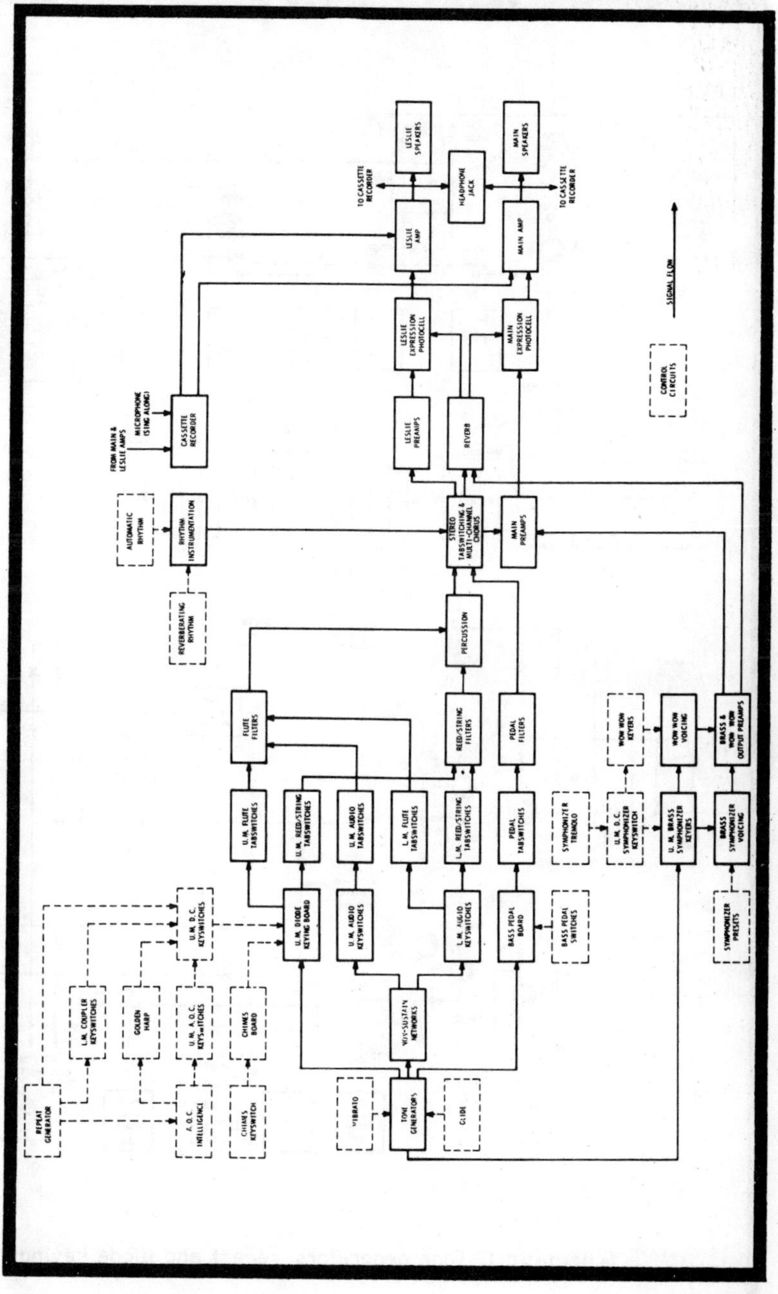

Block diagram of the Lowery Citation Theatre Console.

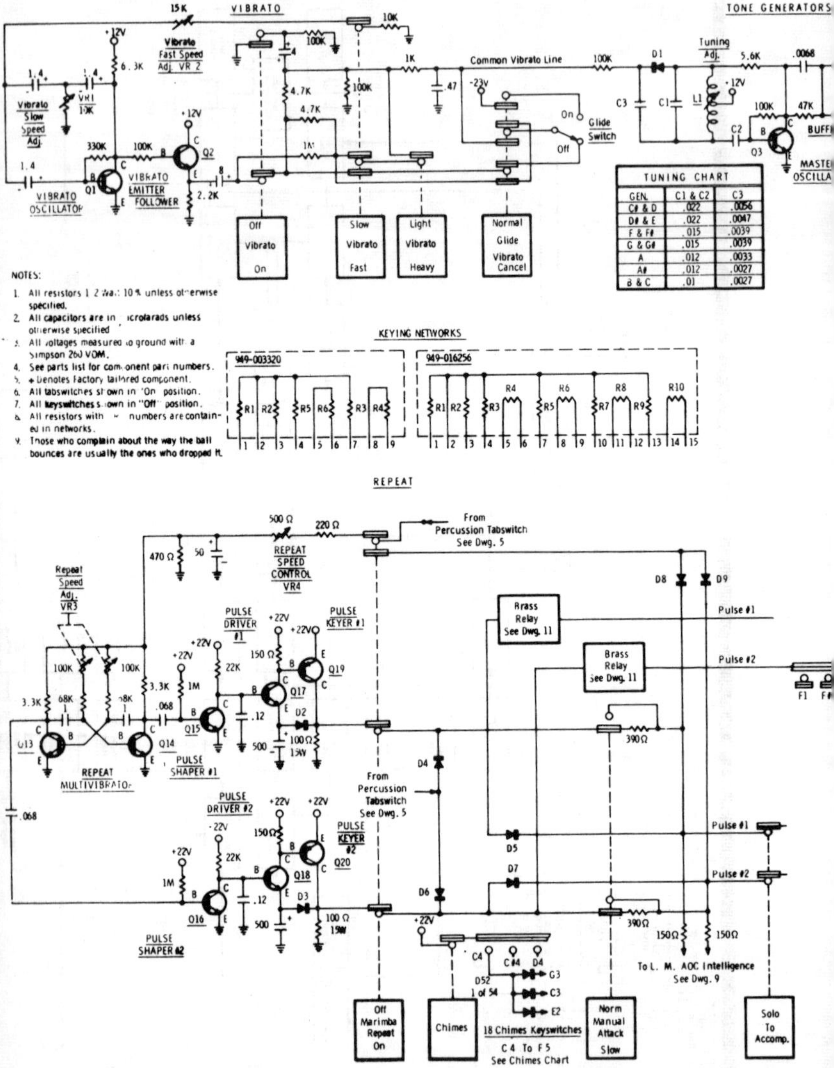

NOTES:

1. All resistors 1 2 Wa.: 10% unless otherwise specified.
2. All capacitors are in microfarads unless otherwise specified
3. All voltages measured to ground with a Simpson 260 VOM.
4. See parts list for component part numbers.
5. + Denotes Factory tailored component.
6. All tabswitches shown in "On" position.
7. All keyswitches shown in "Off" position.
8. All resistors with numbers are contained in networks.
9. Those who complain about the way the ball bounces are usually the ones who dropped it.

TUNING CHART		
GEN.	C1 & C2	C3
C# & D	.022	.0056
D# & E	.022	.0047
F & F#	.015	.0039
G & G#	.015	.0039
A	.012	.0033
A#	.012	.0027
B & C	.01	.0027

Schematic 1. Tone generators, repeat and diode keying.

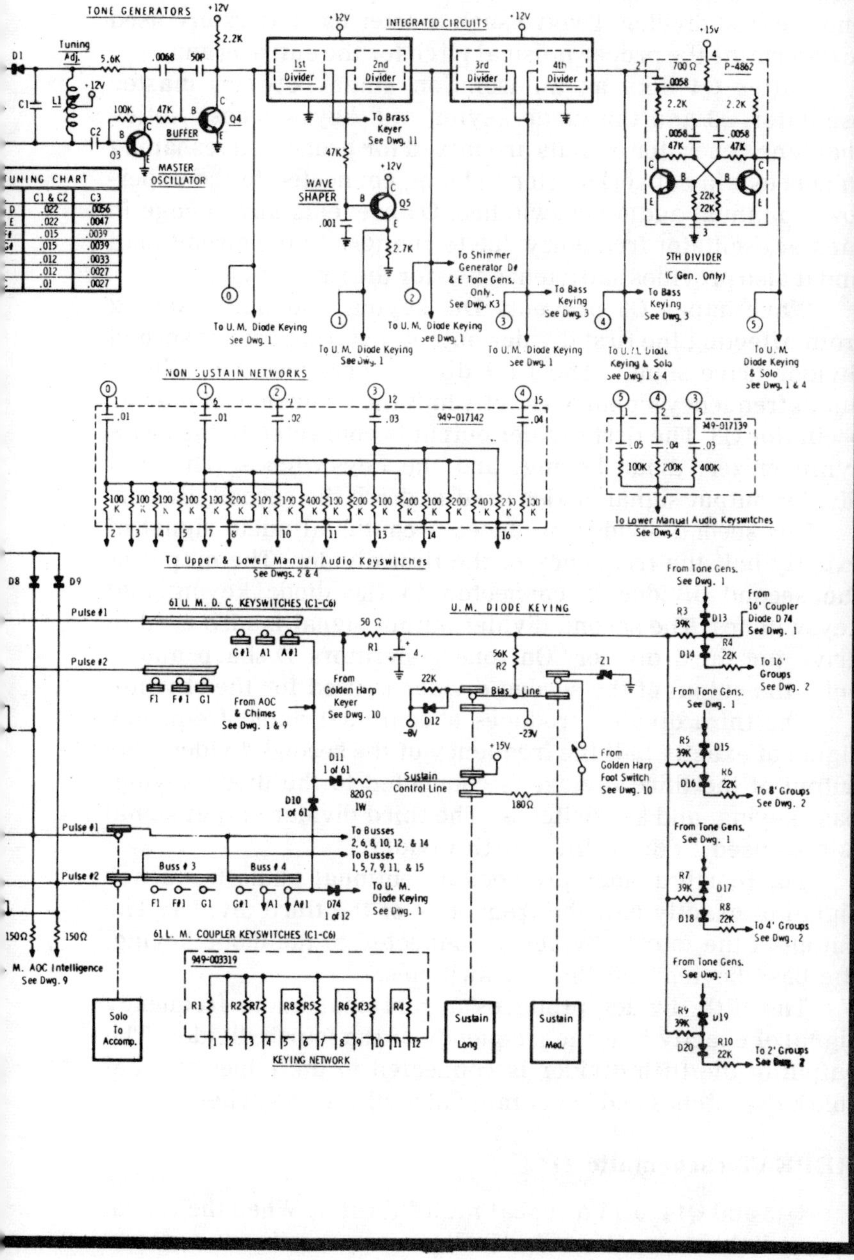

TONE GENERATORS
INTEGRATED CIRCUITS
1st Divider
2nd Divider
3rd Divider
4th Divider
Tuning Adj.
MASTER OSCILLATOR
BUFFER
WAVE SHAPER
To Brass Keyer See Dwg. 11
To Shimmer Generator D# & E Tone Gens. Only. See Dwg. K3
To Bass Keying See Dwg. 3
5TH DIVIDER
(C Gen. Only)
P-4862
TUNING CHART
C1 & C2
C3
To U. M. Diode Keying See Dwg. 1
NON SUSTAIN NETWORKS
949-017142
949-017139
To Upper & Lower Manual Audio Keyswitches See Dwgs. 2 & 4
To Lower Manual Audio Keyswitches See Dwg. 4
61 U. M. D. C. KEYSWITCHES (C1-C6)
U. M. DIODE KEYING
Pulse #1
Pulse #2
From Golden Harp Keyer See Dwg. 10
From AOC & Chimes See Dwg. 1 & 9
Bias Line
Sustain Control Line
From Golden Harp Foot Switch See Dwg. 10
To Busses 2, 6, 8, 10, 12, & 14
To Busses 1, 5, 7, 9, 11, & 15
To U. M. Diode Keying See Dwg. 1
61 L. M. COUPLER KEYSWITCHES (C1-C6)
M. AOC Intelligence See Dwg. 9
949-003319
KEYING NETWORK
Solo To Accomp.
Sustain Long
Sustain Med.
From Tone Gens. See Dwg. 1
From 16' Coupler Diode D74 See Dwg. 1
To 16' Groups See Dwg. 2
To 8' Groups See Dwg. 2
To 4' Groups See Dwg. 2
To 2' Groups See Dwg. 2

TONE GENERATORS (Schematic 1)

Master oscillator Q3 develops a continual audio frequency signal, and the output of this stage is connected to buffer Q4 and the first divider. Twelve such master oscillators are used to determine the proper musical pitch for the entire organ.

Buffer Q4 acts as an isolation stage between master oscillator Q3 and the diode keying and keyswitches. Notice that tone generator outputs are mixed for proper waveshaping in nonsustain networks prior to being connected to the upper-lower manual audio keyswitches. Q4 prevents any change in master oscillator frequency due to changes in the circuit load and it also provides sufficient drive for the first divider.

Waveshaper Q5 prevents DC keying and audio keying from affecting the first divider output, insuring proper second divider drive signal. The first divider produces a continual audio-frequency signal of exactly half the frequency of master oscillator Q3. The first divider output is connected to the brass symphonizer, diode keying, and the keyswitches. The first divider output signal is also used to drive the second divider.

The second divider produces a continual audio signal of exactly half the frequency of the first divider. The output of the second divider is connected to the diode keying and keyswitches. The second divider output signal is also used to drive the third divider. On tone generators D-sharp and E only, the output of the second divider is used for the rhythm.

The third divider produces a continual audio frequency signal of exactly half the frequency of the second divider. The output of the third divider is connected to the diode keying, bass keying, and keyswitches. The third divider output signal is also used to drive the fourth divider.

The fourth divider provides a continual audio frequency signal of exactly half the frequency of the third divider. The output of the fourth divider is connected to the diode keying, the bass keying and the key switches.

The fifth divider produces a continual audio frequency signal of exactly half the frequency of the fourth divider. The output of the fifth divider is connected to the upper manual solo key switches and lower manual audio key switches.

REPEAT (Schematic 1)

Q13 and Q14 form a repeat multivibrator. When the repeat tab switch is on, the circuit alternately produces negative pulses at the collector terminals of each transistor. The alternate negative pulses from the repeat multivibrator are applied to pulse shapers Q15 and Q16, numbers 1 and 2, respectively. Negative pulses from the repeat multivibrator (Q13, Q14) cause the pulse shapers to alternately produce positive-going pulses. The positive voltage pulses are directly connected to pulse drivers numbers 1 and 2 (Q17 and Q18).

Q19 and Q20 are pulse keyers 1 and 2. These circuits operate together to produce alternate positive keying pulses. The keying voltage pulses are applied to the upper manual DC key-switches, coupler and AOC intelligence on busses by way of the AOC attack and coupler (solo-to-accompaniment) tabswitches.

UPPER AND LOWER MANUAL (See Schematics 2 and 4)

Q21 and Q22 are the upper manual 8-foot collector preamp and emitter follower, respectively. Audio signals from the 2-foot, 4-foot and 8-foot upper manual diode keying groups are combined and amplified. The output of these preamps is connected to the trombone, trumpet, oboe, kinura, cello and violin tabswitches.

Q23 is the upper manual 16-foot collector preamp. Audio signals from the upper manual 16-foot diode keying groups are combined and amplified. The output of this preamp is connected to the trombone, clarinet and cello tabswitches.

Q34 (schematic 4) is the lower manual 8-foot reed-string collector preamp. Audio signals from the lower manual 8-foot audio key switch groups are combined and amplified in this preamp. The output of the preamp is connected to the violin, cornet, French horn and English horn tabswitches.

Q114 is the upper manual 16-foot solo divider preamp and 16-foot solo divider network. An audio signal from any one of the first twelve upper manual solo keyswitches is amplified by the upper manual 16-foot solo divider preamp to provide sufficient drive signal for the upper manual 16-foot solo divider, which produces an audio signal of exactly half the frequency at the amplified input. The input frequency is selected by the series opening key switches located on the first twelve upper manual keys. The output of the upper manual solo divider network is connected to the upper manual 16-foot flute tabswitch.

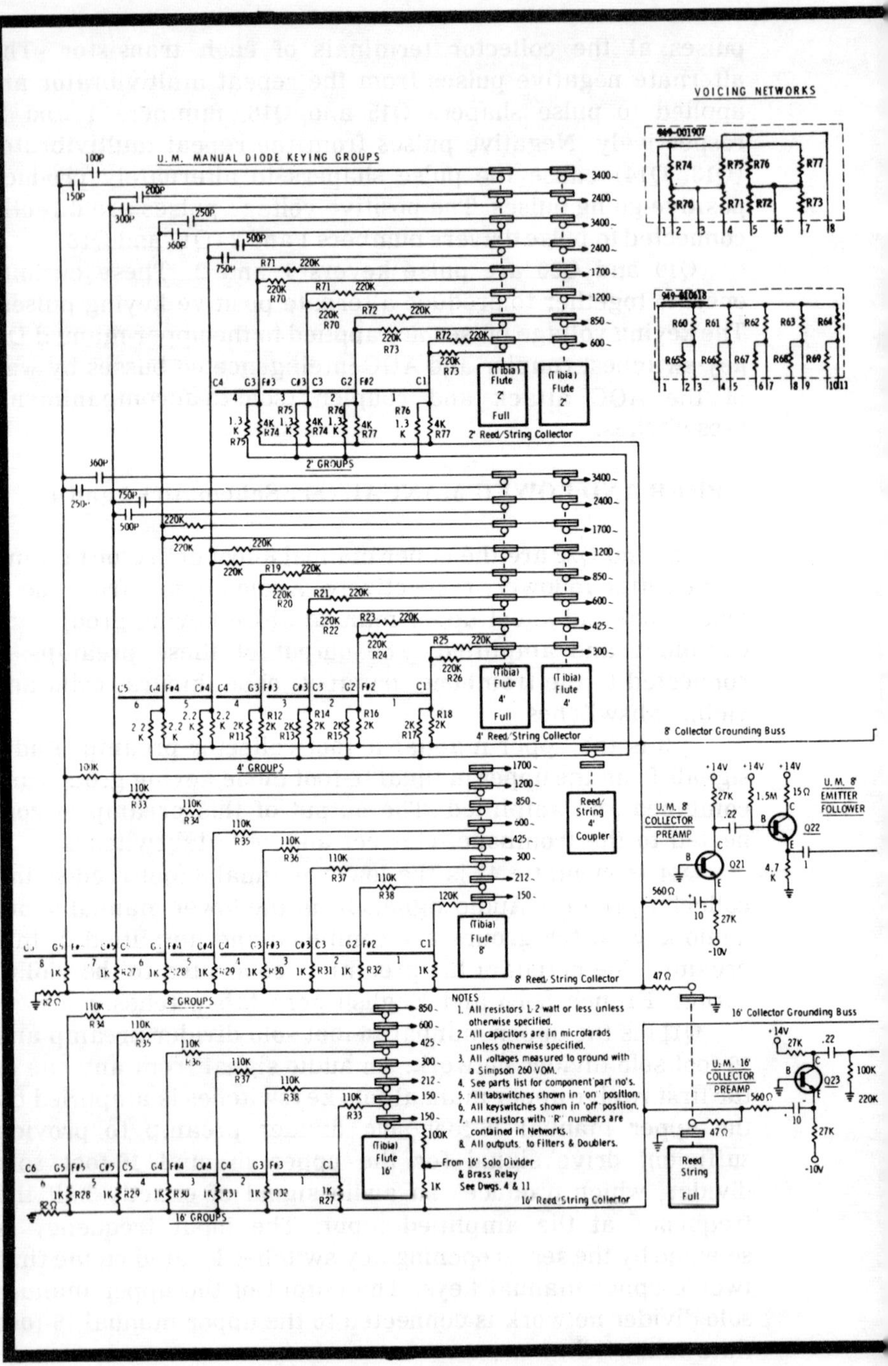
VOICING NETWORKS
949-001907
R74 R75 R76 R77
R70 R71 R72 R73
949-001018
R60 R61 R62 R63 R64
R65 R66 R67 R68 R69
U.M. MANUAL DIODE KEYING GROUPS
(Tibia) Flute 2' Full
(Tibia) Flute 2'
2' Reed/String Collector
2' GROUPS
(Tibia) Flute 4' Full
(Tibia) Flute 4'
4' Reed/String Collector
4' GROUPS
8' Collector Grounding Buss
Reed/String 4' Coupler
U.M. 8' COLLECTOR PREAMP
U.M. 8' EMITTER FOLLOWER
Q21
Q22
(Tibia) Flute 8'
8' Reed/String Collector
8' GROUPS
16' Collector Grounding Buss
U.M. 16' COLLECTOR PREAMP
Q23
(Tibia) Flute 16'
From 16' Solo Divider & Brass Relay See Dwgs. 4 & 11
Reed String Full
16' Reed/String Collector
16' GROUPS
NOTES
1. All resistors 1/2 watt or less unless otherwise specified.
2. All capacitors are in microfarads unless otherwise specified.
3. All voltages measured to ground with a Simpson 260 VOM.
4. See parts list for component part no's.
5. All tabswitches shown in 'on' position.
6. All keyswitches shown in 'off' position.
7. All resistors with 'R' numbers are contained in Networks.
8. All outputs to Filters & Doublers.

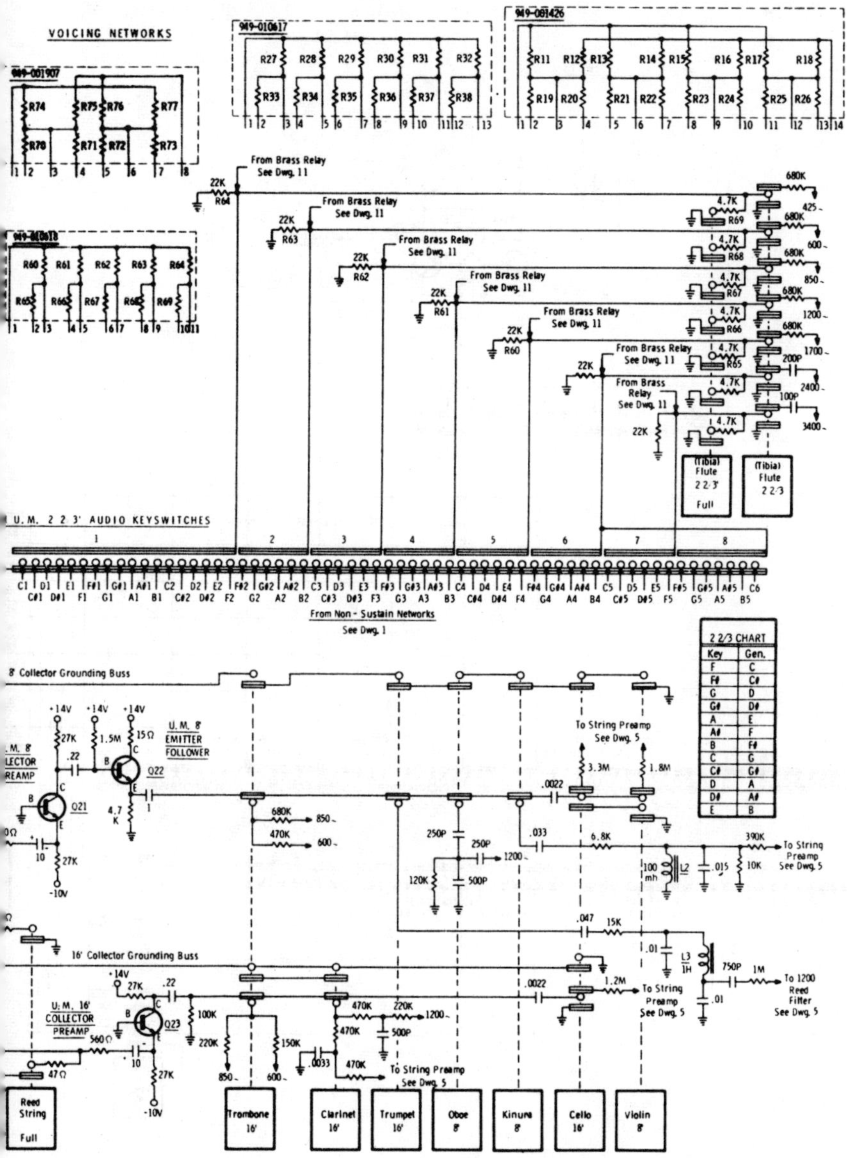

2 2/3 CHART

Key	Gen.
F	C
F#	C#
G	D
G#	D#
A	E
A#	F
B	F#
C	G
C#	G#
D	A
D#	A#
E	B

Schematic 2. Upper manual diode keying groups, 2 2/3 audio key switching and tabswitching.

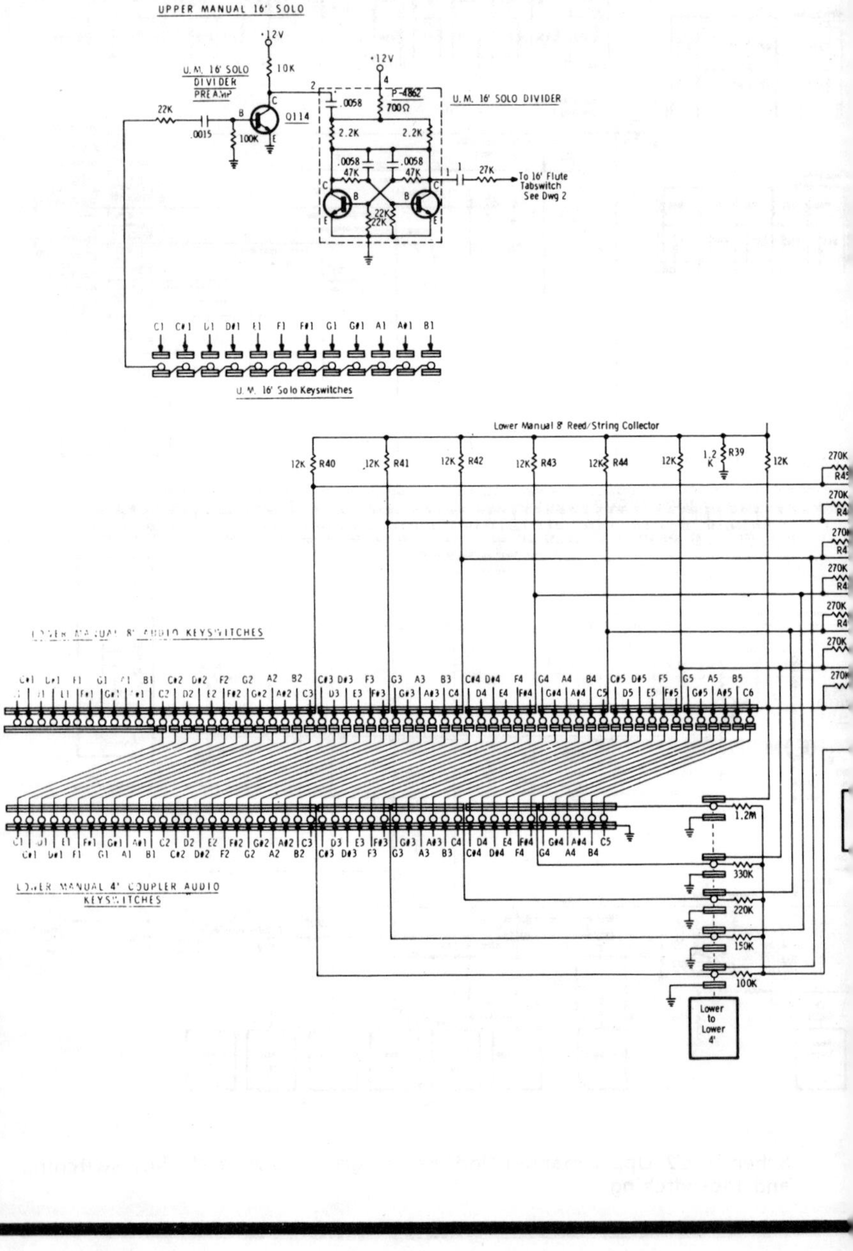
UPPER MANUAL 16' SOLO
+12V
10K
U.M. 16' SOLO DIVIDER PREAMP
22K
.0015
100K
Q114
+12V
P-4862
700Ω
U.M. 16' SOLO DIVIDER
.0058
2.2K
2.2K
.0058
.0058
47K
47K
22K
22K
27K
To 16' Flute Tabswitch See Dwg 2
C1 C#1 D1 D#1 E1 F1 F#1 G1 G#1 A1 A#1 B1
U.M. 16' Solo Keyswitches
Lower Manual 8' Reed/String Collector
12K R40
12K R41
12K R42
12K R43
12K R44
12K
1.2K R39
12K
270K
LOWER MANUAL 8' AUDIO KEYSWITCHES
LOWER MANUAL 4' COUPLER AUDIO KEYSWITCHES
1.2M
330K
220K
150K
100K
Lower to Lower 4'

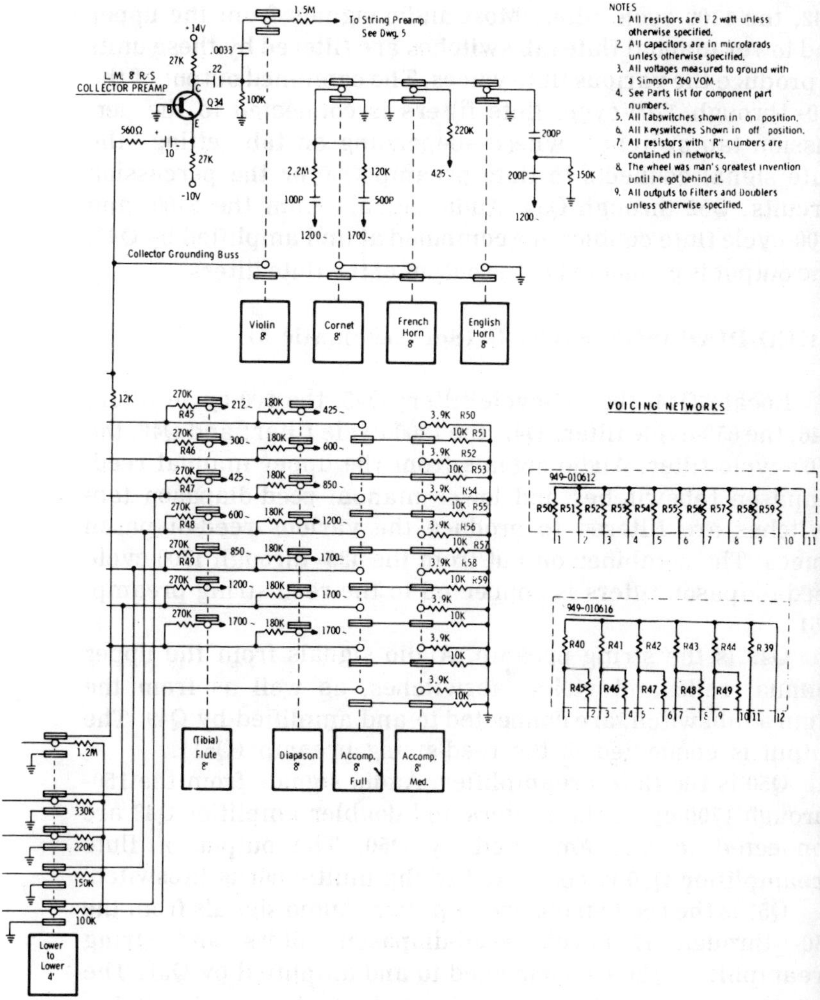

Schematic 4. Upper manual 16′ solo, lower manual keyswitching and tabswitching.

FLUTE FILTERS AND PREAMPS (See Schematic 5)

Locate Q35, the 150-cycle filter; Q36 the 212-cycle filter; Q37, the 300-cycle filter; Q38, the 425-cycle filter; Q39, the 600-cycle filter; Q40, the 850-cycle filter; Q41, the 1200-cycle filter; Q42, the 1700-cycle filter. Most audio signals from the upper and lower manual flute tab switches are filtered by these units to produce the various flute voices. The combined output of the 150- through 1700-cycle flute filters is connected to the percussion tab switches, where—depending on tab setting—the flute signal connects to flute preamp Q50 or the percussion circuits, Q52 through Q54. Audio signals from the 2400- and 3400-cycle flute doubler are combined at and amplified by Q43. The output is connected to the output of the flute filters.

REED-DIAPASON FILTER (See Schematic 5)

Locate Q44, the 425-cycle filter; Q45, the 600-cycle filter; Q46, the 850-cycle filter; Q47, the 1200-cycle filter; and Q48, the 1700-cycle filter. Audio signals from the upper manual reed-diapason tabswitches and lower manual reed-diapason tabswitches are filtered to produce the various reed-diapason voices. The combined output from the 425- through 1700-cycle reed-diapason filters is connected to the reed-string preamp, Q51.

Q49 is the string preamp. Audio signals from the upper manual cello and violin tabswitches, as well as from the kinura tabswitch, are connected to and amplified by Q49. The output is connected to the reed-string preamp (Q51).

Q50 is the flute preamplifier. Audio signals from the 150- through 1700-cycle flute filters and doubler amplifier Q43 are connected to and amplified by Q50. The output of flute preamplifier Q50 is connected to the multi-chorus tabswitch.

Q51 is the reed-string preamplifier. Audio signals from the 150- through 1700-cycle reed-diapason filters and string preamplifier Q49 are connected to and amplified by Q51. The output is connected to the multi-channel chorus tabswitch.

PERCUSSION (See Schematic 5)

Q52 is the bass bypass. Low-frequency audio signals from the flute or reed-diapason filters are amplified by this preamp whenever one of the upper manual keys or lower manual coupler keys is depressed. Output from the bass bypass is connected to the flute or reed-string preamp (Q50 and Q51) through the percussion tabswitch.

Q53 is the percussion modulator. Audio signals from the flute or reed-diapason filters is amplified momentarily by the modulator whenever one of the upper manual keys or lower manual coupler keys is depressed. Output from the percussion modulator is connected to percussion preamplifier Q54. This stage amplifies the audio signal from percussion modulator Q53. The output of this preamplifier is connected to either the flute or reed-string preamplifier Q50 and Q51 by way of the percussion tabswitch.

Locate pulse detectors Q55 and Q56. Depressing any of the upper manual keys or lower manual coupler keys produces positive voltage pulses across the 10-ohm repeat B+ supply resistor. These pulses are connected to the pulse detectors which then amplify the pulses and couple them to the percussion multivibrator, Q57 and Q58. This circuit functions as either a one-shot or combination one-shot and free-running multivibrator, depending on the setting of the percussion repeat switch. When this switch is in the off position, only a single positive output pulse may be produced at the collector of Q58. When in the on position, the multivibrator runs free at the speed set by repeat speed control VR5. Depressing any of the upper manual keys or lower manual coupler keys re-starts the multivibrator from the moment the key is pressed. Since the multivibrator runs free, it produces a series of positive voltage output pulses at the collector of Q58.

Driver Q59 momentarily conducts when triggered by the percussion multivibrator. This controls the momentary gain of percussion modulator Q53. The modulator is turned on the same moment that the driver is turned on. The linear decay of the modulator is determined by the adjustment of the driver circuit, which is controlled by percussion adjustment VR6.

BASS PEDALS (See Schematic 3)

Locate Q24 and Q25, the pedal cancel trigger. Depressing any bass pedal switch creates a pulse which causes the circuit to produce a bigger pulse and momentarily trigger pedal cancel transistor Q26. This transistor momentarily conducts

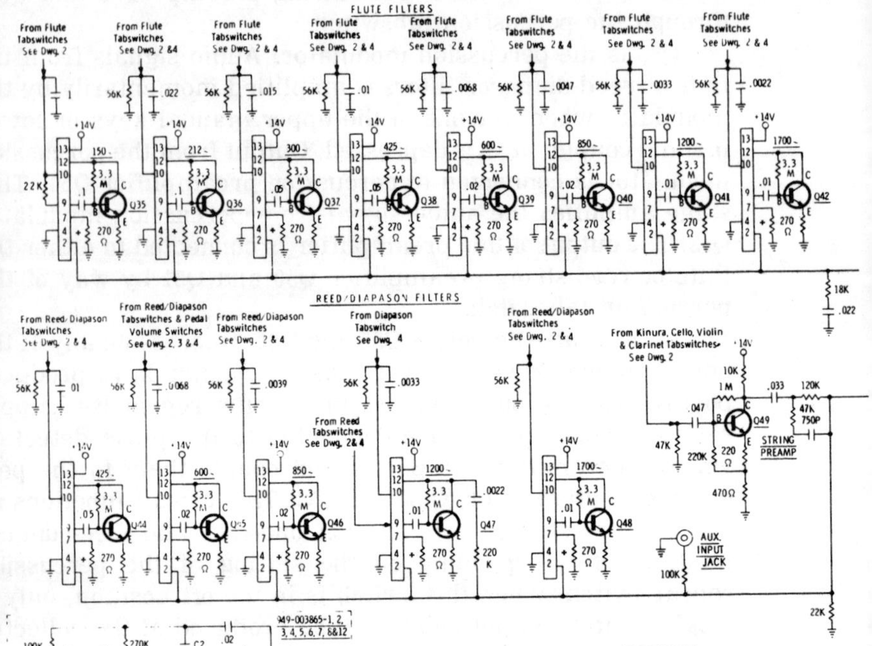

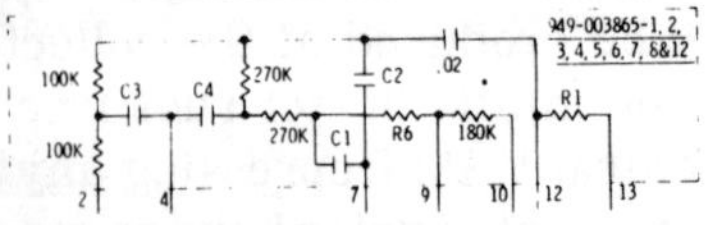

FILTER NETWORK

FILTER VALUE CHART					
PART NO.	FREQ.	C1-C2	C3-C4	R1	R6
949-003865-1	150~	.0047	.01	50K	150K
949-003865-2	212~	.0033	.0068	50K	150K
949-003865-3	300~	.0022	.0047	50K	150K
949-003865-4	425~	.0018	.0033	50K	150K
949-003865-5	600~	.0015	.0022	50K	150K
949-003865-6	850~	.001	.0015	50K	150K
949-003865-7	1200~	750P	.001	50K	80K
949-003865-8	1700~	500P	750P	50K	80K

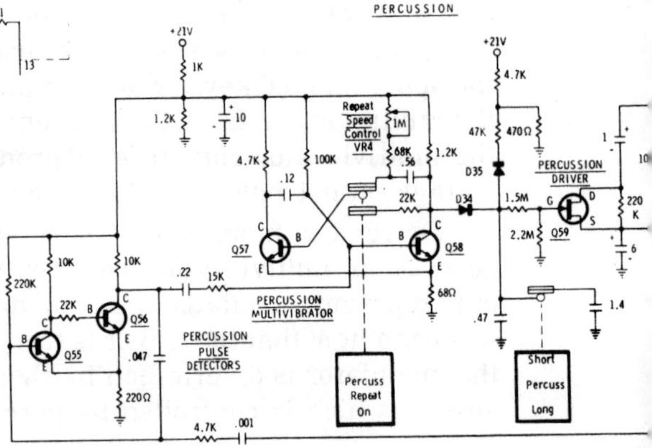

NOTES:

1. All resistors 1/2 watt 10% unless otherwise specified.
2. All capacitors in microfarads unless otherwise specified.
3. All voltages measured to ground with a Simpson 260 VOM.
4. See Parts List for component part numbers.
5. + Denotes factory tailored component.
6. All tabswitches shown in the on position.
8. Life leaps like a geyser for those who drill through the rock of inertia.

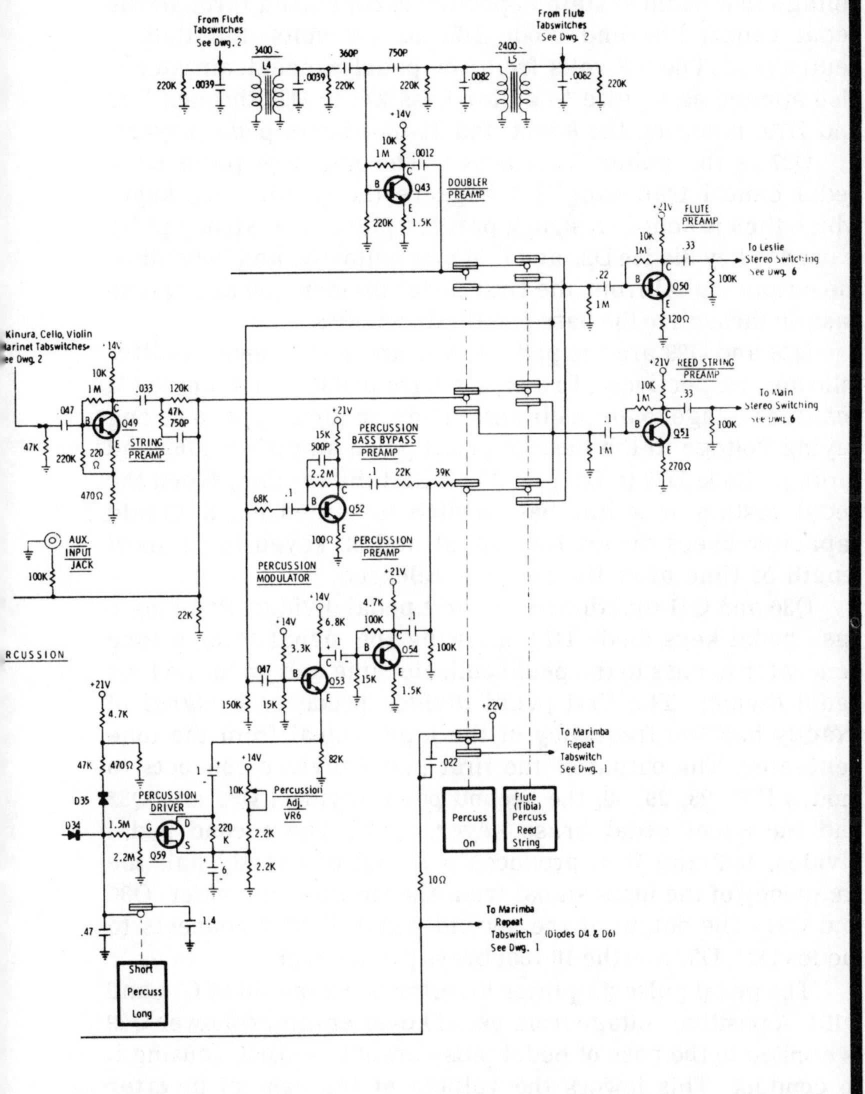

Schematic 5. Flute and reed-string filters, doublers and percussion.

when there is a pulse from the pedal cancel trigger, Q24 and Q25. When the pedal cancel transistor conducts, any positive voltage in a pedal sustain capacitor is conducted through the pedal cancel line and diode D21 to —8 volts and thus is neutralized. The —8 volts from the pedal cancel transistor is also applied as a pulse to guitar bass keyer Q27 through D76 and D79, resetting the 8-foot and 16-foot brass pedal keyers.

Q27 is the guitar bass keyer. The negative pulse from pedal cancel transistor Q26 triggers the guitar bass keyer which then produces a strong positive pulse. This strong pulse is used to key diodes D29 and D30 momentarily, and they allow the output signal from the first pedal divider Q30 and Q31 to pass on through to the bass pedal tabswitches.

Q28 and Q29 are the pedal keyer and pedal keyer emitter follower, respectively. Pressing a bass pedal switch applies a positive voltage to these circuits. They, in turn, apply a strong keying voltage to the base of pedal pulse amplifier Q160 and through diode D75 to D27, 28, 31, 32 and the rhythm. When the pedal sustain or guitar bass switch is turned on, a 15-mfd capacitor keeps diodes D27, 28, 31 and 32 keyed for a short length of time after the pedal is released.

Q30 and Q31 function as the first pedal divider. Pressing a bass pedal keys diode D22, allowing the signal from a tone generator to pass to the pedal collector line and on to the first pedal divider. The first pedal divider produces a signal of exactly half the frequency of the input signal from the tone generator. The output of the first pedal divider connects to diodes D27, 28, 29, 30, the second pedal divider, Q32 and Q33 and the 8-foot pedal brass keyer, Q162. The second pedal divider, Q32 and Q33, produces a signal of exactly half the frequency of the input signal from the first pedal divider, Q30 and Q31. The output of the second pedal divider connects to diodes D31, D32 and the 16-foot brass pedal keyer.

The pedal pulse amplifier inverter is composed of Q16 and Q161. A positive voltage from pedal keyer emitter follower Q29 is applied to the base of pedal pulse amplifier Q160, causing it to conduct. This lowers the voltage at the base of inverter Q161, causing it to conduct, and this allows a positive voltage to be applied to the base of the 8-foot and 16-foot pedal base keyers (Q162 and Q164). A positive voltage from inverter Q161 biases on the 8-foot and 16-foot pedal brass keyers, allowing them to accept the signal from the first and second pedal dividers and pass this on to the pedal brass keyer emitter followers, Q163 and Q165. A signal from the 8-foot and 16-foot pedal brass keyers is converted to a low-impedance output signal that is applied to pedal tabswitches and filters.

Locate Q166 and Q168, the 150-cycle filters. Audio signals from the pedal tabswitches and pedal dividers are filtered to produce various pedal voices, and the output of the 150-cycle filters is then connected to pedal output preamp Q167. Audio signal from the two 150-cycle pedal filters is connected to and amplified by pedal output preamplifier Q167. The output is then connected to the main and Leslie mixing preamps through the pedal volume switches.

STEREO SWITCHING (See Schematic 6)

Audio signals from all rhythm voice circuits are combined at and amplified by Q71, the rhythm emitter follower. The output of Q71 is connected to the main and Leslie mixing preamplifiers Q60-Q63 and to reverb driver Q64.

Q60 and Q61 are the Leslie mixing preamplifiers. Audio signals from the flute and/or reed-string preamplifiers, depending on the setting of the reed-string main-Leslie tabswitches, connect to these preamplifiers. Also, audio signals from the rhythm, bass pedals and brass symphonizer connect to these preamplifiers. The output from Q61 is applied to the Leslie expression pedal photocell, P5A.

Audio signals from the flute and/or reed-string preamplifiers, depending on the setting of the flute and reed-string main-Leslie tabswitches, connect to Q62 and Q63, the main mixing preamps. Also, audio signals from the rhythm, bass pedals and brass symphonizer connect to these preamplifiers. The output of preamplifier Q63 is applied to the main expression pedal photocell, P5B.

REVERB (See Schematic 6)

Q64 is the reverb driver. Audio signals from flute preamplifier Q50, reed-string-diapason preamplifier Q51, rhythm emitter follower Q71, brass symphonizer and cassette output are amplified and connected to the reverb spring unit where the reverb effect is produced.

Reverberating audio signal from the reverb spring unit is amplified for the first time by Q65, reverb preamp No. 1. The

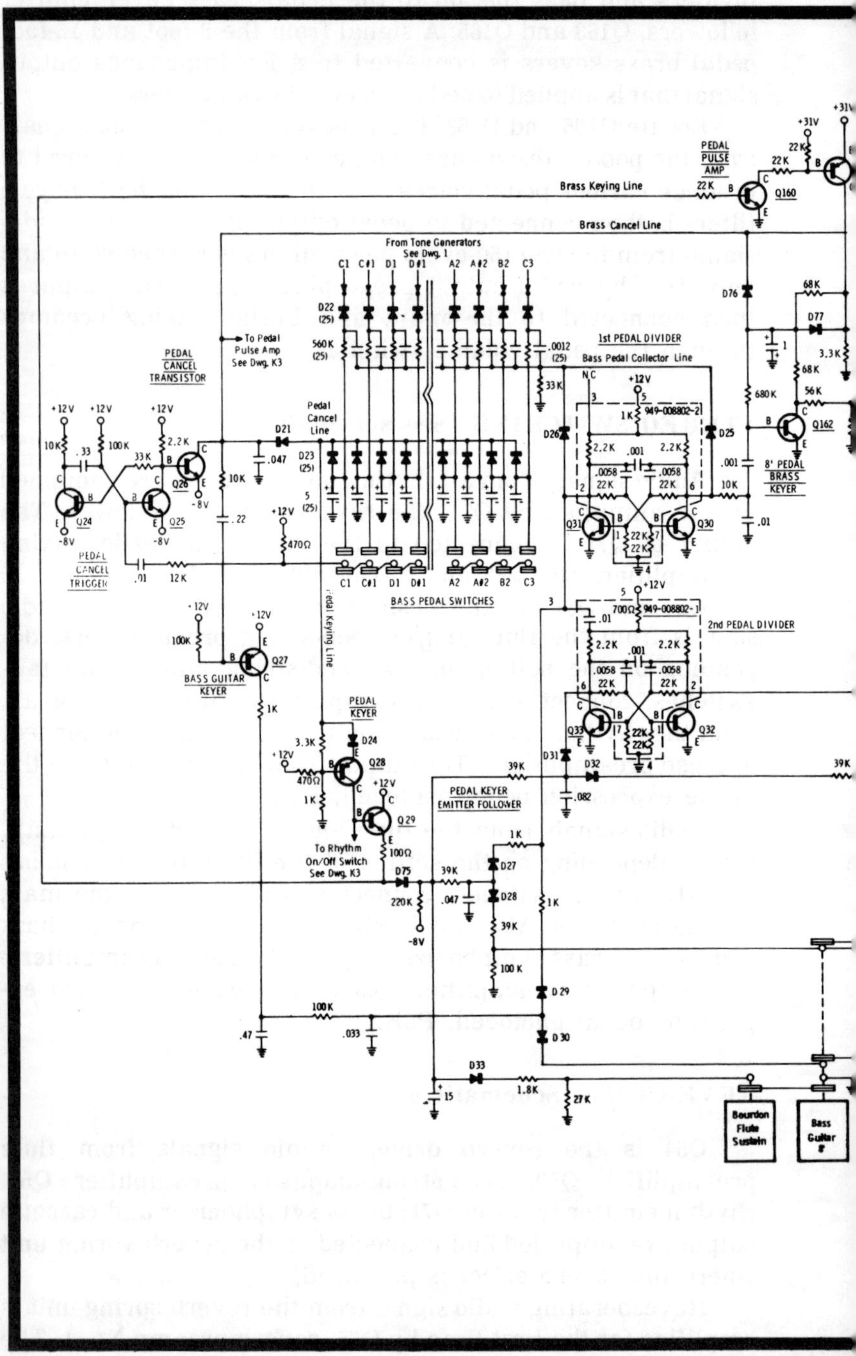
PEDAL PULSE AMP
Brass Keying Line
Q160
Brass Cancel Line
From Tone Generators See Dwg. 1
C1 C#1 D1 D#1 A2 A#2 B2 C3
D22 (25)
560K (25)
.0012 (25)
To Pedal Pulse Amp See Dwg. K3
PEDAL CANCEL TRANSISTOR
1st PEDAL DIVIDER
Bass Pedal Collector Line
949-008802-2
D76
D77
Q162
8' PEDAL BRASS KEYER
Pedal Cancel Line
D21
D23 (25)
D26
D25
Q24
Q25
Q26
Q31
Q30
PEDAL CANCEL TRIGGER
BASS PEDAL SWITCHES
Pedal Keying Line
Q27
BASS GUITAR KEYER
949-008802-1
2nd PEDAL DIVIDER
Q33
Q32
PEDAL KEYER
D24
Q28
Q29
PEDAL KEYER EMITTER FOLLOWER
D31
D32
To Rhythm On/Off Switch See Dwg. K3
D75
D27
D28
D29
D30
D33
Bourdon Flute Sustain
Bass Guitar 8'

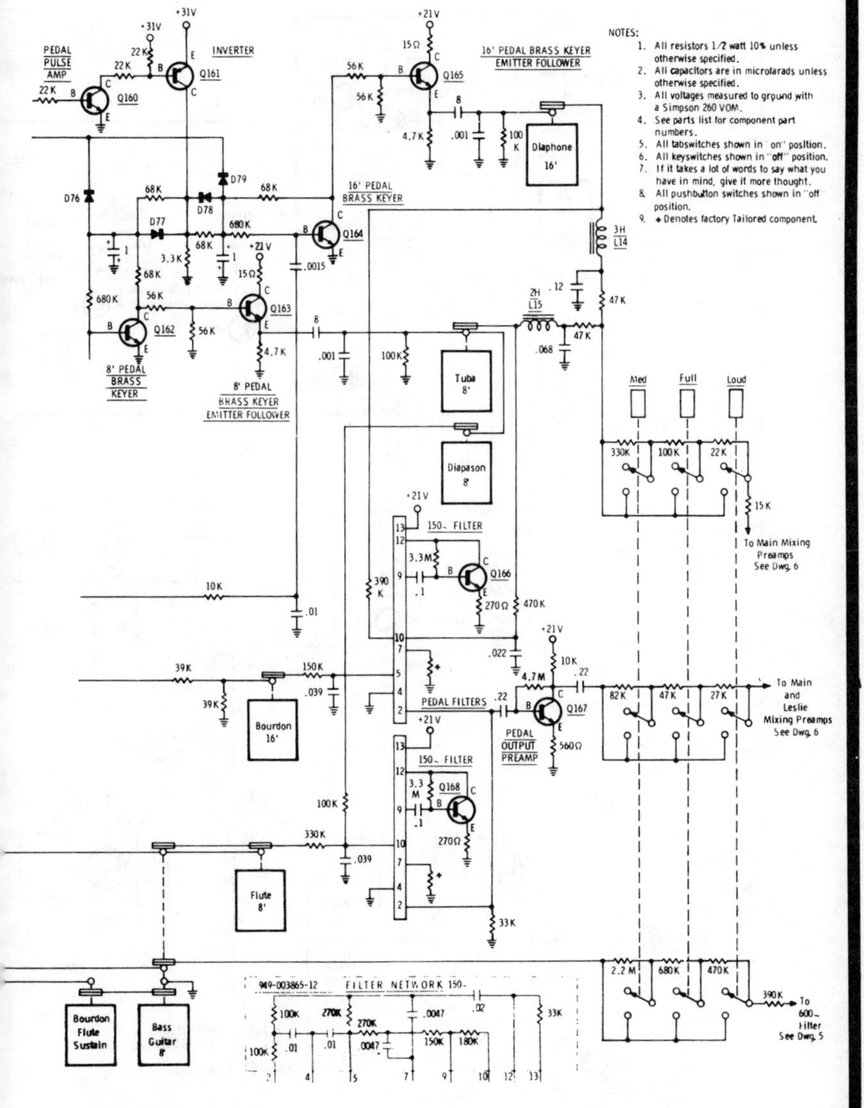

Schematic 3. Bass pedal circuits.

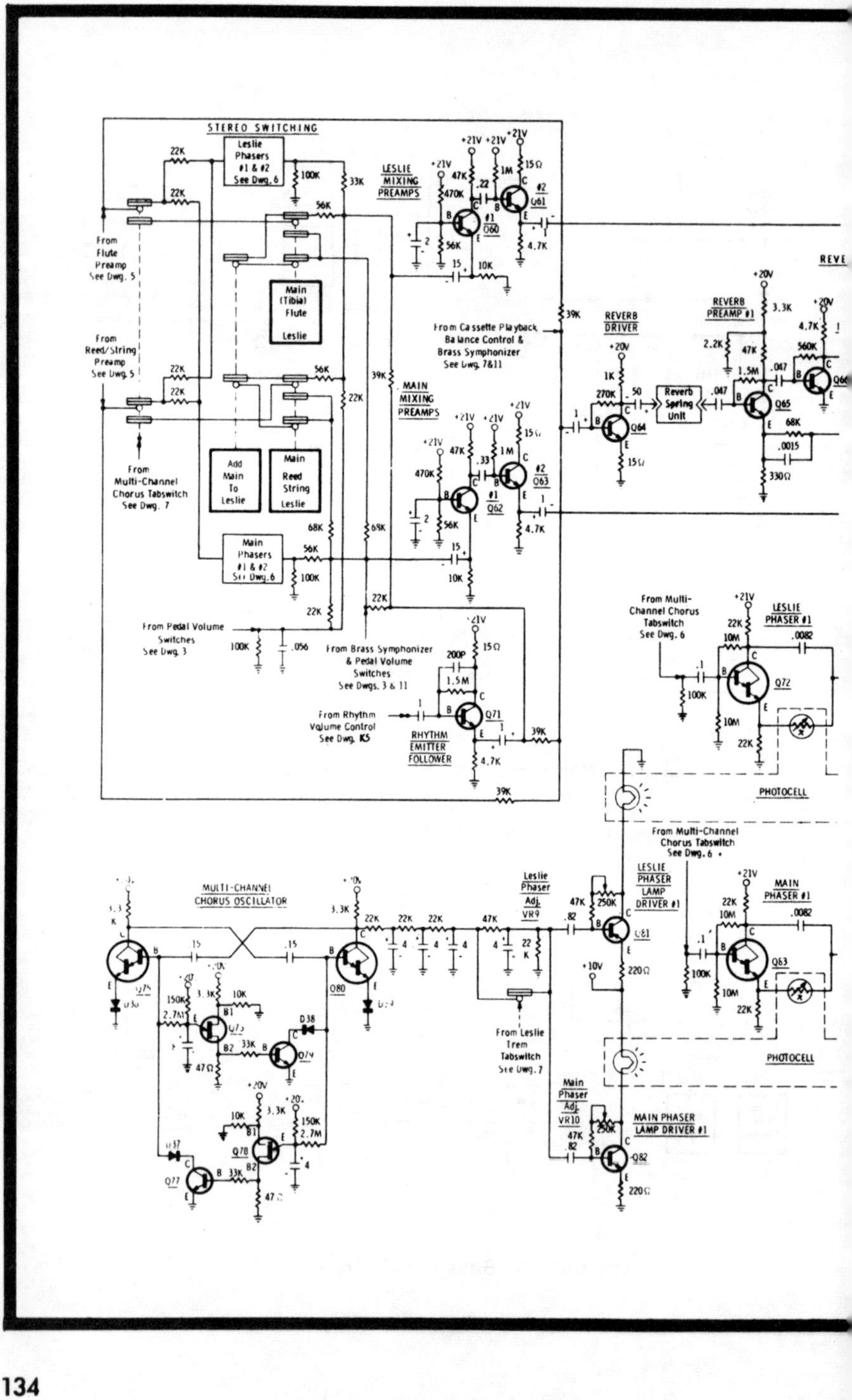
STEREO SWITCHING
Leslie Phasers #1 & #2 See Dwg. 6
Main (Tibia) Flute Leslie
Add Main To Leslie
Main Reed String Leslie
Main Phasers #1 & #2 See Dwg. 6
From Flute Preamp See Dwg. 5
From Reed/String Preamp See Dwg. 5
From Multi-Channel Chorus Tabswitch See Dwg. 7
From Pedal Volume Switches See Dwg. 3
From Brass Symphonizer & Pedal Volume Switches See Dwgs. 3 & 11
From Rhythm Volume Control See Dwg. K5
RHYTHM EMITTER FOLLOWER
LESLIE MIXING PREAMPS
MAIN MIXING PREAMPS
From Cassette Playback Balance Control & Brass Symphonizer See Dwg. 7&11
REVERB DRIVER
Reverb Spring Unit
REVERB PREAMP #1
From Multi-Channel Chorus Tabswitch See Dwg. 6
LESLIE PHASER #1
PHOTOCELL
MULTI-CHANNEL CHORUS OSCILLATOR
Leslie Phaser Adj. VR9
From Leslie Trem Tabswitch See Dwg. 7
LESLIE PHASER LAMP DRIVER #1
From Multi-Channel Chorus Tabswitch See Dwg. 6
MAIN PHASER #1
Main Phaser Adj. VR10
MAIN PHASER LAMP DRIVER #1

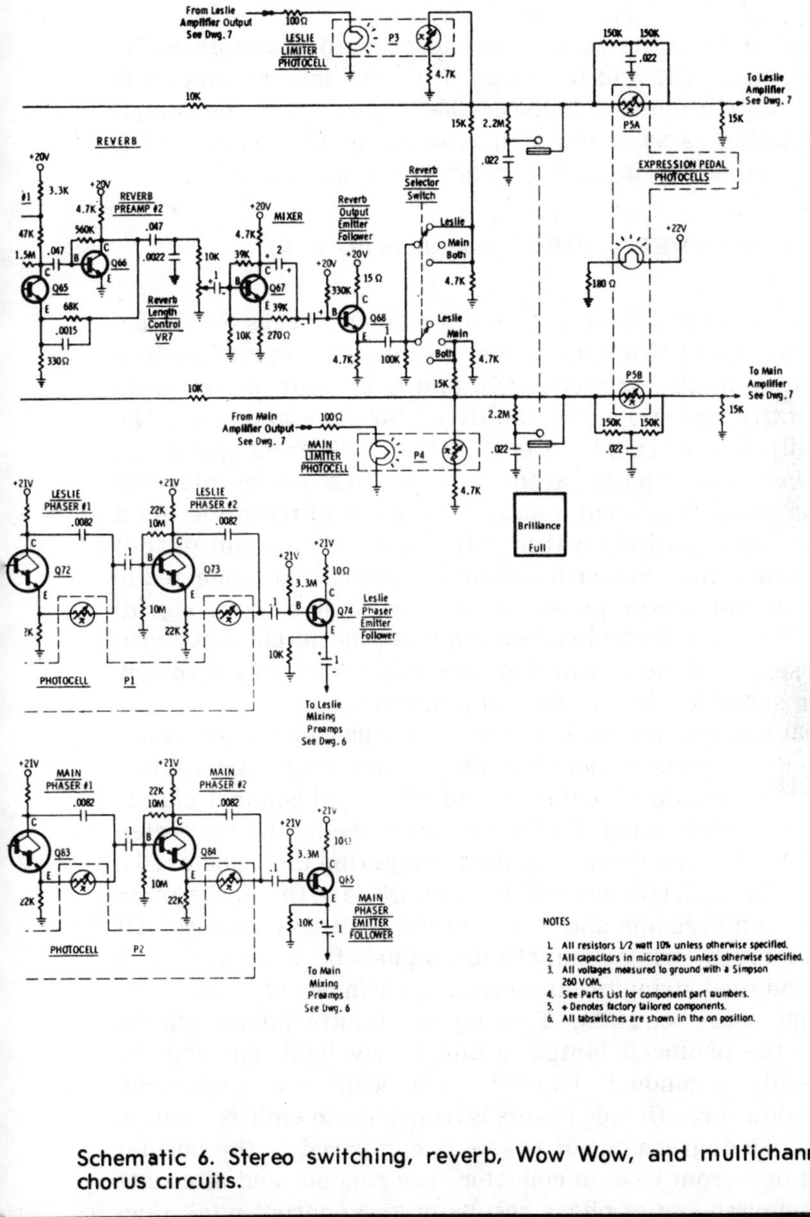

Schematic 6. Stereo switching, reverb, Wow Wow, and multichannel chorus circuits.

amplified signal is then forwarded to reverb preamplifier number two, Q66, where further amplification of the reverberating signal is accomplished. The reverb signal is controlled at the output of this circuit as well. With the reverb control off, all reverb signal is grounded.

Signal from the reverb second preamp is amplified by reverb mixer Q67 and the output from the mixer connects to reverb output emitter follower Q68. Signal from the mixer-preamplifier is switched at the output of this stage and is applied either to the main and/or Leslie amplifiers.

MULTI-CHANNEL CHORUS (See Schematic 6)

Q75 through Q80 form the multi-channel chorus oscillator. This consists of two unijunction circuits each operating in a relaxation oscillator mode (Q76 and Q78), with driver transistors Q77 and Q79 and a multivibrator (Q75 and Q80). The two unijunction oscillators each run at a different speed and produce negative pulses at the drivers. These pulses interrupt the normally consistent operation of the multivibrator. As a result, the multivibrator produces a random-output waveform. This waveform is then RC filtered and connected to the main and Leslie phaser lamp drivers as a drive signal. When the Leslie tremolo tabswitch is on, the output waveform bypasses the stage of filtering, and this results in a stronger driver signal to the phaser lamp drivers.

Q81 and Q82 are the Leslie and main phaser lamp drivers. These two opposite polarity (NPN and PNP) transistors alternately conduct at the rate of the multi-channel chorus oscillator drive signal. As they conduct, the lamps connected to their collectors alternately light, triggering their photocells.

Q72 through Q74 and Q83 through Q85 are the Leslie-main phaser numbers one and two, and the emitter followers. All flute and reed-string channel audio signals from the main and flute and reed-string preamplifiers are connected to and pass through these circuits. Turning on multi-channel chorus allows the photocell lamps to alternately light, causing the photocells to conduct. When the photocells are conducting, signal flow through the phasers is from base to emitter. This is nearly 180 degrees out of phase as compared to the normal signal flow from base to collector. The random and alternate channel changing of phase results in an apparent pitch fluctuation which imitates the effect of a large, multi-tone source organ. The phase-shifted flute and reed-string signals from the phasers connect to the emitter follower circuits and these connect to the main and Leslie mixing preamplifier circuits.

AMPLIFIERS (See Schematic 7)

Q89 through Q104 make up the main and Leslie amplifiers. The circuits in these amplifiers are direct coupled and are identical in operation. The function of the preamplifier and voltage amplifier is to boost signal voltages to a point where they can be used to drive the driver and pre-driver circuits. The pre-driver inverts the audio voltages so that the drivers work in pushpull. The output transistors convert the audio voltages from the drivers to a high-current, low-voltage output signal that is connected by way of the headphone jack to the speakers. The output signal from each of the amplifiers is mixed and connected to the cassette recorder on models that are equipped for this function.

POWER SUPPLY (See Schematic 8)

Positive and negative DC supply voltages are produced by transformer T1 and diodes D42 through D47 and D69 and D70. These voltages are supplied to the various organ circuits as indicated. Zener diodes Z2, Z3, Z4, Z6 and Z11 and Z7 are used as regulators on several voltages as well. The internal Leslie motors are connected across the primary of the power transformer (T1) ahead of the main power fuse and in series with a 5-ampere slo blo fuse. A 2-ampere fuse is included in the DC supply circuit connected to repeat. This prevents component damage in case of a short circuit.

Q111 is the cassette power regulator. The transistor and zener diode, which is attached to its base, insures that a constant +8 volts is always supplied to the cassette recorder speed control. Adjusting the speed control varies the voltage supplied to the cassette recorder between +7 and +8 volts.

GOLDEN HARP (See Schematic 10)

When the Golden Harp footswitch is off, ramp keyer Q105 continually conducts, thus supplying a strong positive voltage

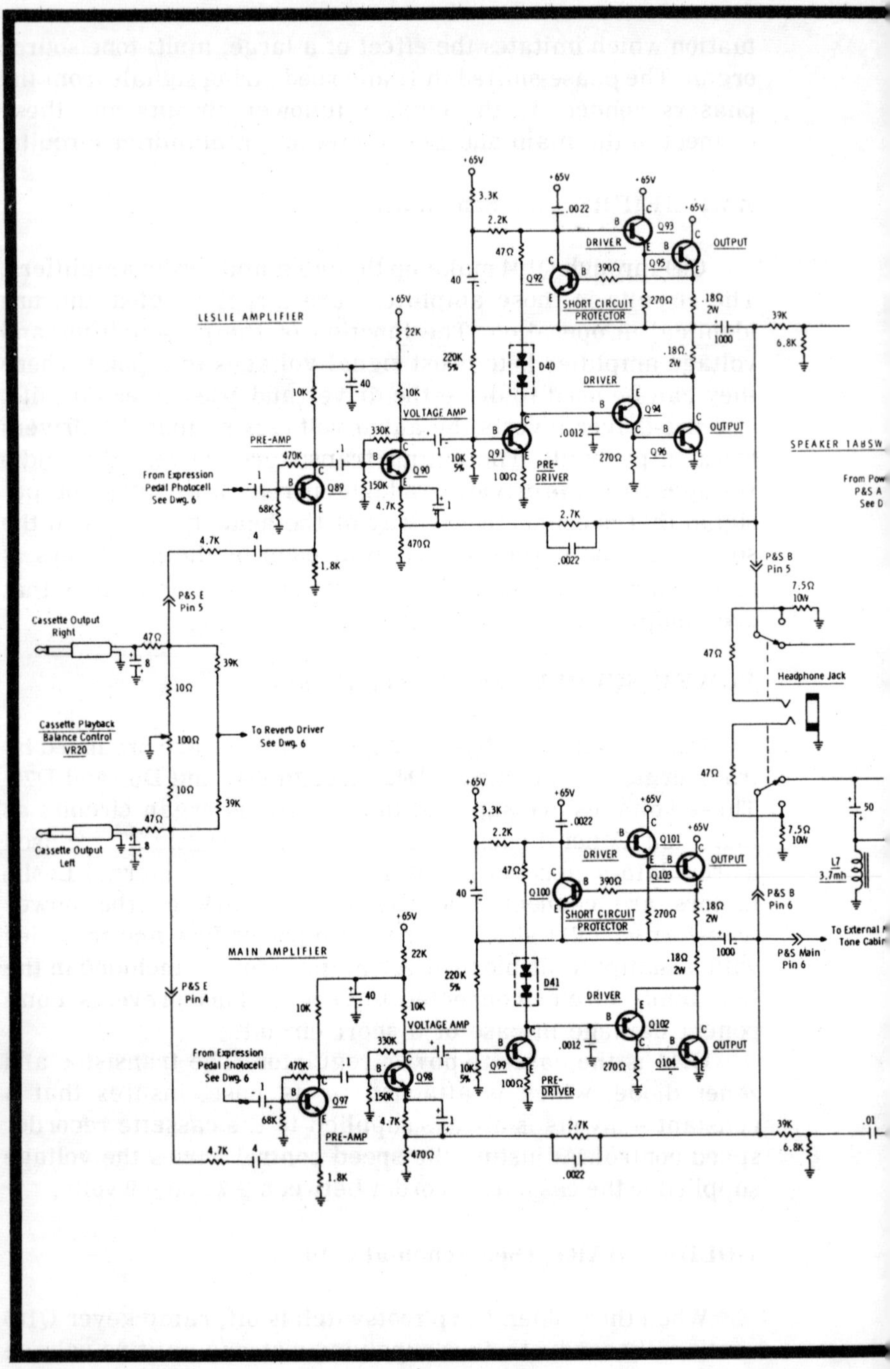
LESLIE AMPLIFIER
MAIN AMPLIFIER
PRE-AMP
VOLTAGE AMP
PRE-DRIVER
DRIVER
OUTPUT
SHORT CIRCUIT PROTECTOR
From Expression Pedal Photocell See Dwg. 6
Cassette Output Right
Cassette Output Left
Cassette Playback Balance Control VR20
To Reverb Driver See Dwg. 6
P&S E Pin 5
P&S E Pin 4
P&S B Pin 5
P&S B Pin 6
P&S Main Pin 6
Headphone Jack
SPEAKER TABSW
To External Tone Cabin
L7 3.7mh
Q89
Q90
Q91
Q92
Q93
Q94
Q95
Q96
Q97
Q98
Q99
Q100
Q101
Q102
Q103
Q104
D40
D41
+65V

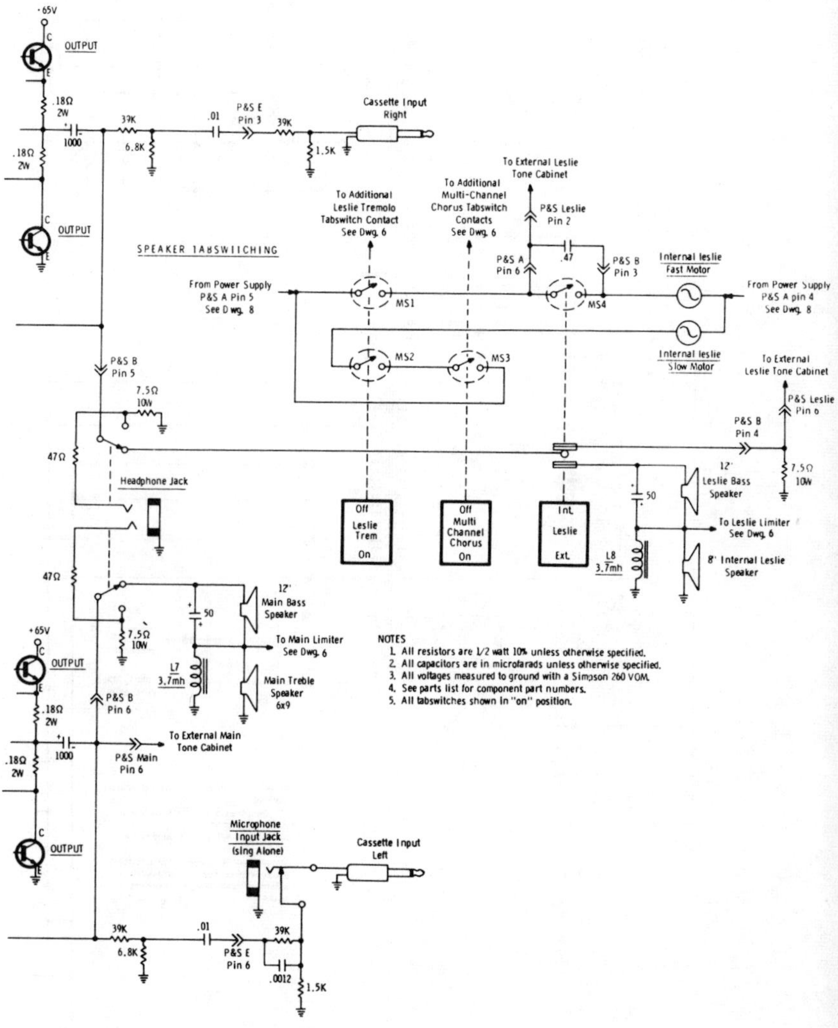

Schematic 7. Main and Leslie amplifiers and speaker tabswitching.

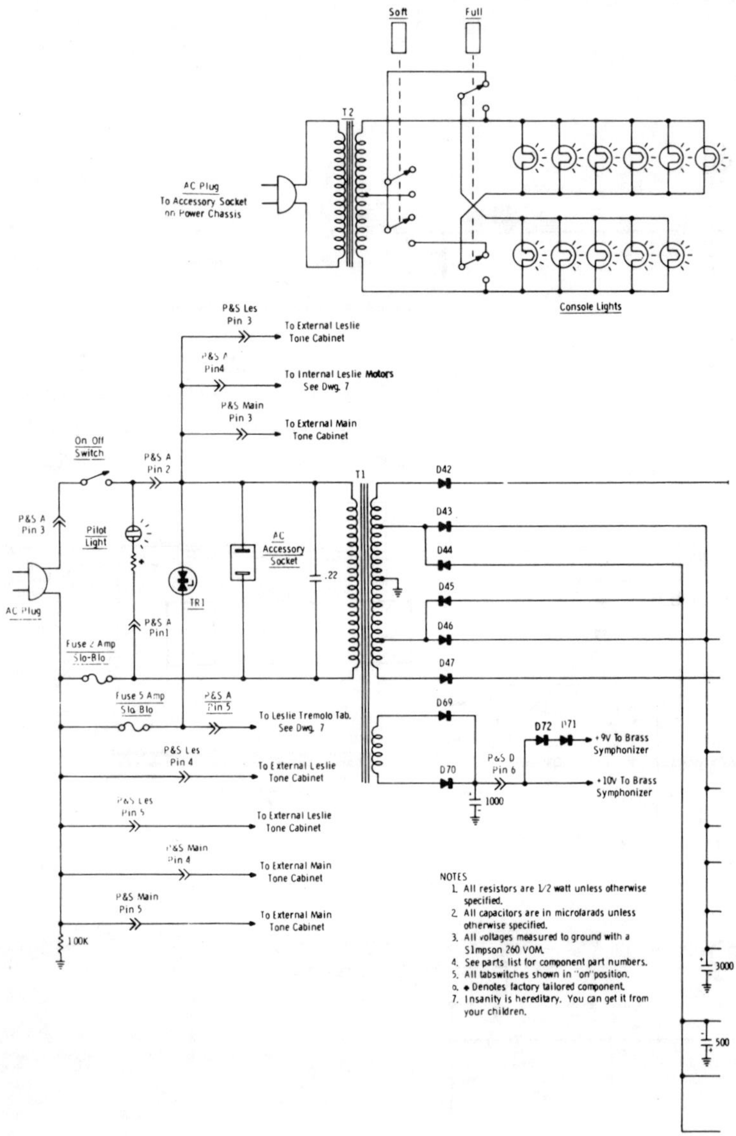

Soft
Full
T2
AC Plug
To Accessory Socket
on Power Chassis
Console Lights
P&S Les
Pin 3
To External Leslie
Tone Cabinet
P&S A
Pin4
To Internal Leslie Motors
See Dwg. 7
P&S Main
Pin 3
To External Main
Tone Cabinet
On Off
Switch
P&S A
Pin 2
T1
D42
D43
D44
D45
D46
D47
P&S A
Pin 3
Pilot
Light
AC
Accessory
Socket
.22
TR1
AC Plug
P&S A
Pin1
Fuse 2 Amp
Slo-Blo
Fuse 5 Amp
Slo Blo
P&S A
Pin 5
To Leslie Tremolo Tab.
See Dwg. 7
D69
D72
D71
+9V To Brass
Symphonizer
P&S D
Pin 6
D70
+10v To Brass
Symphonizer
1000
P&S Les
Pin 4
To External Leslie
Tone Cabinet
P&S Les
Pin 5
To External Leslie
Tone Cabinet
P&S Main
Pin 4
To External Main
Tone Cabinet
P&S Main
Pin 5
To External Main
Tone Cabinet
100K
3000
500
NOTES
1. All resistors are 1/2 watt unless otherwise specified.
2. All capacitors are in microfarads unless otherwise specified.
3. All voltages measured to ground with a Simpson 260 VOM.
4. See parts list for component part numbers.
5. All tabswitches shown in "on" position.
6. ◆ Denotes factory tailored component.
7. Insanity is hereditary. You can get it from your children.

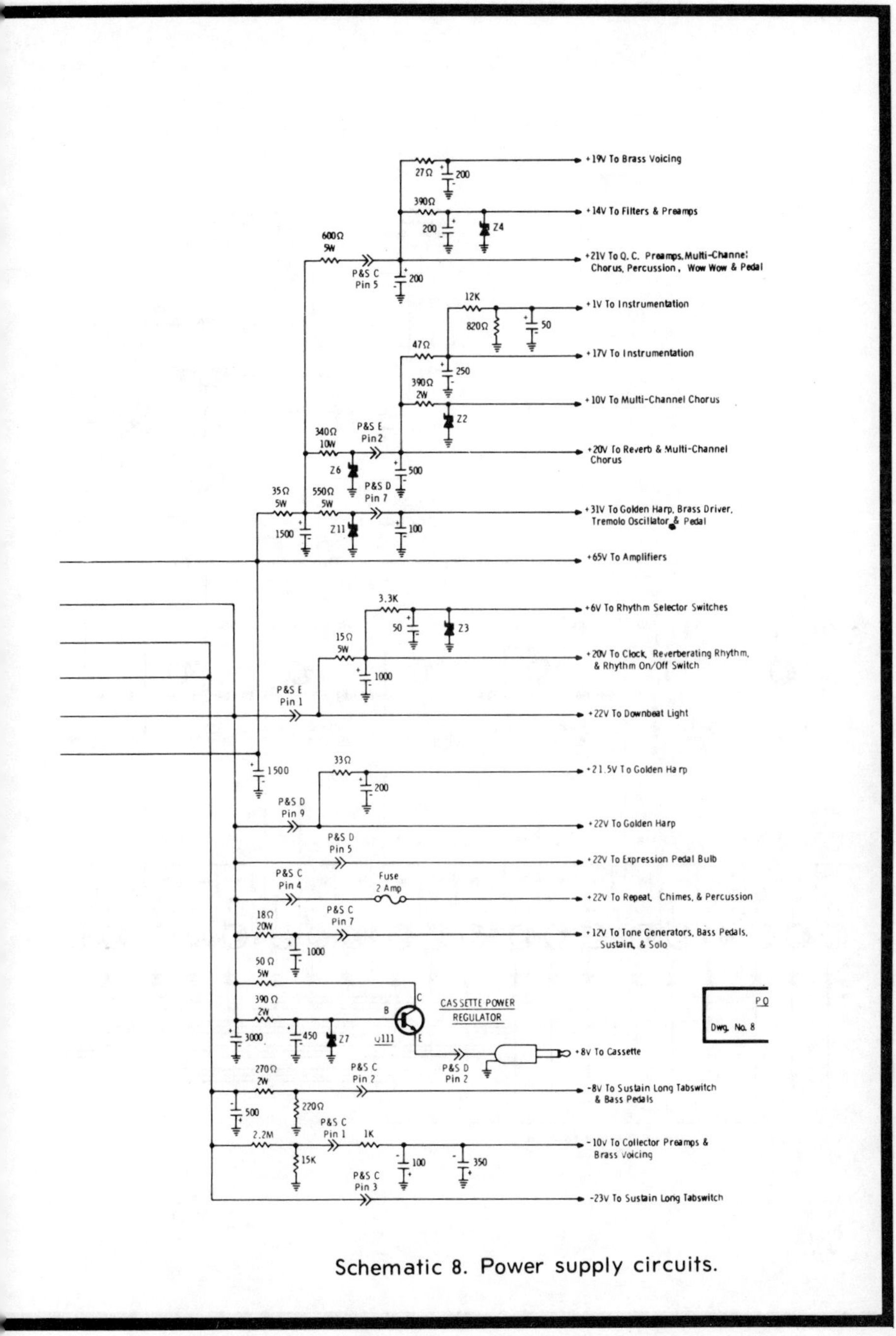

Schematic 8. Power supply circuits.

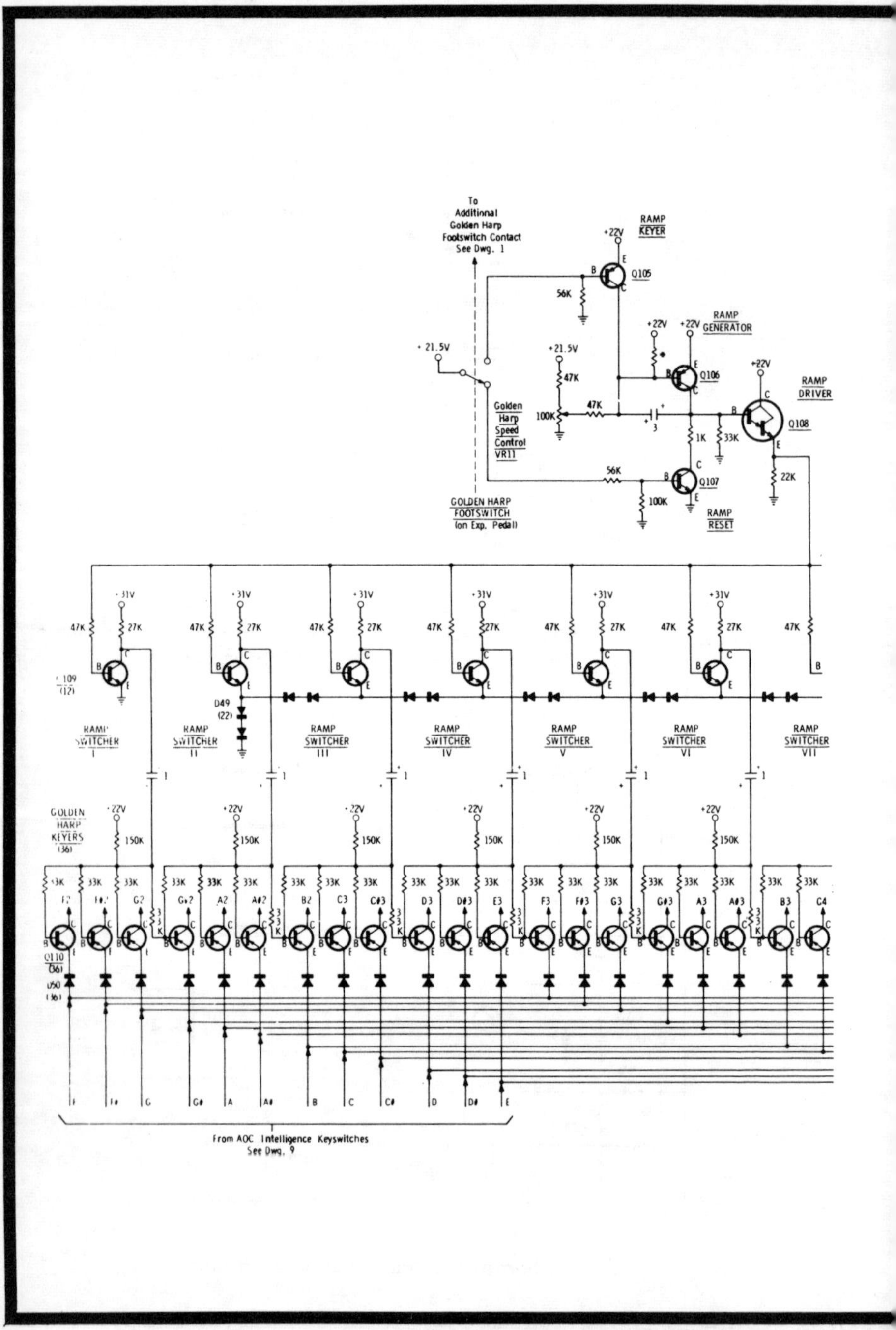
To Additional Golden Harp Footswitch Contact See Dwg. 1
RAMP KEYER
Q105
RAMP GENERATOR
Q106
RAMP DRIVER
Q108
RAMP RESET
Q107
Golden Harp Speed Control VR11
GOLDEN HARP FOOTSWITCH (on Exp. Pedal)
RAMP SWITCHER I
RAMP SWITCHER II
RAMP SWITCHER III
RAMP SWITCHER IV
RAMP SWITCHER V
RAMP SWITCHER VI
RAMP SWITCHER VII
GOLDEN HARP KEYERS (36)
From AOC Intelligence Keyswitches See Dwg. 9

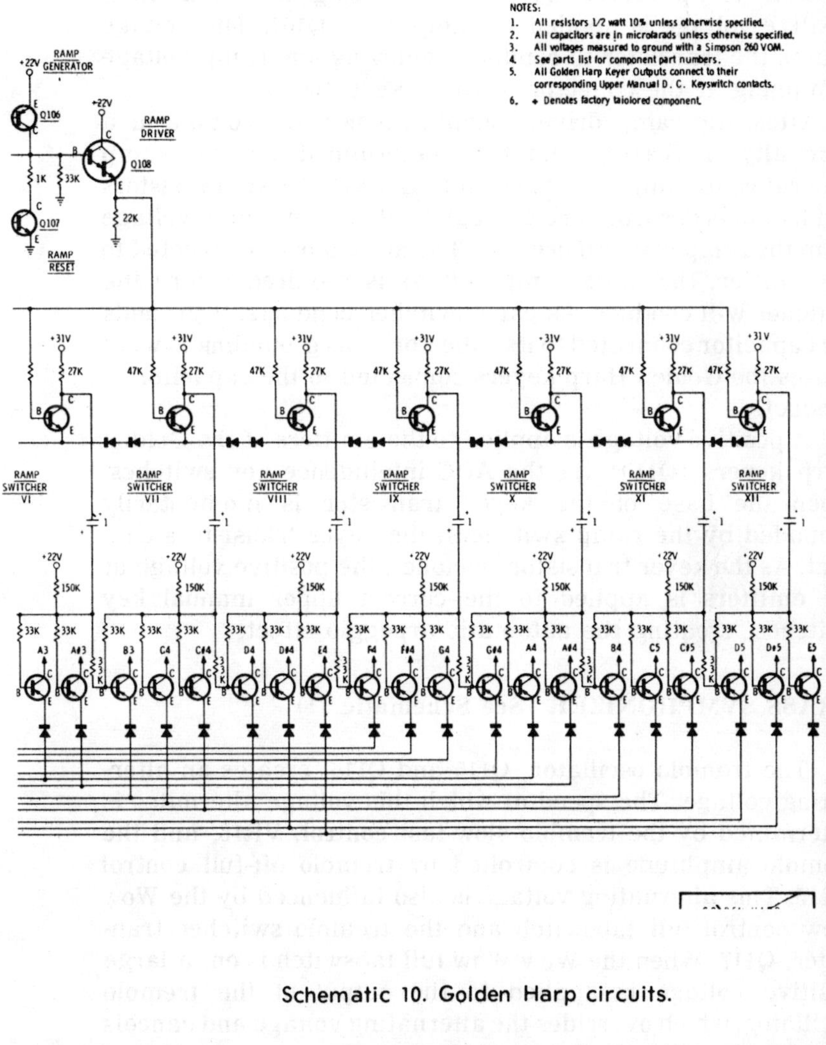

Schematic 10. Golden Harp circuits.

to ramp generator Q106. This positive voltage insures that the ramp generator is normally in its off state. Depressing the foot switch applies positive voltage to the ramp keyer, cutting it off. This allows the ramp generator to begin to conduct. Ramp generator Q106 starts to conduct when Q105 cuts off. The speed at which the ramp keyer goes from zero to full conduction is controlled by the Golden Harp speed control, VR11. It is the gradual voltage rise at the collector of this transistor that controls ramp driver Q108. On releasing the footswitch, positive voltage is applied to ramp reset Q107. The voltage causes the transistor to conduct, removing any ramp voltage remaining at the collector of ramp keyer Q106.

Q108, the ramp driver, supplies a positive voltage in a gradually increasing quantity, determined by the ramp generator, to ramp switchers I through XII. These transistors conduct in order from one through twelve as the ramp voltage from the ramp driver increases. The more diodes connected to the emitter, the more ramp voltage is required before the switcher will conduct. As each switcher conducts, it grounds the capacitor connected to its collector. This grounding is what causes the Golden Harp keyers connected to the capacitor to conduct.

A positive voltage is applied to the emitters of the Golden Harp keyers (Q110) via the AOC intelligence key switches. When the base of the keyer transistor is momentarily grounded by the ramp switchers, the keyer transistors conduct. As the keyer transistors conduct, the positive voltage at the emitters is applied to the correct upper manual key switches, creating the automatic arpeggio effect.

BRASS SYMPHONIZER (See Schematic 11)

The tremolo oscillator, Q115 and Q116, creates an alternating voltage. The speed at which this voltage alternates is determined by the tremolo slow-fast control, VR16, and the tremolo amplitude is controlled by tremolo off-full control VR15. This alternating voltage is also influenced by the Wow Wow control full tabswitch and the tremolo switcher transistor, Q117. When the Wow Wow full tabswitch is on, a large positive voltage is applied to the output of the tremolo oscillator, which overrides the alternating voltage and cancels the tremolo. When the krumet horn preset is pressed, some of the output of the tremolo oscillator will be grounded through the tremolo switcher, Q117. During this time, a steady positive voltage is applied by diode D55, which changes the amplitude of the alternating voltage and produces the proper krumet horn voicing. After the output of the tremolo oscillator has been altered by the various tabs and controls, it is then applied to the base of the brass bus driver, Q118, which conducts and supplies voltage to the upper manual brass and Wow Wow key switches.

When a brass preset is pressed, it momentarily applies a positive voltage to the base of its NPN latching transistor (Q119 to Q128). This causes it to conduct, lowering the voltage at its collector. The drop in voltage causes the PNP transistor connected at the NPN's collector to conduct, applying a constant voltage to the base of the NPN, keeping it on. When the NPN conducts, the positive voltage at its emitter is applied to the base of its associated lamp driver (Q129 to Q133). Positive voltage from one or more of the latching transistors (Q120, etc.) causes these transistors to conduct, grounding one side of the preset indicator lamp, letting it light. The lamp-driver transistors also ground the base of the respective switcher transistors (Q148 etc.). This causes the switcher transistor to stop conducting, removing the ground from the brass voicing circuit and allowing signal to pass from the brass collector preamplifier and emitter follower (Q146, Q147) to the output preamplifier, Q156.

When a brass preset button is pressed, a negative-going pulse is received at the base of Q134 from the common preset indicator lamp supply line. This causes Q134 to conduct, providing a momentary positive voltage to the base of the PNP latching transistors, unlatching any previously-latched preset. This positive voltage is also applied to the base of Q135, causing it to conduct, thus holding Q134 on longer and insuring a strong cancel pulse to the latching circuits.

When a brass preset button is pressed, it lowers the positive voltage at the base of relay switcher number one, Q138. This causes it to conduct and apply a positive voltage to either ground, through relay switcher number two (Q137) or to the base of relay driver Q136 when Q137 is not conducting. When the upper manual cancel preset is pressed, a positive voltage is applied to the base of lamp driver Q133, making it conduct and ground one side of the indicator lamp and the base of relay switcher number two, Q137. Grounding Q137's base

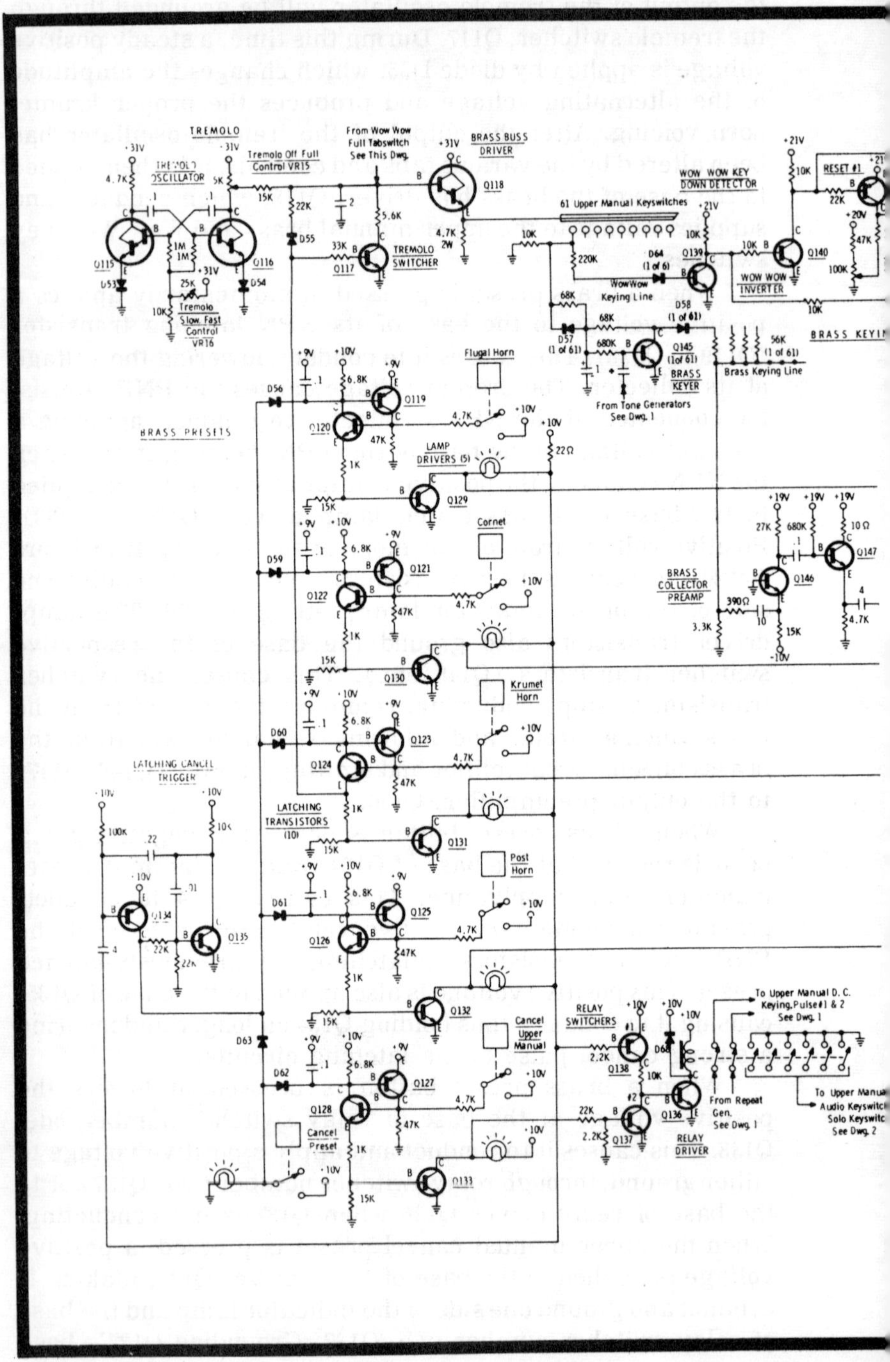
TREMOLO
TREMOLO OSCILLATOR
Tremolo Off Full Control VR15
From Wow Wow Full Tabswitch See This Dwg.
BRASS BUSS DRIVER
Q115
Q116
Q117
Q118
TREMOLO SWITCHER
Tremolo Slow Fast Control VR16
61 Upper Manual Keyswitches
WOW WOW KEY DOWN DETECTOR
RESET #1
WOW WOW INVERTER
WowWow Keying Line
BRASS KEYER
Brass Keying Line
BRASS KEYI
From Tone Generators See Dwg. 1
BRASS PRESETS
Flugal Horn
LAMP DRIVERS (5)
Cornet
Krumet Horn
Post Horn
Cancel Upper Manual
Cancel Preset
LATCHING CANCEL TRIGGER
LATCHING TRANSISTORS (10)
BRASS COLLECTOR PREAMP
RELAY SWITCHERS
RELAY DRIVER
To Upper Manual D. C. Keying, Pulse#1 & 2 See Dwg. 1
From Repeat Gen. See Dwg. 1
To Upper Manua Audio Keyswitc Solo Keyswitc See Dwg. 2

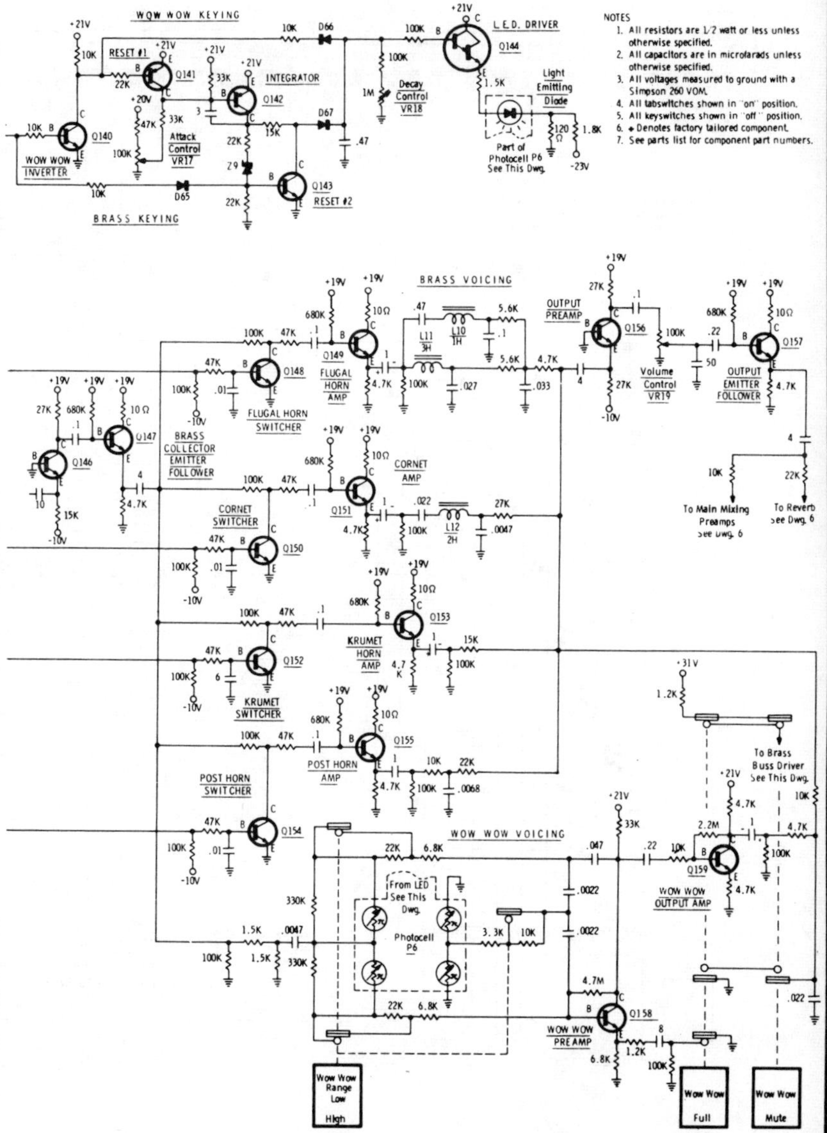

NOTES
1. All resistors are 1/2 watt or less unless otherwise specified.
2. All capacitors are in microfarads unless otherwise specified.
3. All voltages measured to ground with a Simpson 260 VOM.
4. All tabswitches shown in "on" position.
5. All keyswitches shown in "off" position.
6. ◆ Denotes factory tailored component.
7. See parts list for component part numbers.

Schematic 11. Brass symphonizer, tremolo and Wow Wow circuits.

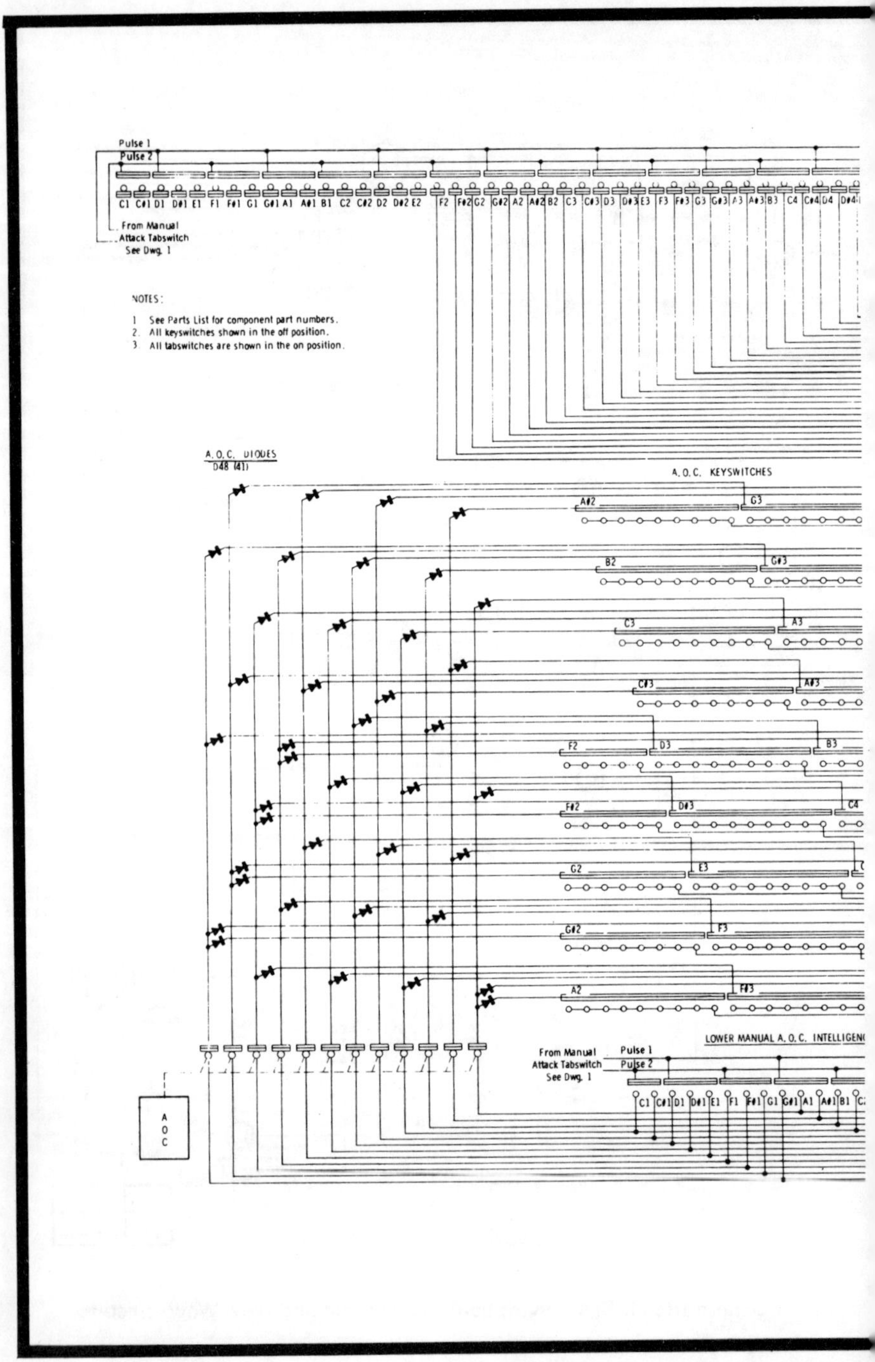
Pulse 1
Pulse 2
C1 C#1 D1 D#1 E1 F1 F#1 G1 G#1 A1 A#1 B1 C2 C#2 D2 D#2 E2
F2 F#2 G2 G#2 A2 A#2 B2 C3 C#3 D3 D#3 E3 F3 F#3 G3 G#3 A3 A#3 B3 C4 C#4 D4
From Manual
Attack Tabswitch
See Dwg. 1
NOTES:
1. See Parts List for component part numbers.
2. All keyswitches shown in the off position.
3. All tabswitches are shown in the on position.
A.O.C. DIODES
D48 (41)
A.O.C. KEYSWITCHES
A#2
G3
B2
G#3
C3
A3
C#3
A#3
F2
D3
B3
F#2
D#3
C4
G2
E3
G#2
F3
A2
F#3
A O C
LOWER MANUAL A.O.C. INTELLIGENC
From Manual
Attack Tabswitch
See Dwg. 1
Pulse 1
Pulse 2
C1 C#1 D1 D#1 E1 F1 F#1 G1 G#1 A1 A#1 B1

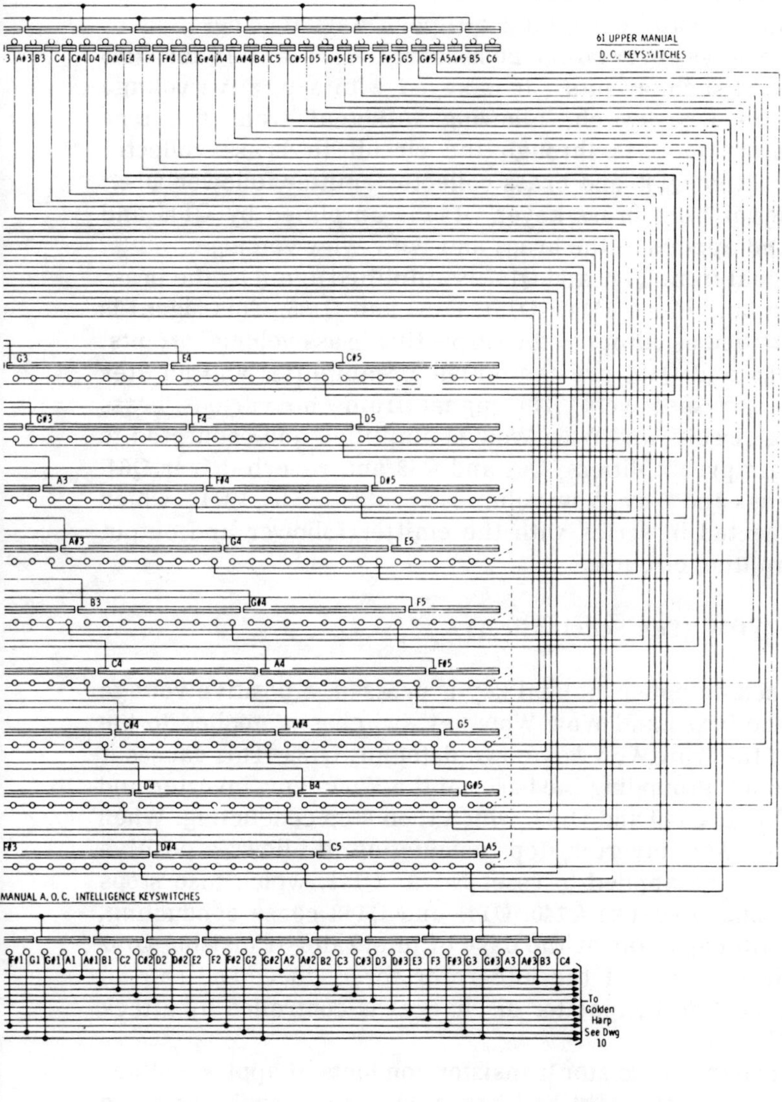

Schematic 9. AOC wiring diagram.

cuts it off, and the positive voltage from relay switcher Q138 is applied to the base of the relay driver, Q136. This causes the relay driver to conduct, grounding the relay and allowing it to operate. When the relay operates, it interrupts pulses 1 and 2 (B+) of the upper manual DC key switches and grounds the 2 2/3 audio groups, cancelling the upper manual voices.

The brass keyer circuit consists of D57, D58, D145 and Q145 (one of 61 such circuits). It is keyed with a positive voltage from the key switch, allowing a signal from the tone generators to pass through the circuit to brass collector preamplifier Q146 and brass collector emitter follower Q147. The signal from brass keyer Q145 is amplified by Q146 and Q147 and applied to the brass and Wow Wow voicing circuits. The signal from Q146 and Q147 is amplified again by the brass voicing amplifiers, Q149, Q151, Q153 and Q155. This signal is then applied as output to the respective brass voicing circuits.

Q156 and Q157 are the output preamplifier and emitter follower, respectively. The signal from the various brass voicing circuits and Wow Wow is amplified and connected to the main preamplifiers, Q62 and Q63 and reverb driver Q64. The brass and Wow Wow volume is controlled by VR19, which is connected in series with the emitter follower and output preamplifier circuits.

WOW WOW (See Schematic 11)

When an upper manual key is pressed, a positive voltage from the brass and Wow Wow key switches is applied to the base of the Wow Wow key down detector, Q139. This causes it to conduct, grounding the bases of the Wow Wow inverter and reset No. 2, Q140 and Q143, which then stop conducting. When the Wow Wow inverter stops conducting, it allows a positive voltage to be applied to reset No. 1, Q141, which also stops conducting. Because Q140, Q141 and Q143 cease conducting, the 3-mfd capacitor at the base of integrator transistor Q142 discharges, causing the integrator to conduct. The rate at which the 3-mfd capacitor discharges is controlled by attack control VR17.

When the integrator transistor conducts, it applies voltage to the base of the light-emitting diode driver while charging the .47-mfd capacitor at its base. This causes the LED driver to conduct, lighting the diode in photocell P6. The rate of discharge of the .47 mfd capacitor is controlled by decay control VR18. Also, as integrator transistor Q142 conducts, it applies a positive voltage to the base of reset No. 1 (Q141) to insure that it does not conduct. Wow Wow preamplifier Q158 changes its resonant frequency as the light-emitting diode lights and the photocells in P6 conduct. The output is connected to Q159, the Wow Wow output amplifier. Wow Wow output amplifier Q159 amplifies the signal from Q158 and applies it to output preamplifier Q156 and output emitter follower Q157.

AUTOMATIC ORGAN COMPUTER (See Schematic 9)

The Automatic Organ Computer (AOC) consists of two switching circuits—AOC key switches and intelligence key switches. Also, 41 isolation diodes are used to prevent cross-keying when chords are played on the upper manual with sustain. Listed below is an example of what happens when a C major chord is held on the lower manual and the C4 upper manual is pressed.

1) With the AOC tabswitch on, hold a major C chord (C, E and G) on the lower manual. This applies a B+ keying voltage from the intelligence key switches to all of the C, E and AOC key switch-on buses via isolation diodes.

2) On pressing the upper manual C4 key:

a) The C4 upper manual DC key switch, as well as the nine AOC key switches, makes contact with the respective on buses.

b) The C4 key switch contact receives B+ keying voltage from its on bus and keys the C4 note.

c) Two of the nine (E3 and G4) AOC key switches contact on buses that have a B+ keying voltage applied to them from the intelligence key switches. This B+ keying voltage is applied to the off buses of the E3 and G4 upper manual DC key switches, thus keying E3 and G4 along with C4.

As you can see by the circuit tracing we've just gone through, and the study we've made, a typical electronic organ is a mass of amplifier and preamplifier stages in mixed configurations, interspersed with additional tone-forming and frequency-divider circuits. While the Lowrey isn't by any means typical, it does cover all of the circuits you are likely to find in any organ. Incidently, the Lowrey people maintain a top-flight technical division that will be happy to assist a technician, and they have a vast assortment of technical literature to go along with any servicing needs you may come up against. Don't hesitate to call on them for any assistance you may require. The following troubleshooting charts were taken from the manufacturer's service manual.

TROUBLESHOOTING GUIDE

Q1 VIBRATO OSCILLATOR

No Vibrato

Q2 VIBRATO EMITTER FOLLOWER

No Vibrato

Q3 MASTER OSCILLATOR

All notes of a given tone (C for example), are dead or out of tune.

Q4 BUFFER

All notes of a given tone (C for example), are dead or out of tune.

Q5 WAVESHAPER

1. 2' tabs; 3rd octave of a given note (C for example), dead, weak or garbled.
2. 4' tabs; 4th octave of a given note (C for example), dead, weak or garbled.
3. 8' tabs; 5th octave of a given note (C for example), dead, weak or garbled.
4. 16' tabs; 6th octave of a given note (C only), dead, weak or garbled.

1ST DIVIDER

1. All notes of a given tone (C for example), are dead or out of tune.
2. 2' tabs; 1st, 2nd and 3rd octave of a given note (C for example), dead or weak.
3. 4' tabs; 1st, 2nd, 3rd and 4th octave of a given note (C for example), dead or weak.
4. 8' tabs; 1st, 2nd, 3rd, 4th and 5th octave of a given note (C for example), dead or weak.
5. 16' tabs; 1st, 2nd, 3rd, 4th, 5th and 6th octave of a given note (C for example), dead or weak.

2ND DIVIDER

1. 2' tabs; 1st two octaves of a given note (C for example), dead or weak.
2. 4' tabs; 1st three octaves of a given note (C for example), dead or weak.
3. 8' tabs; 1st four octaves of a given note (C for example), dead or weak.
4. 16' tabs; 1st five octaves of a given note (C for example), dead or weak.
5. 16' Pedal of a given note (C for example), dead or weak.
6. 8' Pedal of a given note (C for example), dead or weak.

3RD DIVIDER

1. 2' tabs; 1st octave of a given note (C for example), dead or weak.
2. 4' tabs; 1st two octaves of a given note (C for example), dead or weak.
3. 8' tabs; 1st three octaves of a given note (C for example), dead or weak.
4. 16' tabs; 1st four octaves of a given note (C for example), dead or weak.
5. 16' and 8' Pedals on 1st two octaves of a given note (C for example), dead or weak.

4TH DIVIDER

1. 2' tabs; 1st octave of a given note (C for example), dead or weak.
2. 4' tabs; 1st two octaves of a given note (C for example), dead or weak.
3. 8' tabs; 1st three octaves of a given note (C for example), dead or weak.
4. 16' tabs; 1st four octaves of a given note (C for example), dead or weak.
5. 16' and 8' Pedals on 1st two octaves of a given note (C for example), dead or weak.

5TH DIVIDER

1. 8' tabs; 1st octave dead or weak (C only).
2. 16' tabs; 1st and 2nd octave dead or weak (C only).

Q13 REPEAT MULTIVIBRATOR

No Marimba repeat and every other group of 3 notes is dead or weak on upper keyboard with repeat off or on.

Q14 REPEAT MULTIVIBRATOR

No Marimba repeat and every other group of 3 notes is dead or weak on upper keyboard with repeat off or on.

Q15 PULSE SHAPER #1

Repeat works on every other upper keyboard 3-note group.

Q16 PULSE SHAPER #2

Repeat works on every other upper keyboard 3-note group.

Q17 PULSE DRIVER #1

Repeat works on every other upper keyboard 3-note group.

Q18 PULSE DRIVER #2

Repeat works on every other upper keyboard 3-note group.

Q19 PULSE KEYER #1

Repeat works on every other upper keyboard 3-note group.

Q20 PULSE KEYER #2

Repeat works on every other upper keyboard 3-note group.

Q21 UPPER MANUAL 8' COLLECTOR PREAMP

1. Trumpet 8', Oboe 8', Kinura 8' and Violin 8', dead or weak.
2. Reed String 4' Coupler dead or weak.
3. Trombone 16' and Cello 16' lack highs.

Q22 UPPER MANUAL EMITTER FOLLOWER

1. Trumpet 8', Oboe 8', Kinura 8' and Violin 8', dead or weak.
2. Reed String 4' Coupler dead or weak.
3. Trombone 16' and Cello 16' lack highs.

Q23 UPPER MANUAL 16' COLLECTOR PREAMP

1. Trombone and Cello voices sound weak and one octave high (8').

TROUBLESHOOTING GUIDE

2. 16' Clarinet voice is dead.

Q24-Q25 PEDAL CANCEL TRIGGER

1. All pedals rumble, but if one is held down, it sounds normal after 15 seconds.
2. No pedals.

Q26 PEDAL CANCEL

Pedals dead

Q27 BASS GUITAR KEYER

1. No Guitar Bass Harmonic.
2. Guitar Bass Harmonic sustains at a constant volume for 10 seconds.

Q28 PEDAL KEYER

1. Pedals sustain at a constant volume for 10 seconds.
2. No pedal except Guitar Bass Harmonic.

Q29 PEDAL KEYER EMITTER FOLLOWER

1. Pedals sustain at a constant volume for 10 seconds.
2. No pedal except Guitar Bass Harmonic.

Q30-Q31 1ST PEDAL DIVIDER

Dead pedals, rumble in all pedals, or pedal tone one octave high.

Q32-Q33 2ND PEDAL DIVIDER

No Pedal 16', rumble in all pedals 16' only.

Q34 LOWER KEYBOARD REED STRING COLLECTOR PREAMP

Violin 8', Cornet 8', French Horn 8' and English Horn 8' dead or weak.

Q35 150 CYCLE FILTER

1. Upper keyboard 16' Flute C1 thru F#3 dead or weak.
2. Upper keyboard 8' Flute C1 thru F#2 dead or weak.

Q36 212 CYCLE FILTER

1. Upper keyboard 16' Flute G3 thru C4 dead or weak.
2. Upper keyboard 8' Flute G2 thru C3 dead or weak.
3. Lower keyboard 8' Flute C1 thru C3 dead or weak.

Q37 300 CYCLE FILTER

1. Upper keyboard 16' C# 4 thru F# 4 dead or weak.
2. Upper keyboard 8' Flute C# 3 thru F# 4 dead or weak.
3. Upper keyboard 4' Flute C1 thru F# 2 dead or weak.
4. Lower keyboard 8' Flute C# 3 thru F# 3 dead or weak.

Q38 425 CYCLE FILTER

1. Upper keyboard 16' Flute G4 thru C5 dead or weak.
2. Upper keyboard 8' Flute G3 thru C4 dead or weak.
3. Upper keyboard 4' Flute G2 thru C3 dead or weak.
4. Upper keyboard 2-2/3' Flute C1 thru F2 dead or weak.
5. Lower keyboard 8' Flute G3 thru C4 dead or weak.

Q39 600 CYCLE FILTER

1. Upper keyboard 16' Flute G4 thru F# 5 dead or weak.
2. Upper keyboard 8' Flute C# 4 thru F# 4 dead or weak.
3. Upper keyboard 4' Flute C# 3 thru F# 3 dead or weak.
4. Upper keyboard 2' Flute C1 thru F# 2 dead or weak.
5. Upper keyboard 2-2/3' Flute F# 2 thru B2 dead or weak.
6. Lower keyboard 8' Glute C# 4 thru F# 4 dead or weak.

Q40 850 CYCLE FILTER

1. Upper keyboard 16' Flute G5 thru C6 dead or weak.
2. Upper keyboard 8' Flute G4 thru C5 dead or weak.
3. Upper keyboard 4' Flute G3 thru C4 dead or weak.
4. Upper keyboard 2' Flute G2 thru C3 dead or weak.
5. Upper keyboard 2 2/3' Flute C3 thru F3 dead or weak.
6. Lower keyboard 8' Flute G4 thru C5 dead or weak.

Q41 1200 CYCLE FILTER

1. Upper keyboard 8' Flute C# 5 thru F# 5 dead or weak.
2. Upper keyboard 4' Flute C# 4 thru F# 4 dead or weak.
3. Upper keyboard 2' Flute C# 3 thru F# 3 dead or weak.
4. Upper keyboard 2-2/3' Flute F# 3 thru B3 dead or weak.
5. Lower keyboard 8' Flute C# 5 thru F# 5 dead or weak.

Q42 1700 CYCLE FILTER

1. Upper keyboard 8' Flute G5 thru F# 5 dead or weak.
2. Upper keyboard 4' Flute G4 thru C5 dead or weak.
3. Upper keyboard 2' Flute G3 thru C4 dead or weak.
4. Upper keyboard 2-2/3' Flute C4 thru F4 dead or weak.
5. Lower keyboard 8' Flute G5 thru C6 dead or weak.

Q43 DOUBLER PREAMP

1. Upper keyboard 4' Flute C# 5 thru C6 dead or weak.
2. Upper keyboard 2' Flute C# 4 thru C6 dead or weak.
3. Upper keyboard 2-2/3' Flute F# 4 thru C6 dead or weak.

Q44 425 CYCLE FILTER

1. Lower keyboard Diapason 8' C1 thru C3 dead or weak.
2. Lower keyboard French Horn 8' dead or weak.

Q45 600 CYCLE FILTER

1. Lower keyboard Diapason 8' C# 3 thru C4 dead or weak.

Q46 850 CYCLE FILTER

1. Lower keyboard Diapason 8' G3 thru C4 dead or weak.

Q47 1200 CYCLE FILTER

1. Lower keyboard Diapason 8' C# 4 thru F# 4 dead or weak.
2. Upper keyboard Trumpet 8' dead or weak.
3. Upper keyboard 16' Clarinet lacks highs.

Q48 1700 CYCLE FILTER

1. Lower keyboard Diapason 8' G4 thru C6 dead or weak.
2. Lower keyboard Cornet 8' dead or weak.
3. Lower keyboard English Horn 8' dead or weak.
4. Upper keyboard Oboe 8' dead or weak.

TROUBLESHOOTING GUIDE

Q49 STRING PREAMP

1. Upper keyboard Kinura 8' dead or weak.
2. Upper keybaord Violin 8' dead or weak.
3. Upper keyboard Cello 16' dead or weak.
4. Lower keyboard Violin 8' dead or weak.

Q50 FLUTE PREAMP

1. Upper keyboard 16' Flute dead or weak.
2. Upper keyboard 8' Flute dead or weak.
3. Upper keyboard 4' Flute dead or weak.
4. Upper keyboard 2' Flute dead or weak.
5. Upper keyboard 2 2/3' Flute dead or weak.
6. Lower keyboard 8' Flute dead or weak.

Q51 REED STRING PREAMP

1. Upper keyboard Trombone 16', Clarinet 16', dead or weak.
2. Upper keyboard Trumpet 8', Oboe 8', Kinura 8', Violin 8' and Cello 16' dead or weak.
3. Lower keyboard Diapason 8', Violin 8', Cornet 8', French Horn 8' and English Horn 8' dead or weak.

Q52 PERCUSSION BASS BYPASS

With Percussion tab on, voices percuss completely (no sound after percussion.)

Q53 PERCUSSION MODULATOR

1. No percussion or very weak percussion.
2. No percussion repeat.

Q54 PERCUSSION PREAMP

1. No percussion or very weak percussion.
2. No percussion repeat.

Q55-Q56 PERCUSSION PULSE DETECTORS

No percussion, but repeat works.

Q57-Q58 PERCUSSION MULTIVIBRATOR

No percussion and no repeat, or no repeat but percussion O.K.

Q59 PERCUSSION DRIVER

No percussion or repeat or weak percussion and repeat.

Q60-Q61 LESLIE MIXING PREAMP

All voices dead or weak when in Leslie.

Q62-Q63 MAIN MIXING PREAMP

All voices dead or weak when in Main.

Q64 thru Q68 REVERB DRIVER, PREAMPS, MIXER & EMITTER FOLLOWER

No Reverb or weak Reverb.

Q71 RHYTHM EMITTER FOLLOWER

All rhythm voices, reverberation and automatic, dead or weak.

Q72 thru Q85 MULTI-CHANNEL CHORUS AND LESLIE & MAIN PHASERS

Failure of any of the above transistors will cause a change in the amount of Chorus or complete loss of Chorus. When checking for Chorus, it is best to keep the Leslie from rotating and with no vibrato, check for phase shift.

To repair or adjust, other than complete circuit board replacement, refer to the Lowrey Repair Procedure Manual.

Q89 thru Q96 PREAMP (LESLIE), VOLTAGE AMP, PRE-DRIVER, SHORT CIRCUIT PROTECTOR, DRIVERS & OUTPUTS

Entire organ dead, weak or distorted, and may blow fuses in Leslie position.

Q97 thru Q104 PREAMP (MAIN), VOLTAGE AMP, PRE-DRIVER, SHORT CIRCUIT PROTECTOR, DRIVERS & OUTPUTS

Entire organ dead, weak or distorted in Main position, and may blow fuses.

Q105 RAMP KEYER

No Golden Harp and/or only one not sounds when Golden Harp switch is depressed.

Q106 RAMP GENERATOR

No Golden Harp

Q107 RAMP RESET

Golden Harp does not give full spectrum of chord being played.

Q108 RAMP DRIVER

No Golden Harp

Q109 (12) RAMP SWITCHER

When using Golden Harp, one tone will be silent from the 3-tone sequence. (Example - F1 missing from F2 & F3.)

Q110 (36) GOLDEN HARP KEYERS

One tone missing from 3-tone sequence, or notes will play when keys are depressed on lower keyboard with upper keyboard tabs on. (Golden Harp switch does not have to be activated.)

POWER SUPPLY

D42, D43, D44, D45, D46 & D47
T1 Transformer
1. Entire organ dead, weak, distorted and/or constant power hum.
2. Loss of entire section of organ (example - Reverb, Rhythm, Vibrato etc.)
3. Organ blows fuses.

Q111 CASSETTE POWER REGULATOR

Constant hum, unstable Cassette speed or no Cassette.

Q114 UPPER MANUAL 16' SOLO DIVIDER AND UPPER MANUAL 16' SOLO DIVIDER NETWORK

1. First 12 upper manual notes an octave high on 16'.
2. First 12 upper manual notes dead or weak, or rumble on 16'.

TROUBLESHOOTING GUIDE

Q115, Q116 TREMOLO OSCILLATOR

1. Brass Symphonizer voices weak when Tremolo control in full position.
2. No Tremolo.

Q117 TREMOLO SWITCHER

1. Brass Symphonizer voices weak, loss of highs.
2. Tremolo depth more pronounced.

Q118 BRASS BUSS DRIVER

1. No Tremolo.
2. Symphonizer voices weak or dead.

Q119—Q126 LATCHING TRANSISTORS

1. Particular preset voice does not turn off.
2. Preset lamp on constantly.
3. Voice does not play unless preset button is held on.

Q127, Q128 CANCEL UPPER MANUAL

1. Upper manual cancel lamp on constantly; Upper manual does not play.
2. Upper manual cancel preset does not function unless held on.

Q129—Q132 LAMP DRIVERS

1. Preset lamp is on constantly; preset voice plays all the time.
2. Preset lamp does not come on; preset voice does not play.

Q133 LAMP DRIVER UPPER MANUAL CANCEL

1. Upper manual cancel lamp on constantly; Upper manual does not play.
2. Upper manual does not cancel when preset is depressed.

Q134, Q135 LATCHING TRIGGER

1. Preset voices will not play unless preset button is held on.
2. Upper manual cancel functions only when held on.

Q136 RELAY DRIVER

1. Relay energized all the time, cancelling upper manual.
2. Relay will not energize, and upper manual cancel preset has no effect.

Q137, Q138 RELAY SWITCHERS

1. Upper manual cancel preset does not energize relay; Lamp stays on.
2. Upper manual voices are dead.
3. Upper manual voices can be cancelled even though presets are not on.

Q139 WOW-WOW KEYDOWN DETECTOR

1. No Wow, but Wow-Wow voice plays.

Q140—Q143 WOW-WOW INVERTER, RESET NO. 1 & 2 and INTEGRATOR

No Wow-Wow.

Q144 LED DRIVER

1. No Wow-Wow; Highs are more pronounced.
2. No Wow-Wow; No highs.

Q145 BRASS KEYER

One note weak or dead when using Symphonizer.

Q146 BRASS COLLECTOR PREAMP

1. Brass Symphonizer and Wow-Wow weak in volume.
2. Brass Symphonizer and Wow-Wow dead.

Q147 BRASS COLLECTOR EMITTER FOLLOWER

1. Brass Symphonizer and Wow-Wow dead.
2. Brass Symphonizer and Wow-Wow weak in volume.

Q148, Q150, Q152, Q154 PRESET SWITCHERS

1. Preset lights when depressed, but voice is dead.
2. Preset plays at all times, and will not cancel..

Q149, Q151, Q153, Q155 PRESET AMPS

Preset voices weak or dead.

Q156 OUTPUT PREAMP

Brass Symphonizer and Wow-Wow dead or weak.

Q157 OUTPUT EMITTER FOLLOWER

Brass Symphonizer and Wow-Wow dead or weak.

Q158 WOW-WOW PREAMP

1. Wow-Wow weak.
2. Wow-Wow voice sounds but no Wow-Wow effect.

Q159 WOW-WOW OUTPUT AMP

Wow-Wow weak or dead.

RELAY

1. Upper manual diode keyed voices dead — or play in 3-note groups, due to open diode keying relay contacts.
2. Some or all groups of 2-2/3' voices play when upper manual cancel preset is on, due to open 2-2/3' relay contacts.

7 Modifications

The younger generation is moving more and more into the great outdoors, and this may help alleviate the fear shared by many otologists that the high decibel rating of modern music will play havoc with the kid's eardrums. Outdoors, there's more room for dispersion of the sound, so that can't hurt a bit. However, when you get a bunch of kids who are used to hearing electrically amplified sound when they are indoors, sure enough you're going to get requests to "rig something up" so they can amplify outdoors as well.

One of the easiest things to rig up is a long extension cord. We've managed this nicely, for even in many public parks you can find either a concealed weatherproof outlet, and the park department officials can sometimes tip you on where to locate these, or, again with permission and some common sense, you can tap into public park lighting fixtures.

That's all well and good, when the kids are performing with and at the behest of the park commission. The kid that goes to the park or beach with his guitar, however, is another story entirely, and the department is not about to let you wire into a lamp or outlet just for this guy's amusement! But if the guy has a good radio in his car, you can easily solve his problem. And you're entitled to an extra fee for a specialized job like this.

Start by pulling the radio out of the car. (You earn a goodly reward for this in itself, for some of the new dashboard designs make the job difficult! With the radio on the bench, you add a double-pole, double throw toggle switch wherever you can fit it. At the same time, find a place for two different kinds of jacks. We like a simple 2-conductor phono jack for the input and an RCA-type phone jack for the output. Place both of these where they can conveniently be reached by the musician. If the radio is accessible from under the dashboard, place them there. Make sure he can get at the switch, too.

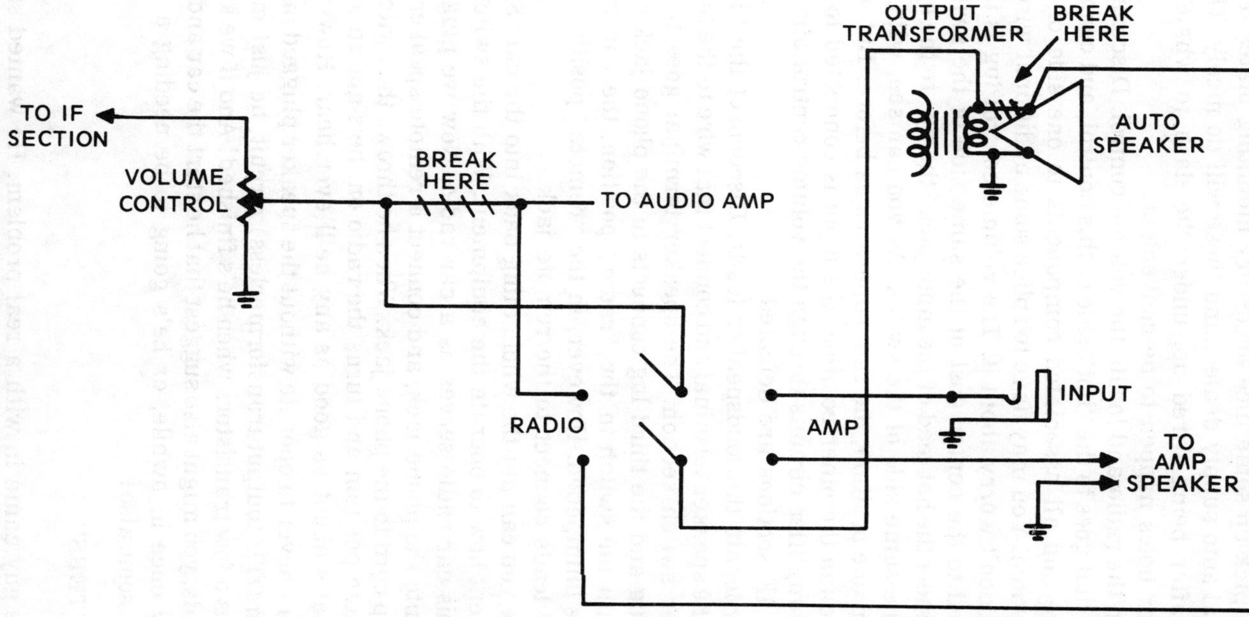

Schematic showing the wiring needed to adapt a car radio to a guitar amplifier.

If the chassis is a small one, and there just isn't room for these extras, or if you can't fit them in easily, don't despair. You can pick up some nice accessory mounting plates from your local auto supply dealer, and these will do nicely. They attach, after being wired up, under the dash to whatever screws or holes happen to be convenient.

Open the radio and locate the volume control. Disconnect the wire that goes to the "hot" side of this control, and connect that wire and all associated components to one side of the toggle switch. You may have to splice some additional wire to this, but don't worry about it. The volume control lug is then connected to the center post of the same side of the switch. Now connect the hot lead of the input jack (the tip) to the open lug on the same side of the switch. As you can see, with the switch in one position, the radio operates as before. But with the switch in the other position, the input is connected to the radio's amplifier circuits through the volume control and the RF and IF sections are defeated.

Now locate the loudspeaker leads. Disconnect the "hot" lead to the speaker terminal and connect that wire to the top of the other switch section. The speaker terminal goes to the center lug and the third lug connects to the phono jack's hot side. With the switch in the "radio" position, the car radio operates unimpeded. However, in the "remote" position, the speaker leads connect to the remote jack.

Now you can put the whole thing back into the car. Show your client how to operate the equipment. With the switch in radio, his car radio serves as a car radio. Now we plug his guitar into the phone jack, and connect a remote speaker via some zip cord to the phono jack. When he throws the switch to the remote position and turns the radio on, he's got an amplifier that's about as good as any he'll ever hear. However, warn him never to operate without the speaker plugged in, for if it's an OTL (output transformerless) circuit, he just might be minus a few transistors when he's finished! And if we know these kids, you might also suggest that he start the car and run it every once in awhile, or he's going to be needing a new battery soon also!

"ADAPTERS"

One guy came in with a real problem. He wanted some guitar music in his car, which he and his friends used all the time. He invested a few bucks in one of those "AC converters" that plugs into a cigarette lighter and provides a source of alternating current in the car. Following the instructions carefully, he mounted the unit, plugged it into the cigarette lighter, and then plugged his electric razor into the unit. A flip of his thumb, and the razor whirled away, giving him as good a shave as he ever got. Happy with the results up to that point, he tried going a step further. He brought out his amplifier, plugged the monster into the little outlet, and turned it on. The fuse blew. He couldn't understand why, and he wanted something **done** about it. You know, he didn't like our explanation about current, either. And he didn't like the price of converter units that could handle his amplifier. There are other ways out of this dilemma, though, and the guy who can offer these youngsters something a bit different can really score in the marketplace.

With the new transistorized technology, and a little ingenuity, you can really make it big. Offer a youngster a battery-operated, completely self-contained amplifier with some decent output, and you've got it. To simplify things, we always start with those ready-made preamplifiers and low-power amplifiers. We then couple this to a couple of good push-pull output transistors, using the ready-mades as preamps and drivers. What we have then is a battery-operated amplifier that, while it won't provide the ultimate in fidelity, will nonetheless offer the youngster the opportunity to take his guitar wherever he goes and still have an amplified sound.

When you get a musician to try one of these units, it's an easy matter to sell him on rechargeable ni-cad batteries and a charger pack as well. These are commercially available in a goodly assortment of voltages and power ratings, and the chargers are sold commercially also. Contact any of the manufacturers for more information, and watch the profits stack up.

ADDING PICKUPS

Sometimes, a musician becomes a musician simply because of necessity. He might start out with a nice acoustic guitar, and when his friends find out that he can play—that he might even be able to read music—he finds himself in urgent need of an electrically amplified instrument.

Many youngsters who start out with guitar teachers, learn on simple, acoustical guitars, and sooner or later they learn the meaning of the word "combo." At this point, if they are sufficiently well-heeled, they go out and buy the flashiest electric guitar with all kinds of knobs, controls and pickups, and along with it the biggest amplifier they can manage to locate. And big does not necessarily mean high powered, for on opening some of these units you're going to find that most of the space is filled up with loudspeakers. However, some of the youngsters still have to rely on Dad for the "bread," and if Dad has any smarts, he'll advise the youngster to go out and earn the necessary instruments.

At this point, permit me to digress to explain what happened in my own case, for it's fairly typical of the latter course. When the author was about 13 years old, the big-band era was upon us, and I hankered for a musical instrument—any musical instrument. A birthday was upcoming, and I made it known that my sole and total joy would come only from a musical instrument. We meandered down to musical-instrument row, and Dad asked to see—to my absolute horror—an Ocarina, a "sweet potato" that could be had for under a buck.

The next least expensive instrument was a guitar... a cheap one, for only five dollars. In a mad moment of magnanimity, I got the guitar. I also got an extra dollar to spend at the local music school for 25 cents a lesson. After four lessons, paid for in advance, and separated by a week each, I "joined" an orchestra formed of other kids like myself. We saved our school lunch money and bought stock orchestrations of current popular songs. We had only one requirement, that they be in the key of C, F or B-flat since none of us could read in other keys as yet!

We got jobs, too. We played bar-mitsvahs, weddings—we even played at the opening of a Brooklyn fish market. And we made enough money at it so I could afford lessons that cost two bucks a half hour, at a time when two bucks was really two bucks!

However, it wasn't long before the realization struck that classic guitar might be educational, but it didn't have the mass appeal that the orchestral type did. But to get a decent job with a decent band meant an electric guitar, and more expense than I could afford.

I remember that I had about 15 dollars, and the local music emporium offered to fit my guitar with a pickup and sell me an amplifier. First, we tried assorted pickups, plugging them into an old amplifier that was facing the wall in the shop. We finally decided on one, and then started trying out amplifiers that were within my price range. Frankly, I could have built a better one in a cigar box, for none of these sounded like more than a 5-tube radio. I asked about the price of the old job facing the wall, and the guy—offhandedly—offered to let it go at a price I could afford. When he turned it around to dust it off and saw the name GIBSON on the front, he tried to back out of the deal. But I held him to it, and went home proudly with my "electric" guitar on my lap in the subway.

That's essentially how the kids get started today also. You will find yourself asked to fit an electrical pickup to a guitar, and this may take a bit more doing than appears on the surface.

To add a pickup to a guitar, you've got to consider the type of guitar that you're dealing with. Many of the flat-top guitars available today for folk music do not have a separate bridge and tail piece. Rather, the strings are mounted directly to the bridge. There's no way to friction-fit a pickup under the strings behind the bridge, since there are no strings behind the bridge. If a contact microphone is desired for an instrument such as this, one of many commercially available clamp brackets must be used to hold the pickup to the guitar. These contact pickups work with acoustical guitars only, and must be in firm contact with the instrument's body. There are two types, both encased in rubber, either with or without a volume control. The clamps are fitted with special felt pads that will not mar the guitar's body finish.

The other type of add-on pickup is a magnetic type, usually fitted to a pick shield made of plastic. If the guitar already has such a shield, it must be removed so the new one can be added. If you can manage to use the screw holes from the previous pick shield, all well and good. If not, you're going to have to provide new holes, and there's a right and a wrong way to do this. The screws are generally No. 4 round-head wood screws, and you should start by drilling a pilot hole which will prevent the screw from cracking the guitar body. Usually, one screw goes through an adjustable L bracket into the guitar's side, and the other goes through a ¼-inch spacer into the top of the guitar, near the neck piece. Do not tighten the screws fully at the time of installation, since you must allow some leeway to adjust the pickup so its pole pieces are under the strings. These pickups usually come all wired and ready to go, with assorted controls for volume, tone and balance right on the pick shield.

Occasionally, you run into a guitarist who wants an acoustic guitar converted completely to an electric, with the pickups mounted directly to the guitar body. Contrary to common belief, there is no need to dismantle the guitar to accomplish this. Determine the number of pickups to be added, and set them on the guitar body under the strings, properly centered. Mark the locations of the two mounting screws for each, and then remove the pickups. Drill the pilot holes for the mounting screws, and then, using a wood brace and bit, drill a ¼-inch hole for the wires from each pickup to pass through into the guitar's body. These holes should be placed so they are covered by the pickup when it is mounted. Necessary controls are available in miniature sizes with shafts requiring a five-sixteenths inch clearance hole or in standard 3 8-inch shaft sizes. Locate the positions for these controls and, using wood bits, drill the holes for them.

Mount the uppermost pickup first; "snake" its lead wires into the access hole. Attach the pickup with the small screws, and then, reaching into the second pickup's access hole, using a mechanical "grab," pull the first unit's wires out and connect them to the second pickup. Continue with this same procedure until all of the pickups are in place, with the wires appearing through the f-slot or the center hole in the guitar. Wire the controls and the plug-in socket at this time. Using the "grab" through the first potentiometer hole, grasp the pot's shaft and pull it into place. Add the trim washer, the lockwasher and nut. Repeat for the other potentiometers and the socket. The guitar is now an electric.

To prevent the unit from developing an unwanted buzzing, you'll have to turn the nuts down tight with a lockwrench. Usually, the pickups come with small rubber pads that will prevent them from developing a mechanical buzz, but be sure to use small lockwashers under the screw heads, just to make sure.

Other Pickups

You're going to be asked to do some strange repairs in your career, and if you approach these with the right attitude, you will be appreciated for your efforts. This appreciation can pay off also. Take the youngster who plays a trumpet and who wants its sound amplified. Because the body of a trumpet or other rigid instrument will not vibrate sufficiently to pick up the sound through a contact or dynamic pickup, you've got to do something else.

What we've had the best results with, after much experimentation, is the ordinary acoustic microphone element. This picks up the actual sound waves from the instrument's bell or mouth and feeds them to the amplifier. What you need, however, is a way to attach the pickup to the instrument. We've had success with two different methods. The first system is to epoxy-cement the microphone element directly to the bell, and then epoxy cement a small bracket to hold the connecting jack. Wire the pickup to the jack, supply a connecting cord, and you are all set.

Another way to go is to actually mount the jack through the bell of the instrument. Drill a small hole for the jack, and then wire the pickup to the inside of the jack. If you work carefully enough, you can solder the ground connection of the jack directly to the ground side of the microphone element for support. Wire the hot side to the jack's hot side, and the installation is complete.

We've also provided some classy installations by "potting" the job when it's finished. You can obtain an RTV silicone rubber that's used for caulking, and, using a small plastic form that fits around the element, make a mold. Insert a plug in the jack so the jack won't leak the silicone, and coat the plug with a mold-release agent before doing this. Coat the inside of the mold form with the same stuff. Now, squeeze the silicone out of its tube and into the form, keeping the instrument in a position so the form is level. Do NOT put in so much that the pickup is covered! Allow the stuff to dry, after poking it with a toothpick to make sure it's well-filled. When it dries, remove the mold form, remove the plug, and the job is done. The instrument will have a shaped rubbery lump in its throat. This will usually not interfere with unamplified, acoustical playing, but it will provide excellent amplified sound when connected to an amplifier.

Let's face it. The musician that wants a pickup on his instrument could also be a possible customer for an amplifier—if you can provide the pickup. Fail to provide the pickup, and the customer will walk out the door!

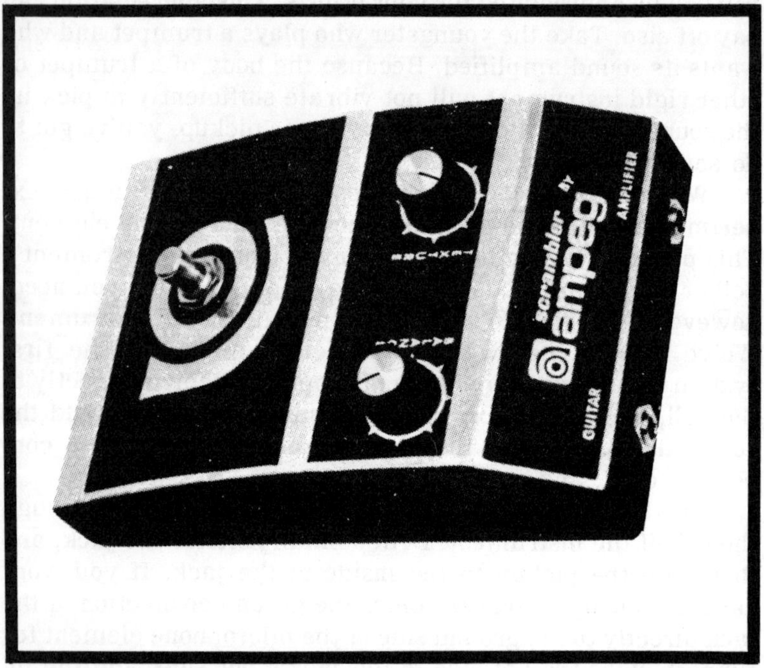

Ampeg Model SC-1 Scrambler.

Recently, a group came in with a problem. They sang, they played, and they liked to move around at the same time. The problem was that you can't hold an instrument and play it with two hands, and still hold a microphone. Sure, floor stands and fixed mikes could be used, but this would necessarily curtail some of the movement that they felt was so important to their act.

The solution came in the form of a bunch of throat microphones. With the mikes tightly fastened to each player's throat, they could move, play and sing, with the only problem being one of keeping from tangling themselves up in the cords and strangling one another. The fidelity is of a level meant more for communication than for music reproduction, but the musicians loved the new mikes.

AMPLIFIER MODIFICATIONS

Many youngsters will spend every last dime and most of next year's allowance on the best amplifier they can buy.

Usually, this is a stripped-down model with few if any appurtenances. Consequently, you may be asked to install such capabilities as tremolo or fuzz.

Making such an addition is relatively simple. Check the amplifier schematic and then check one of the manufacturer's other models that has the same circuit configuration but includes the additional capability. This will usually give you an excellent clue as to where, electrically, it should be installed. Many electronic distributors carry such devices separate and apart from the amplifiers they sell. You can order the additional device, and follow the instructions packaged with it to make the installation. However, there are certain things you should do as well.

These devices are generally connected through a plug-in arrangement to the amplifier's panel. Assuming that the amplifier never had a facility such as the one you are adding, there will be no jack for it, and no place to mount it. Chances are that you will find ample space inside the cabinet to place the unit, but do check the positions of the connecting cords, and if any operating rather than pre-set controls are required,

Heathkit Model TA-28 "fuzz booster."

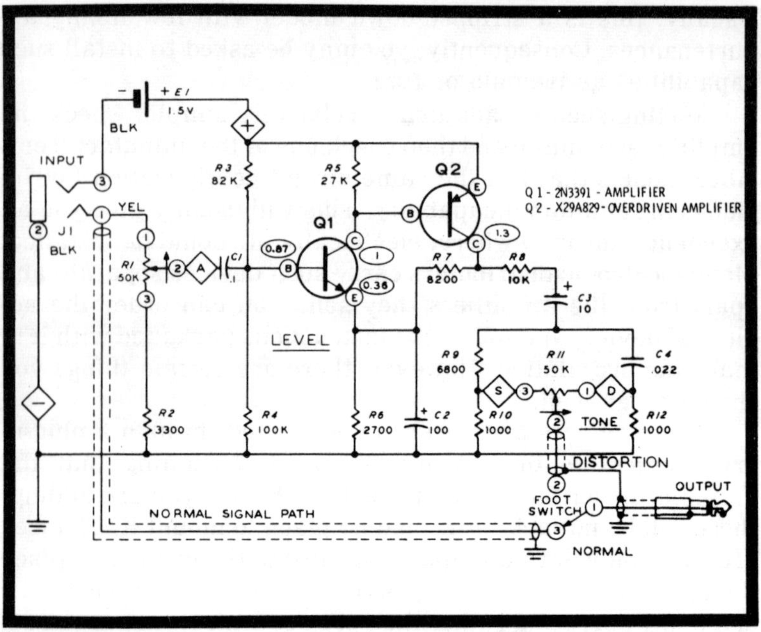

Schematic of the Heathkit Model TA-28 "fuzz booster."

you will have to mount them where they can be reached. We have solved this problem handily with ordinary control shaft extensions that run through a small drilled hole in the amplifier's back plate.

Wire the unit into the amplifier, and add a suitable jack for the foot-control switch. Ordinarily, a simple phone jack is used. This can usually be located on the amplifier's control panel. There's always enough room for one of those. Run the wiring along the side of the cabinet to the added chassis.

To complete this kind of modification, we always go one step further, and it's a nice touch the clients appreciate. Using the white rub-off type lettering available at any electronics supply outlet, add some identification for the new controls and connectors. It's usually an unexpected touch that pleases the client.

Many of these units, such as the various reverberators, have controls that the musician may be called upon to adjust during a performance. Obviously, he cannot be expected to pick up a screwdriver and make such adjustments while his audience waits. If this is the case, you will generally find that the added chassis comes with a metal panel plate that can be

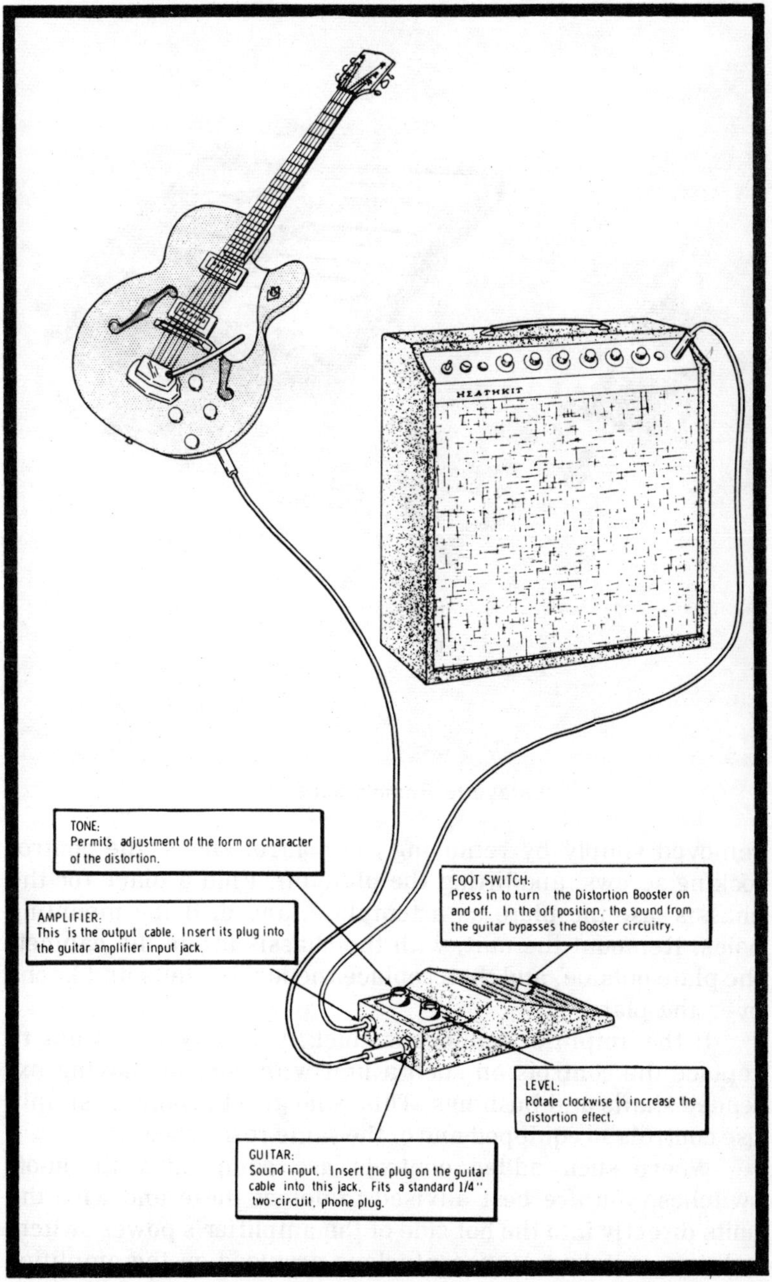

Drawing showing the "fuzz booster" plugged into the circuit.

Lafayette Radio's Super Fuzz.

removed simply by removing the control knobs, the control locking screws, and lifting the plate off. Find a place for the chassis, use the plate as a template, and drill the mounting holes. Remount the unit, with the chassis inside the cabinet, the plate outside, and then replace the locking nuts and knobs over the plate.

If the amplifier cabinet is thick, you may also want to replace the controls on such a unit with controls having extended shafts and bushings. This is no great problem; simply use controls so equipped and of the same resistance.

Where such added controls are equipped with on-off switches, you are best advised to defeat these and wire the units directly into the hot side of the amplifier's power switch, unless a switched AC receptacle is provided on the amplifier itself. We haven't seen many of these, so the hot side of the power switch is usually the best method.

The only problem we've ever run into with these units is that some clients feel that in asking for such an installation they are entitled to more than a simple addition of a commercially available unit. What seems to be most disturbing is the fact that there's a "name" on the panel plate. We have bypassed this problem by removing such plates and reversing them. Add a bit of black lacquer, some rub-off type, and everybody's happy!

DAMPERS, REFLECTORS AND DIRECTORS

Sometimes there are major things you can do to improve an amplifier's performance without actually touching the amplifier. If the room is "soft" and has little in the way of reverberation, you might offer your client a bit of acoustic design in the form of some bounce panels to liven the room. These can be easily constructed by cutting one-half inch plywood to interesting free-form shapes, and covering one side with formica or a similar reflective material. By suspending these boards from the ceiling, you will create an interesting and unusual ceiling pattern that also functions to reflect sound. These are especially suitable where a room has inordinately high ceilings that allow the sound to get lost in the heights.

Conversely, if the room is too live, where it sounds like the performers are singing in the bathtub, you can use the same techniques and cover the boards with acoustic tile which will absorb some of the sound and create the kind of deadness that a too-live room requires.

If this sounds at all like a superficial treatment, don't underestimate it. It really does work, and it works well. In fact, you would be well-advised to consider putting these up one at a time, so you don't overdo it and find yourself pulling them down again!

This process is called "tuning the room," and is essential in most public rooms, where designers and architects have not considered the use of electronic amplifiers. Unfortunately, many operators of these rooms are looking only for noise and entertainment, and couldn't care less about the acoustic problems. This is the problem of the musicians who play there. Many musicians are well aware of the problem, and will come to you for help, but they play limited engagements and aren't about to pay you to redecorate a room for a one-night performance.

We've run into this problem, and have helped at least one group by setting up collapsible panels for acoustical control. Prepare plywood boards, measuring four feet square, with acoustic tile on one side and formica on the other. All that's needed now are a few easel mounts, and by turning the boards either this way or that way, and then directing and placing them where they're needed, the room can be softened or livened as required. The boards and easels then collapse for transport to the next job.

THE "HARD" SOUND

When the author was a good deal younger, during the swing era, it was the fashion for a guitar to be an aid to the overall sound of an orchestra; the sound was "wooden," produced by an acoustical guitar, rich in overtones and harmonics. The amplifier's biggest problem in those days was that it, to some extent, curtailed those rich harmonics that gave depth and timbre to the instrument.

Today's youngsters want a hard sound, and they sometimes think that "hard" rock has to do with hard in the sense that it applies to drugs. It just isn't so! The so-called hard sound is just what it says. The basic note played is heard by itself with minimal overtone and no harmonics. To achieve this end, they use acoustical guitars only rarely, preferring the far less resilient solid-body types.

If you want to give a youngster a harder sound from his amplifier, here are some simple tricks that will help suppress the harmonics. We've had a good measure of success with heavily shellacking the loudspeaker cone just for starters. Do both sides for the best effect.

Incidentally you can deliberately distort a loudspeaker by taping any of a number of items across the cone so as to produce rattle or added vibration. We have seen everything used from loose springs to rubber bands or bits of paper. The trick here is to use a relatively small loudspeaker, and bring a set of terminals out to the back so that the speaker can be connected by means of a switch, thereby giving the musician the option of introducing this sound or not. A convenient way to switch this is with an open-circuit plug-in jack and a foot switch connected via a cord and a phono plug.

Another good solution for the acoustical guitar is to fill the body so it won't properly reverberate. We've done this with expanding plastic foam, available in a pressurized aerosol can. It sounds like a pretty-drastic step, and indeed it is. But if that's what the customer wants, explain what's involved, explain further that it's irrevocable once he's committed to this course, and then spray away.

There's no fixed rule where music is concerned, and while the rock types look for the extremely hard sound, some of the kids who are into folk guitar can tolerate a little more in the way of softness. A good way to learn how to talk about sound with the kids is to take a glance at the instrument. You'll find that, for the most part, the kids who are into modern music will use steel strings. The youngsters who like the folk type generally use gut strings or nylon.

"SUBDUING" THE AMPLIFIER

Sometimes glare problems are present, especially when a musician is going to be photographed. The problem is caused by "hot spots" or reflected light from an instrument or an amplifier's shiny surfaces. If one of your customers gets a bid to appear on television, chances are that you can be of great help to him before his appearance. Reflected light can create all kinds of flares and halos, which can virtually ruin his image.

To prevent such reflections, television studio people often use ordinary milk, which, when it dries, will keep light from bouncing aimlessly. Of course, what the heck do they care? When the musician leaves at night, he takes his milk-coated equipment with him, and then it's his problem!

Instead, pay a visit to any well-equipped photography shop, where you can buy a glare-killing liquid in an aeresol can that will not only do the required job, but it won't smell, either. However, do use it sparingly, for it leaves a fine residue that feels greasy.

LOCKS

Many musicians play permanent jobs, and frequently leave their equipment at the job rather than lug it back and forth between performances. If a musician has a job with a small combo, and he plays regularly every weekend night at the same place, chances are that he will leave his amplifier (at least) on the stage so he won't have the added problem of carrying it around.

Unfortunately for him, anyone is at liberty to turn it on simply by operating the switch. If the amplifier is also used with a microphone, you can depend on some well-lathered bar patron to turn the unit on and use the microphone to generate his own entertainment on the nights that the musicians are off. Maybe that's OK with the owner of the bar and the other patrons, but it is your customer's amplifier!

You can solve the problem for him by installing a key-operated switch. These are readily available at any electronic supply house at a moderate cost, and you'll usually find them where they sell burglar-alarm systems. Mount the key switch either on the panel or in an out-of-the-way place where it won't be too visible. Usually, the best bet is a location convenient to the line cord, for that's where you will have to wire it.

To mount the key switch, first examine it, and see what sort of hole is needed. These usually require a D-shaped hole, but since we aren't building in a maximum security system (more of a deterrent), a round hole will do as well. Most key switches usually require a hole of between ¾ inch and one inch, but you should measure the hole in the mounting nut that comes with the switch to get the correct hole size. You can best measure the opening size needed by placing the nut on a ruler and measuring the hole diameter, using two of the opposing points of the nut as references.

Next, locate the place for the switch. If it is to be panel mounted, find a place where there is ample room for the switch, and then drill a pilot hole. We generally start with a ⅛-inch hole, and then use a tapered hand reamer to enlarge the hole to ⅜-inch diameter. A chassis punch of the correct size is used next to give a nice, clean hole.

If you choose to mount the keyswitch through the body of the amplifier housing, you will find that this is usually a leatherette or vinyl-covered wood. A hole saw of the correct diameter must be used to make the hole for the switch. Drill the hole, and then deburr it with a small round file.

To install the switch, first remove the nut and lockwasher. You may find it expedient to also remove one or more of the terminal screws. Leave the trim washer in place. Put the switch into the hole, aligning the keyhole vertically in the off position. Replace the lockwasher and nut and tighten firmly.

You must now break the AC line in the amplifier where it goes to the on-off switch, which may be on one of the controls. Connect the line to the keyswitch, and then connect it from the keyswitch to the terminal the line went to. With the keyswitch off, nothing will turn the amplifier on.

Some instrumentalists dislike the idea of two switches, and they want the keyswitch used in place of the on-off switch. You can do this also, so that turning on the keyswitch will turn on the amplifier. Of course, this means defeating and removing the existing on-off switch. If it is attached to a control, simply disconnect the switching contact wires and, with a small screwdriver, lift the holding tabs so the switch can be lifted off the control. Connect the two switched wires together, and the job is done. If the on-off switch on the amplifier is a toggle type, you can simply remove it entirely, connecting its wires to the keyswitch, and then replace the toggle with a small snap hole plug.

MISCELLANEOUS MODIFICATIONS

In your work, you're sure to run into more than your share of unusual requests, and quite frankly, I like to think that anybody who invests in a book of this nature is of more than a casual experimental turn of mind. When somebody comes in asking if you can "do" something special, chances are that you'll listen to his idea and then maybe even waste a lot more time than the job will pay, trying to implement the request.

You may run into a guy who wants his amplifier and loudspeaker built right into the guitar. Is it possible? Sure it is. Can you do it? Sure you can. Should you try to? No. This is a case where the technology is there, where you can really satisfy the customer's needs, and give him exactly what he wants. So why do we say that you shouldn't do it? Because it doesn't pay, from a financial point of view. And it isn't the lack of electronics that stands in your way either. Frankly, a guitar makes an ideal loudspeaker enclosure for guitar music. Modern transistorized amplifiers can be fit in with no trouble at all. And there's scarcely a musician who isn't willing to connect a short length of 2-conductor cable between a 9-volt battery in his hip pocket to a simple power plug on his guitar.

The problem is getting the stuff into the guitar. There's only one right way to do this, and it means taking the guitar apart. You have to start by removing the celluloid binding around the guitar's edge, and then carefully take the bottom of the guitar off the sides. And no matter how careful you are, chances are that you'll split the wood before you get too far. The first thought is to use a solvent of some sort to soften the glue and remove the bottom of the guitar that way. However, most guitars are finished with a lacquer that not only shows off the wood grain nicely but actually **forms** the wood grain. The solvent will play merry old Ned with that lacquer, so don't try it.

The next usual solution is to do a little studying, and you find that the glue used is a hide glue, and that boiling water, a teaspoonful at a time, is the best way to soften that glue. It's a painstaking process, and chances are that the boiling water won't help the guitar's finish either. The best way that we've found is to actually cut the wood with a very fine saber saw, and then cement it back and refinish over the cut later on. It's a tough job, and not one that we recommend.

A far better solution to the problem, and one that makes a lot more sense, is to remote the amplifier. Get one of those inexpensive FM wireless microphones and fit it with a small plug that matches the microphone connector jack. If you mount this plug directly to the wireless mike, it will also serve to support the mike at the same time.

With this plugged into the guitar's mike jack, and a small transistorized FM receiver connected to the amplifier input, the musician can stroll idly through his audience with no wire connection to his amplifier, yet the sound is amplified and he has complete and total freedom, which is what he really wanted in the first place. You haven't laid the guitar to waste, and the guitar and amplifier can still be used in normal fashion.

This brings to mind another incident. A non-musician customer came into the shop one day with a strange request. Money was no object—he wanted a couple of nice looking guitars. He examined several models, and apparently what he was after was a classic model, with a center hole instead of f slots. He found one he liked, asked for another, and then, satisfied, payed the price. Now he wanted to know if we could mount loudspeakers inside the guitars and bring the wiring out to the bottom hole that was used for the peg. We agreed, and at a nice price, too. He picked up his guitars a week later, seemed well satisfied with the job. He explained that he was furnishing his apartment, and the two guitars were to hang on the wall as components of his stereo system.

We got a call recently from a would-be night club operator, who had an idea, and wanted to know could we do it. Here's what he came up with. Lots of night club patrons want to talk instead of just listen to the music. Why can't we rig up a "silent" music group that could play live, but could be heard only if you put earphones on at your table.

Sound like a fun job? It was. We rigged up a big plexiglass booth that was soundproofed, so the musicians could be seen but not heard. Then we wired up some microphones, an amplifier, and wired each table with a set of four phone jacks with individual volume controls. It cost the new nightclub owner a pretty penny, and the pretty penny went into our cash register.

The club was an instant success. But there were some problems, too. If two patrons were sitting at the same table and wanted to talk while they were listening to the music, they first had to tap one another on the arm to get their attention, and then motion for the other to take the earphones off. As an alternative, you could reach across the table and turn down your partner's volume control.

Well, we solved that problem in what proved to be a uniquely appealing way. We added small intercom-type amplifiers and microphones, so that those people at any given table could still hear the music, yet could comfortably talk to each other also. It worked, and worked well. More tinkle in the register, too.

We figured that we had seen the last of this particular night-club owner, but he came back with another question. People wanted to dance. How could we help? We were starting to play with magnetic telephone pickups dangling from earphones, and a huge coil of wire circling the room to carry the signal, when the owner called up and said to forget the whole thing—he had solved the problem himself. So intrigued had we become that we went over to see how. He had simply ripped out all of the wiring and taken down the plexiglass sound-proof booth!

Speaking of night clubs, they've got a club in Britain called the "Telephone Lounge" or some such thing. Each table is equipped with a dial telephone. If you see a pretty girl at a table, you simply pick up the phone, dial a 2-digit number corresponding to her table, and try to strike up a conversation. It's a nice way to meet people, and the fun is in trying to guess where and who the party is that is calling you. Asking somebody to wave a hand doesn't help, because everybody tries that, and the room is full of waving hands.

To modernize this, we had a club operator ask if we couldn't set up a similar system, but with intercoms! Sure we could, and we did. After it was installed, we moved from table to table to test it, and frankly, had only one callback. Seems some of the patrons found that you could pull the little black knobs off the units, and couples who were meeting here were taking the plastic knobs as souvenirs. We replaced the knobs, socking them in with a good coat of epoxy, and everybody, especially the manager, was very happy ever after.

Back in the late 30s and early 40s, big bands were all individualized by what were called "band stands"—music stands with fronts emblazoned with either the name of the band or its monogram. Many of the smaller "kid" bands who really hadn't made it yet could purchase corrugated cardboard stands that folded up for storage, and at reasonable cost. They'd lug these from job to job, setting them up wherever they got a job. The band members effected some uniformity by wearing the same jackets, either an off-white, or a maroon.

Today, the small combo does the same thing, but in a different way. They select a name first, a name that will have some meaning or appeal to them, or just be obtuse enough to have meaning only to those who are "in." Even the solo performer tries to publicize his name. You can offer any or all of these the opportunity to do so.

To personalize an instrument or an amplifier, start by obliterating the manufacturer's name from the amplifier. You can usually do this either by resurfacing the face of the amplifier, or by applying some properly colored paint over it. Do not try to dissolve the name, as the name is usually hot-stamped and any such attempt will also dissolve the surfacing material.

Obtain fairly-large press-on letters in a contrasting color. These are available at your local art-supply store in a variety of colors, type faces and sizes. Carefully add the press-on letters, and then burnish them down tightly. A coat of wax at this time usually helps to seal them in place.

The instrument is another matter entirely. While many guitarists and bassists would like the name on the fingerboard, this is not a good idea, since the constant string pressure will abrade the name shortly, leaving just a mess. A better place is on the body of the instrument. Start by cleaning the instrument thoroughly, and then, using the press-type, apply the name. Be careful not to use too much pressure in doing this, or you may dig into the wood and score the instrument. After the name is applied and burnished down, again use a good coat of wax to seal it in place.

One friend who went into the amplifier repair business suddenly found himself in the customizing business instead! He was asked to add a few flamboyant decorations to a guitar, and did such a great customizing job on it that others soon began to come to his shop. When he saw how much of his income was derived from this, he simply pushed the test equipment to the back of the bench and he hasn't touched a soldering iron since!

He makes best use of, believe it or not, a local automotive-supply shop. They provide him with all sorts of self-adhering vinyl stripes and decorations in a multitude of colors and for easy application to any car—or guitar. He has done well by adding "racing stripes" to musical instruments. When four musicians get together to form a combo, chances are that they will all have different instruments. My friend's racing stripes makes all of them look a little more alike.

You may have observed that today's rock group depends on more than just music. They sing, and they dance. Many appear to be very agile acrobats as well. With horizontal stripes on the guitars, the simultaneous movements of the group are enhanced and stressed. Whatever they do, they look better while they're doing it when the instruments are striped.

The fancy stripes are simple enough to apply. Peel away the backing paper, stretch the stripe a bit to make sure there are no wrinkles or bubbles, align it and press it down. With the passage of time, the cement sets up and the stripes are permanently bonded to the instrument, just as they become binded to the surface of a car.

Why should an electronics technician have to know about this if he's going into the amplifier repair field? Because there's a good buck to be made in doing this work, and the effort-profit factor is high!

Many guitar manufacturers do not make provision for a neck cord, and this is a handy adjunct for a guitarist. To affix a neck cord, all you have to do is drill (very carefully) a ¼-inch hole at the bottom of the guitar, and insert the peg with some good wood cement. These pegs are tapered, so tap it gently with a small hammer to insure a tight fit, and the job is done.

Have you ever had a young musician practicing in your home? One technician had purchased an electronic organ for his daughter, and he soon tired of the sour notes and clinkers that she hit. When she wasn't producing those awful sounds, she was practicing scales. He found himself with his teeth on edge waiting for the next note. It was wearing him to a frazzle. Finally, he hit on a solution. He brought home a set of those big, cushiony stereo earphones, and clamped them on his head while his daughter practiced. He heard nothing at all, and she could play up a storm while he enjoyed his newspaper.

Then the neighbors started to complain. He couldn't very well buy earphones for all of the neighbors, so he took another tack. He got a deep-throated earphone jack, drilled a five-eights hole with a wood hole saw in a convenient place on the organ's panel, and mounted the jack to the organ's panel. The jack, in a closed-circuit configuration, was than wired into the speaker system. With no connection to the jack, the organ played through the built-in loudspeaker. However, when a practice session was needed, his daughter put the head-phones on, plugged into the jack, and could practice her clinkers to her heart's content, for only she would hear them. It solved another family problem, too, for all she could hear was the organ while the rest of the family was able to enjoy the hi-fi or television without disturbing her.

LIGHT SHOWS

Many rock musicians include light shows as a part of the act. The object of a light show is to automatically produce light effects that respond to the variations in frequency and amplitude that are produced by the instrument. Generally, these devices are sold separately and need only be connected in parallel with the loudspeaker system. A typical system of this sort is Edmund Scientific's "Music-Vision" system. Here's how it works:

An 8-inch loudspeaker is furnished, and a thin, flexible rubber sheet is stretched across the speaker's front, cemented in place with a plio-bond like liquid cement. Small, front-surface mirrors are then attached to the rubber sheet. They can be cemented directly to the rubber, or they can be attached by strings of varying length. A slide projector is focused on the rubber sheet, and a 4-colored transparent color wheel, which is motor driven, is placed in the projector's light path.

With everything turned on, the wheel slowly turns, changing the color of the light. The loudspeaker with the rubber sheet is connected to the amplifier's loudspeaker. As the musician plays, light is reflected from the mirrors to nearby walls and ceilings. The mirrors that are cemented directly to the rubber sheet will produce circular light patterns, and those attached by string will produce elliptical or figure-eight patterns. As the speaker vibrates, the rubber sheet also vibrates, so the patterns change constantly as the amplitude and frequency of the music changes. It's a rather startling effect, and when used in combination with other light show effects, such as stroboscopic lights, it can be quite imaginative and effective as well.

TAPE RECORDERS

Maybe you don't feel that tape recorders count as an amplifier function, but simply by demonstrating a few simple tricks with them, we've sold lots of recorders to musicians. Les Paul, the noted guitarist, pioneered multiple-voice recordings, along with his wife, Mary Ford. While they used top-quality recorders, you can duplicate their efforts with any good recorder that offers a voice-over feature.

To start with, demonstrate to your client that he can use a tape recorder to improve his fingering technique. We start with a complex classic, such as the Malaguena, and, playing it a full octave lower than it was written, we record it at 3.75 inches. We then play it back at 7½ inches, and it sounds just fantastic. The speed is doubled, the tonal range comes up to the full frequency that it's supposed to have, and the sound is simply fantastic. We then slow the recorder to 3¾ again, and, using a tremolo technique, play another piece, such as "Return to Sorrento," a full octave higher than it's supposed to be. Playing this back at 7½ makes it sound exactly like a mandolin. Rewind, let the musician monitor this track and record on track two a guitar chord accompaniment to it. With sound-on-sound, you can marry the new chording with the mandolin; of course, this is recorded at 7½.

Now, before he becomes too entranced, rewind and let him hear this combined track, then add a solo guitar voice playing single string obbligato over both. We usually finish by making another recording using the guitar's bass notes to provide some added rhythm and set off the mandolin. Now play the blended track back to him at 7½, and watch his face light up as he hears himself sounding like an entire Mummers parade!

METRONOME

There are other devices you're going to have to service also, and some of these can be real head-scratchers. Recently, electronic metronomes have become popular. The standard metronome contains a clockwork mechanism that you wind with a key. It is really a clock that's built sort of upside down. A pendulum with a graduated arm extends upward from the bottom, and a sliding weight moves on the pendulum. To operate this unit, you flip the pendulum with a finger, and it swings in an arc, back and forth, beating out the time for a music student with a regular "tick-tock" sound. You can move the weight downward, closer to the fulcrum, to make it faster, or upward and away from the fulcrum, to slow it.

The electronic pendulum is different. It consists of a small, transistorized flip-flop with a variable resistor that determines the pulse rate. The output of the flip-flop is fed to an audio amplifier and then to a small loudspeaker. An on-off switch in series with the built-in 9-volt battery controls the power to the unit. What usually goes wrong with these things is that the battery runs down. We always replace these with 9-volt alkaline types which provide better life expectancy.

The truth of the matter is that to most music students, there is no need for a dead-on measure of accuracy, just a relative indication will be enough. Don't bother trying to cycle the electronic metronome against a stop watch or a pulse rate counter; just check it at a couple of positions along the dial against a stop watch, which should be quite enough.

ELECTRONIC TUNERS

The average piano is rich in harmonics, and as a result, is difficult to use to tune an instrument. Yet most musicians will tune their instruments against a piano for the simple reason that you can easily tune a guitar or bass, but tuning a piano is a job and a half. They assume that the piano is in good tune, and then tune the other instruments to it. Pitch pipes are available, and many guitarists buy these and tune the guitar to the pipe when they're playing alone or practicing. When they get to where a piano is, they have to retune anyway.

There is an electronic tuning device that operates with a motor-driven stroboscopic wheel, a neon lamp, and a microphone. You connect the microphone (or the instrument's pickup) to the unit, plug it in and turn it on. Then you select the note to which you are attempting to tune, pluck your string, and observe the dial. When you are in tune, the dial will seem to "freeze" and hold position. If you are just slightly below the note, the note on the dial will appear to be climbing up the scale; if you are above the note, it will appear to be descending.

These units operate by comparing the input frequency from the instrument against the 60-Hz line current. They are most accurate, and are used for tuning electronic organs, among other things. However, if you are tuning up a combo that uses a piano as part of the group, make sure (by checking with this unit and a microphone) that the piano is in proper tune first.

ELECTRONIC BONGOS

Bongos are those small drums that come attached in pairs, one with a larger diameter than the other. Well, we now have them in an electronic version, and they are played in exactly the same way. However, rather than acoustically echoing, the way the real ones do, the electronic versions use the capacity introduced by the player's thumbs to create the sound which is then amplified. Interestingly enough, the capacitor of the sensing element on top of the drum is sensitive to where the surface is struck, and the differences in capacity result in a different tone which is then amplified.

Again, the biggest problem with these devices is the fact the batteries go sour. Unfortunately, these units are equipped with such low-level amplification and such small loudspeakers that they are really designed for use as party novelties and not

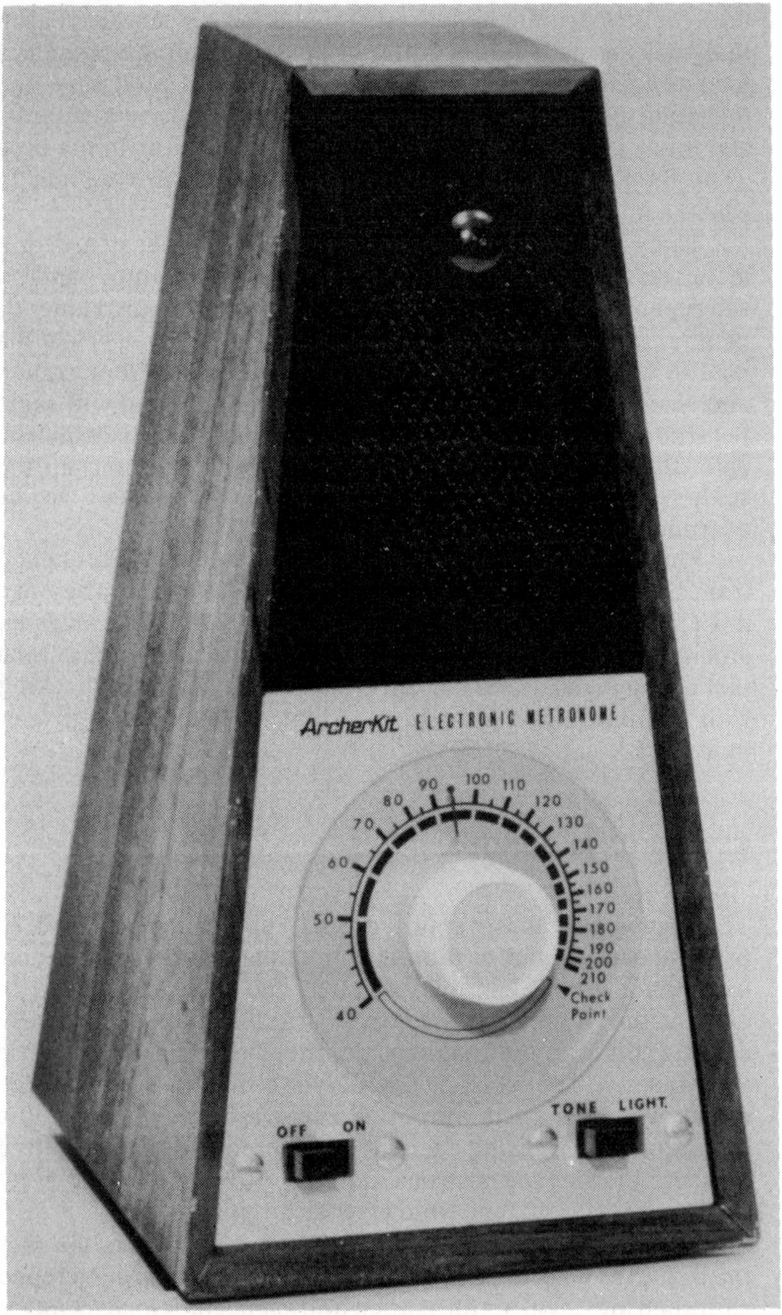

ArcherKit electronic metronome. Courtesy Allied Radio Shack.

really for group or orchestral work. However, we have been able to play a few interesting games by using the internal battery-operated amplifiers as low-level drivers to feed into the main group amplifier. The result is a more respectable sound than you could get with "live" bongos.

Naturally, when this sound is heard, there's always a stampede of people wanting the same, more and better. We've managed to rig up contact mikes to unamplified bongos and give the musician a better or at least an amplified sound. Other south-of-the-border instruments that you may be called on to amplify will include maraccas, claves, and a host of other rhythm and percussion instruments, including an oddly-shaped gourd that has been cut with serrations, and is played by rubbing rhythmically with a stick. This is usually accompanied by a lot of smiling and toe-tapping.

We put a contact unit on one, and held it in place with double-sided tape, of the type available from many burglar-alarm installers. Our initial tests consisted of connecting the mike to an amplifier, and then taking a few unskilled and hasty rubs with the stick. Sounded good, if we say so ourselves. But the thing spent almost as much time being repaired as it did in making music. After a few repairs, we asked the musician for a couple of free tickets to the next performance. He was flattered, and handed them over. He smiled almost as broadly as he did when he was playing.

It only took one set to know what the problem was. He rubbed away at that stick like he was trying to light a fire with a boy scout's bow and spindle. Then all of a sudden he screamed "Ariba!" and began whacking away at the pickup with the stick. The sound that came out was a sharp clackety-clack-clack and then all was silent again. Somehow, he learned by accident that tapping the pickup gave him a different kind of sound, and the tapping grew to a walloping, and that pickup just wasn't designed to take that for too long. He caught my eye in the audience and shrugged his shoulders. He was turned off, and didn't like it.

COMPLEX SPEAKER SYSTEMS

Sometimes several speakers are used in a musical instrument amplifier system. They can be directly connected to the amplifier system, or can be switched at the operator's pleasure. We saw an interesting system several years ago, in

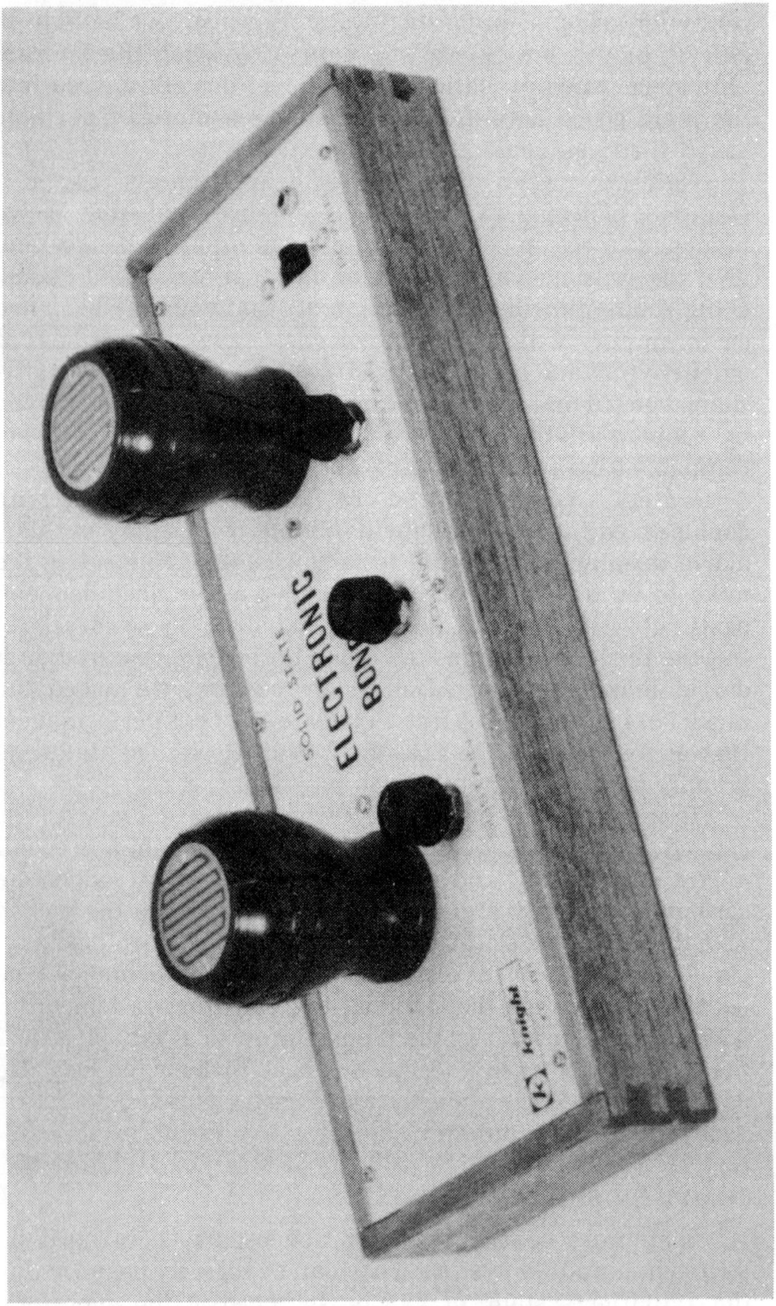

Knight electronic bongo. Courtesy Allied Radio Shack.

which a series of switch mats, each about four inches square, were placed in a semicircle in front of the guitarist. By placing his foot on one or more, he could trigger almost any combination of six different speakers that he wanted. He could play a phrase that came from one side of the room, and then answer this with another phrase at the other side of the room. In other systems, multiple speakers are used, and frequently, these are added, not as part of the original design, but as an afterthought on the part of the musician, as his affluence dictated.

Unfortunately, you may find that in adding loudspeakers indiscriminately, and adding them with little or no knowledge of electronics and balancing, a degradation of quality can occur. Always make sure that you check the output impedance of the amplifier terminals to which additional loudspeakers are connected, and be sure to total the impedance of the load as well.

Typical of this is the young man who brought an amplifier in for repair, and had two separate loudspeakers connected to it. The original speakers were connected to the loudspeaker output terminals of the amplifier, to the screws marked "GND" and "8 ohms." The added loudspeaker was connected to the two remaining screws, the ones marked "4" ohms and the one marked "16 ohms." Naturally, the thing wasn't working right. The technician observed that both speakers were 8-ohm types. He connected them between ground and four ohms, in parallel, and things sounded a little bit better.

Text (Chapter 8) Continues on Page 249 →

SCHEMATIC SECTION

The intervening schematic and foldout section contains the following:

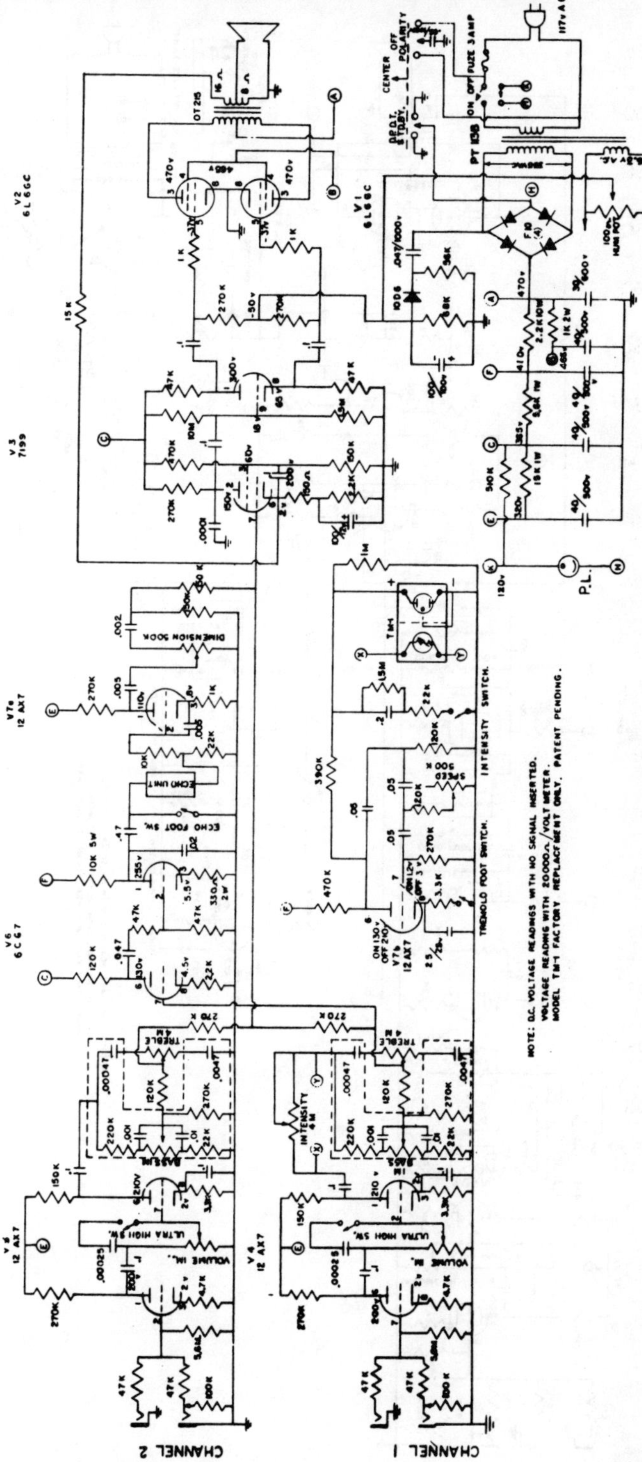

Ampeg Model G-15.

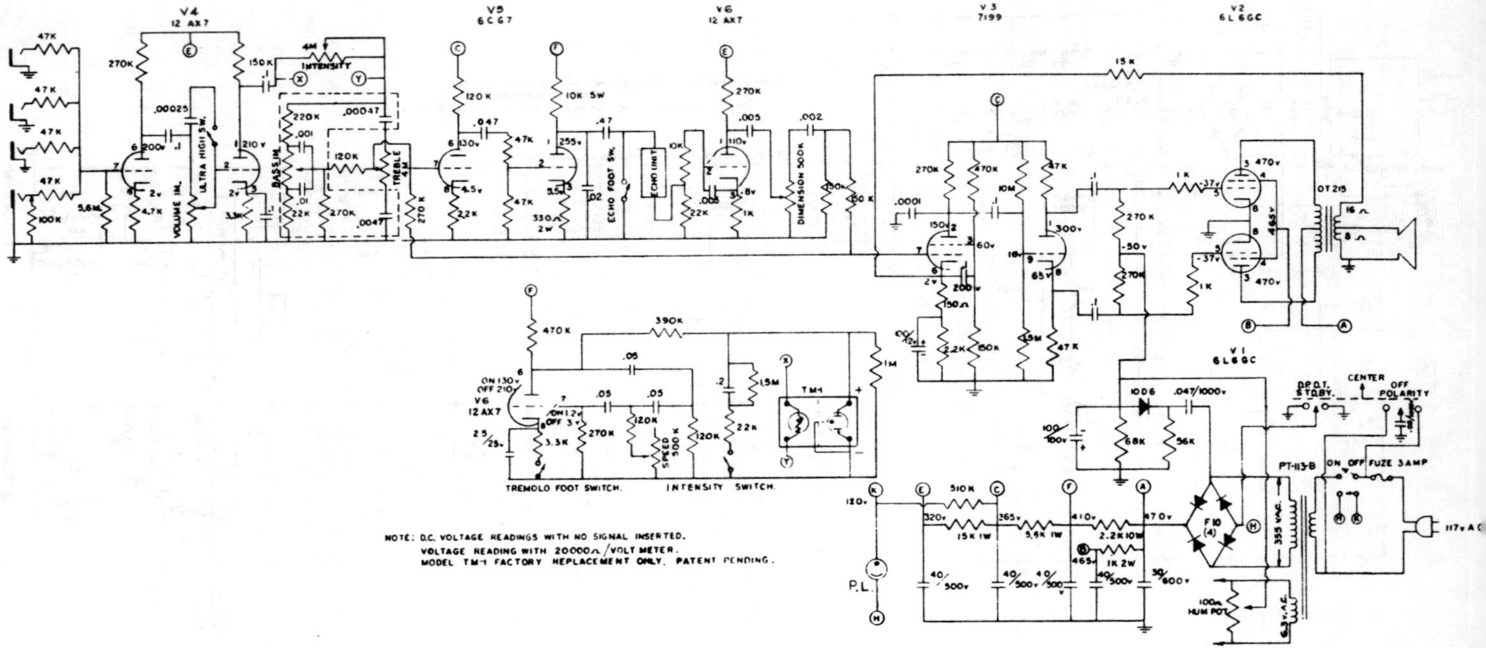

NOTE: D.C. VOLTAGE READINGS WITH NO SIGNAL INSERTED.
VOLTAGE READING WITH 20000 Ω/VOLT METER.
MODEL TM-1 FACTORY REPLACEMENT ONLY. PATENT PENDING.

Ampeg Model GS-15R.

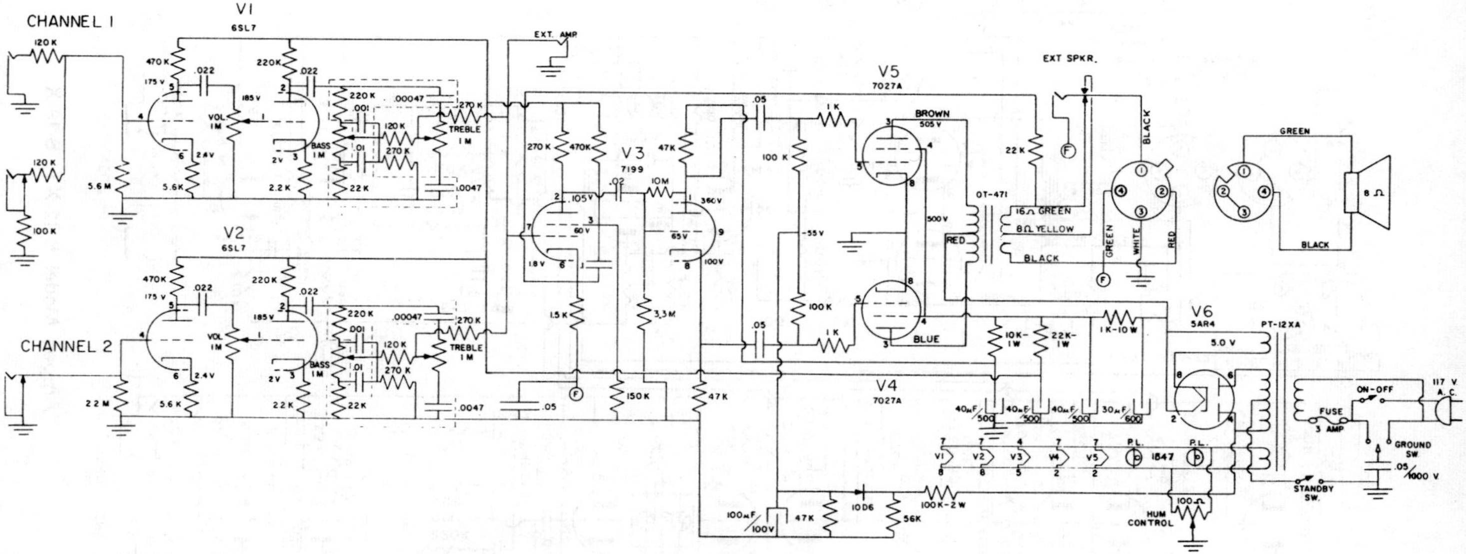

Ampeg Model B-18-N, B-15-ND.

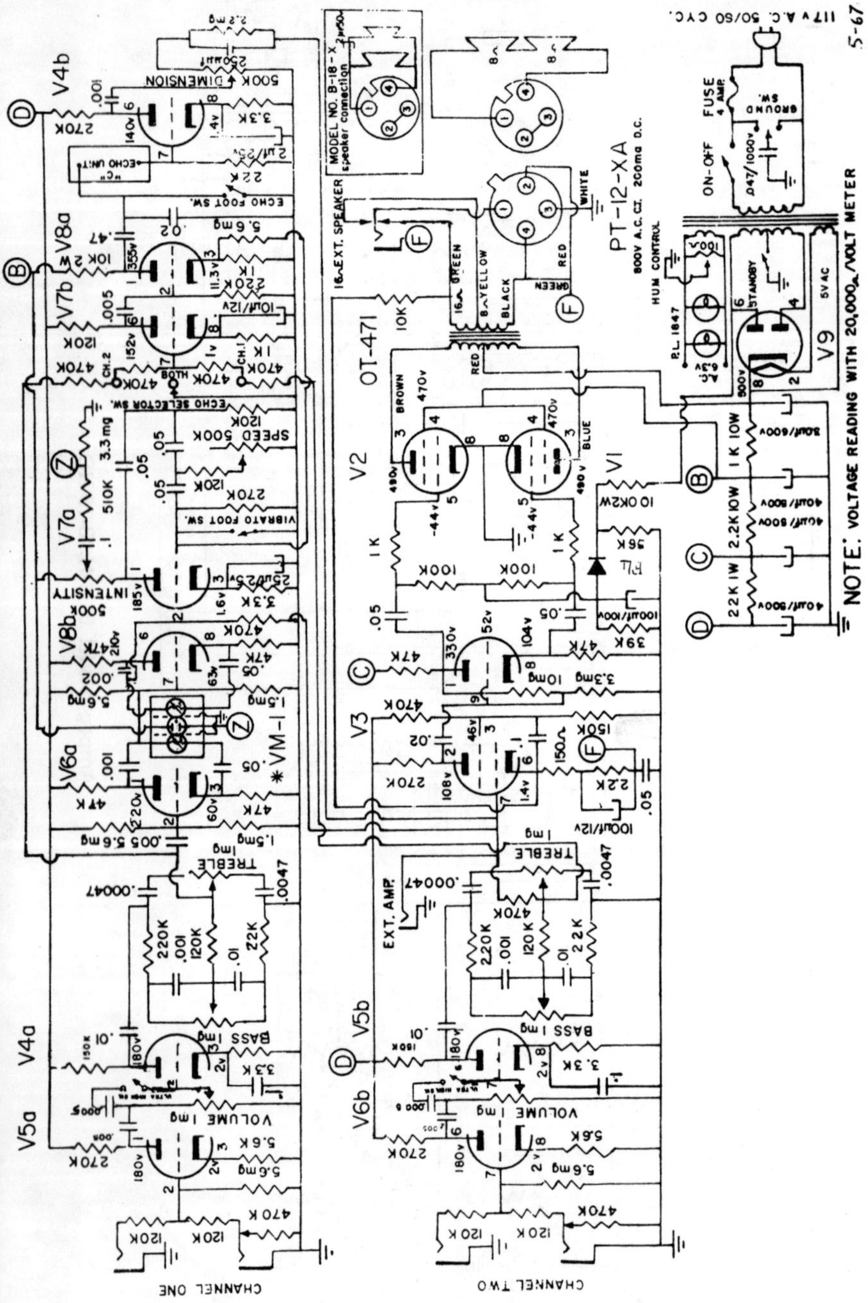

Ampeg Model B-12-XT, B-18-X.

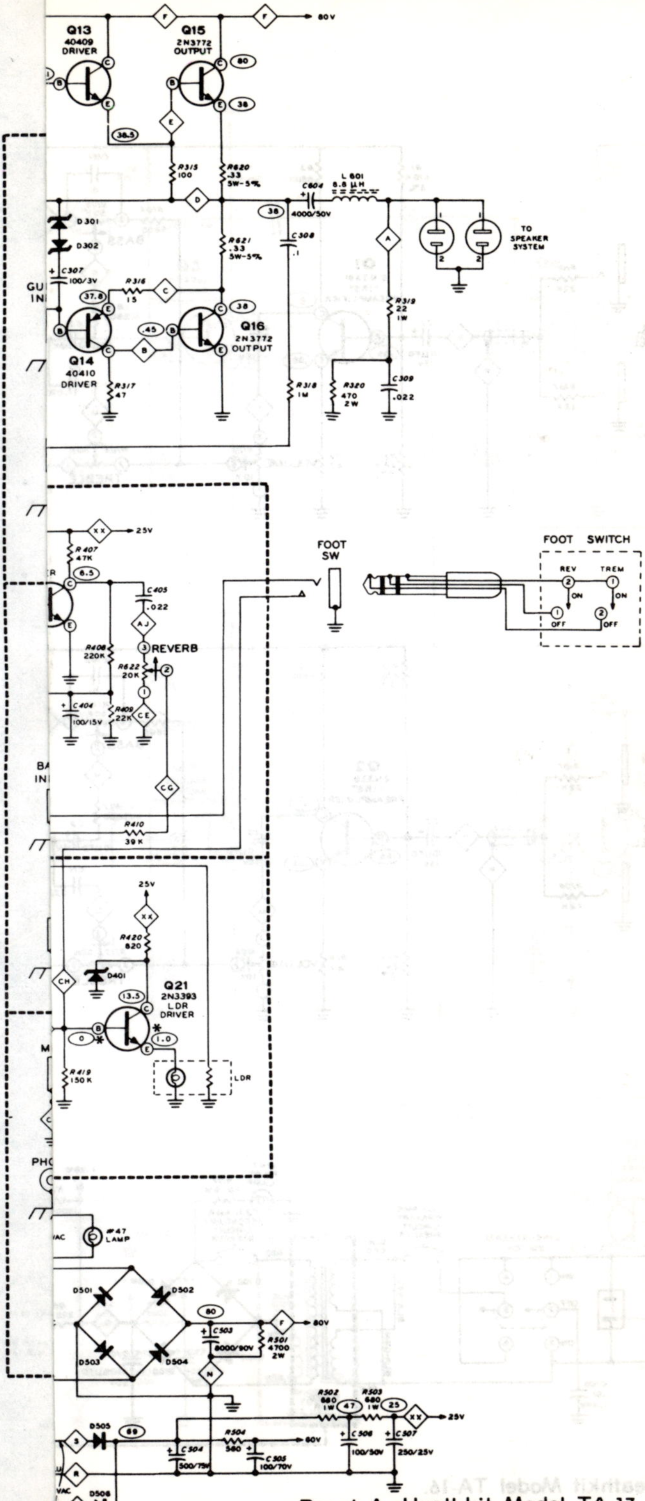

Panel A. Heathkit Model TA-17.

'S:

VE ARE IN pf,

T, TAKEN WI
UND. VOLTAG

FROM

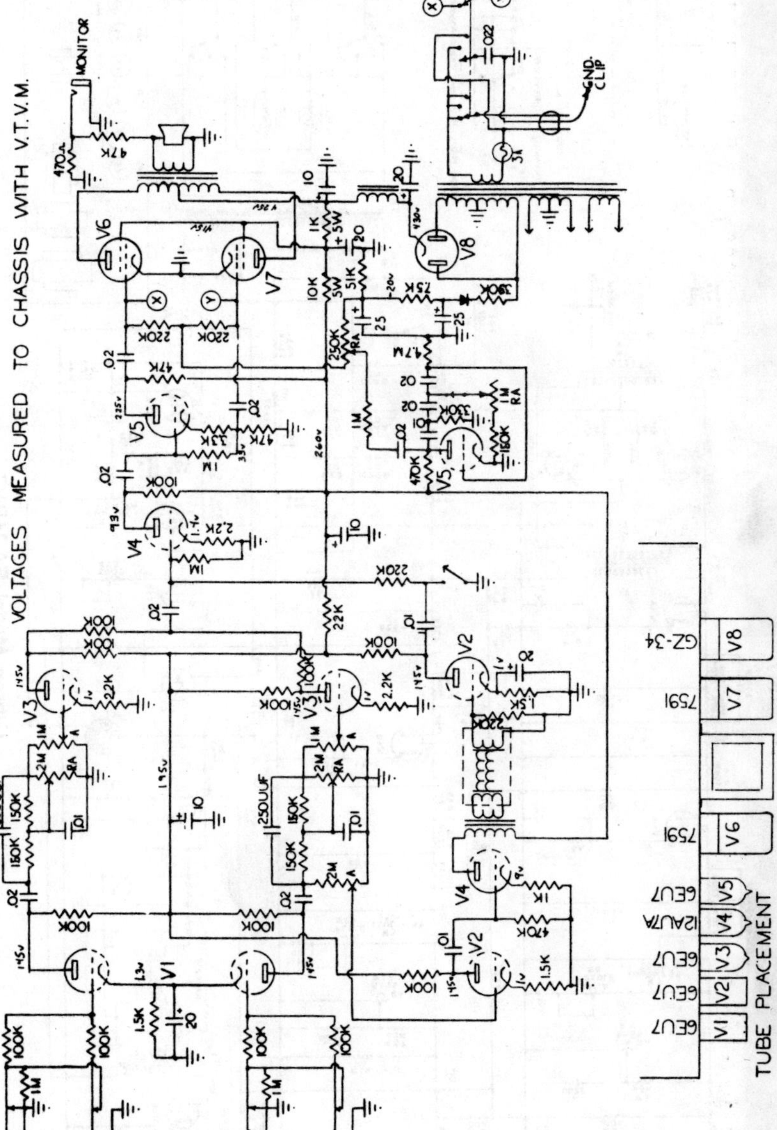

Gibson Model EA-12RVT.

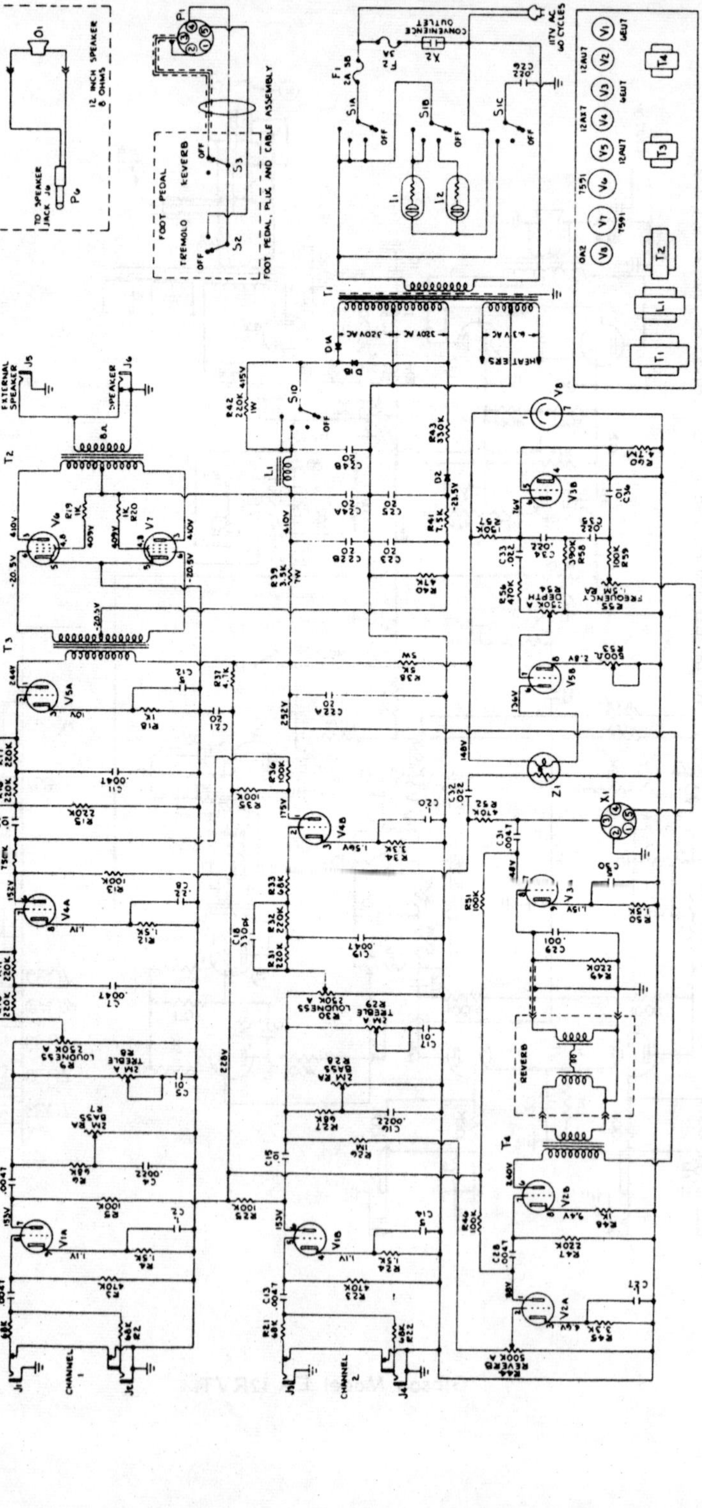

Gibson Model EA-16RVT.

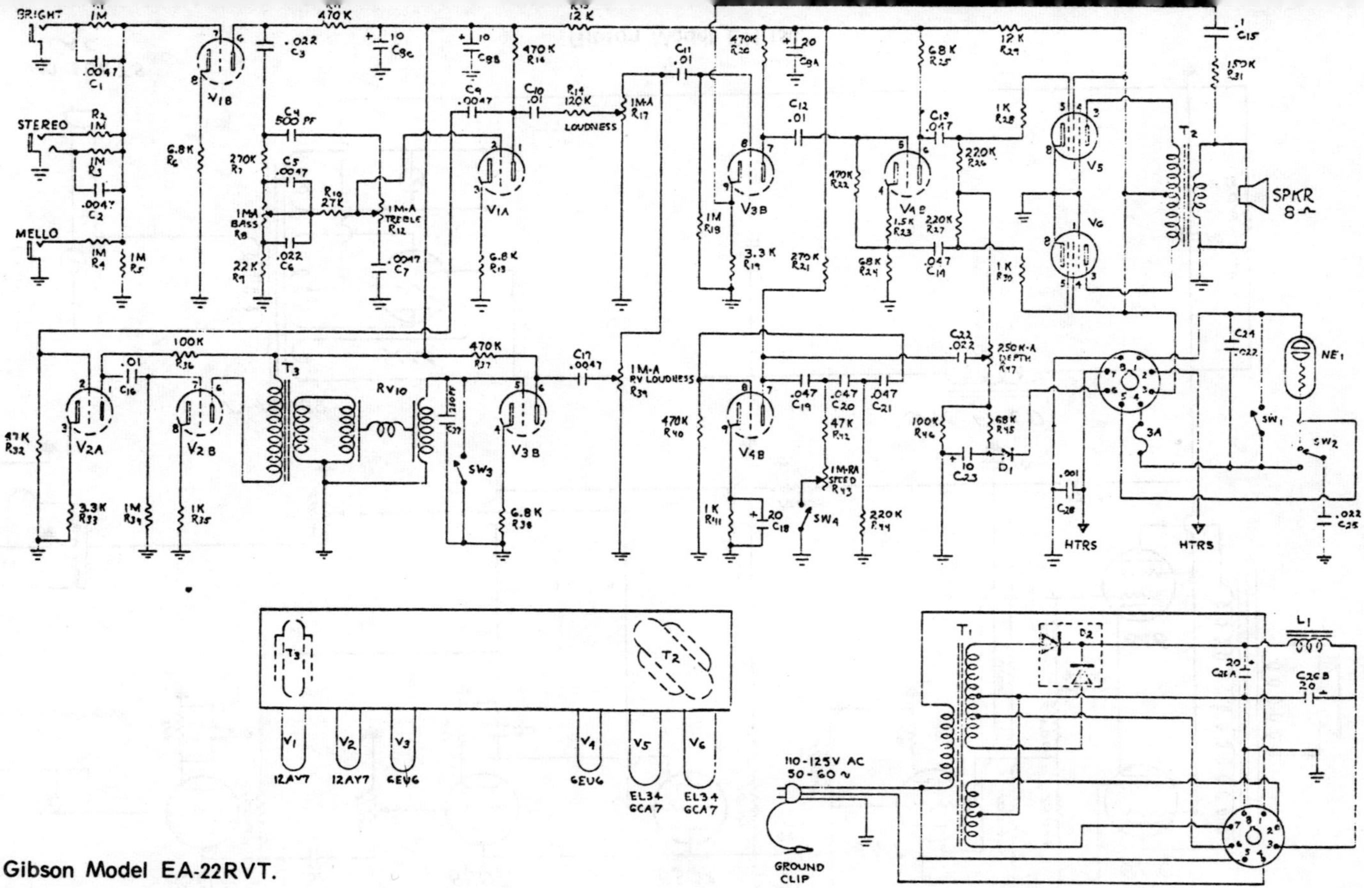

Gibson Model EA-22RVT.

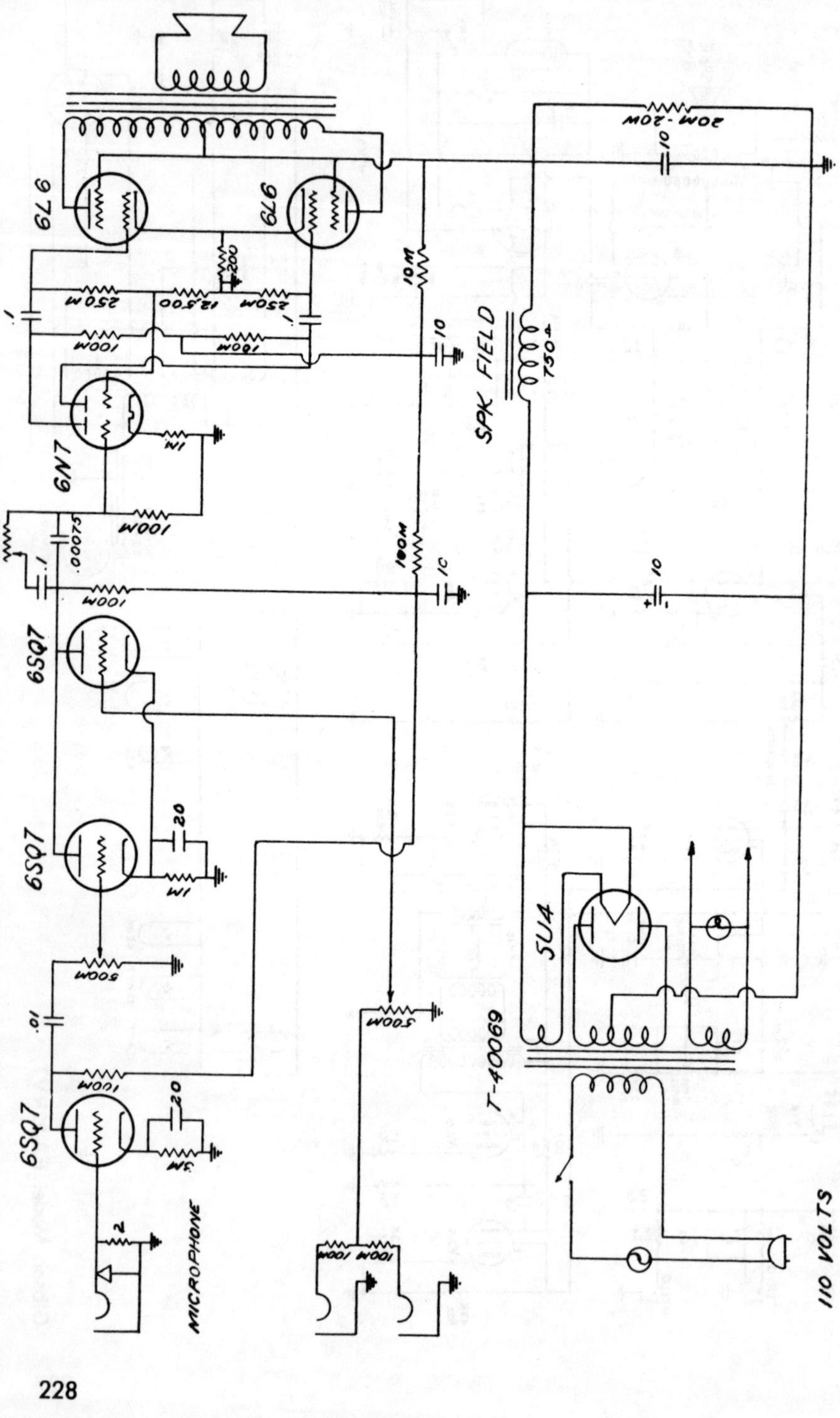

Gibson Model EH-150.

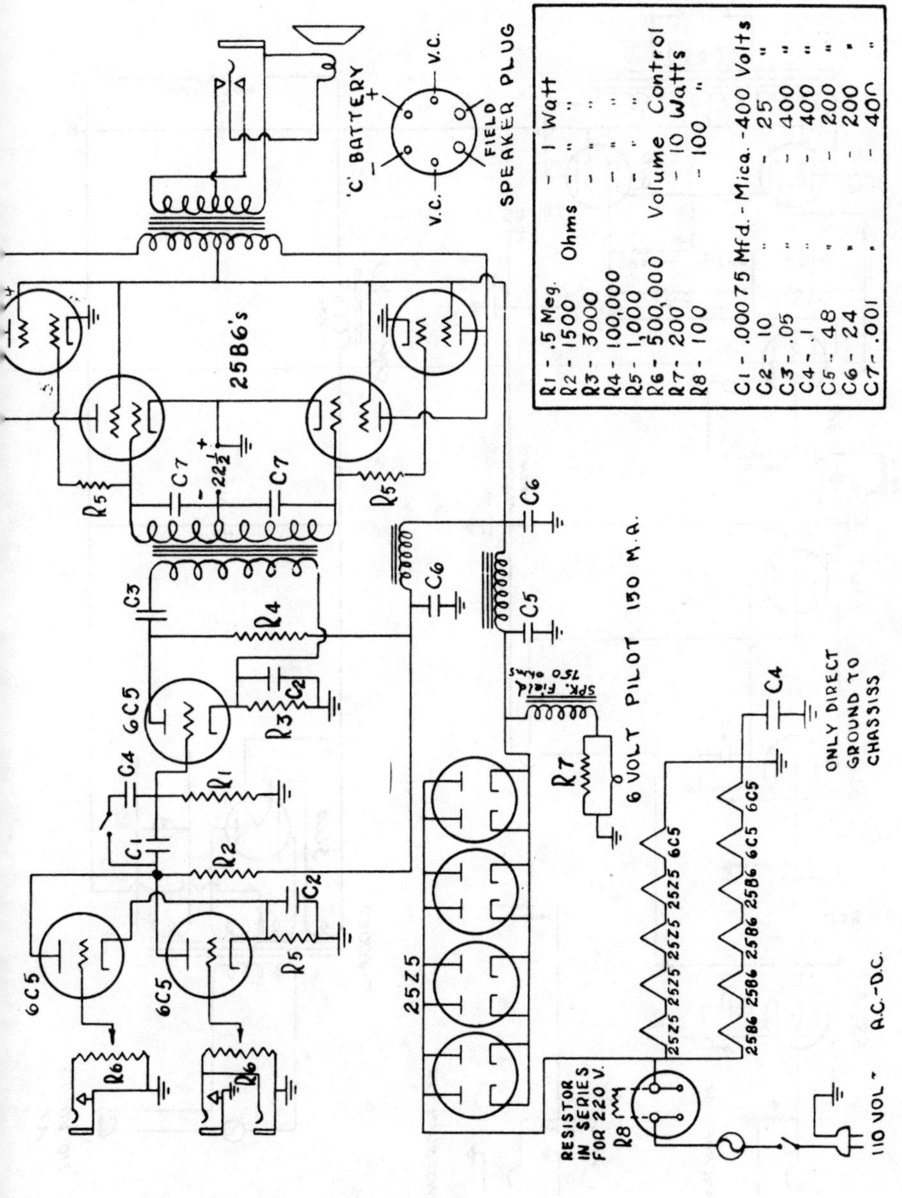

Gibson Model EH-160.

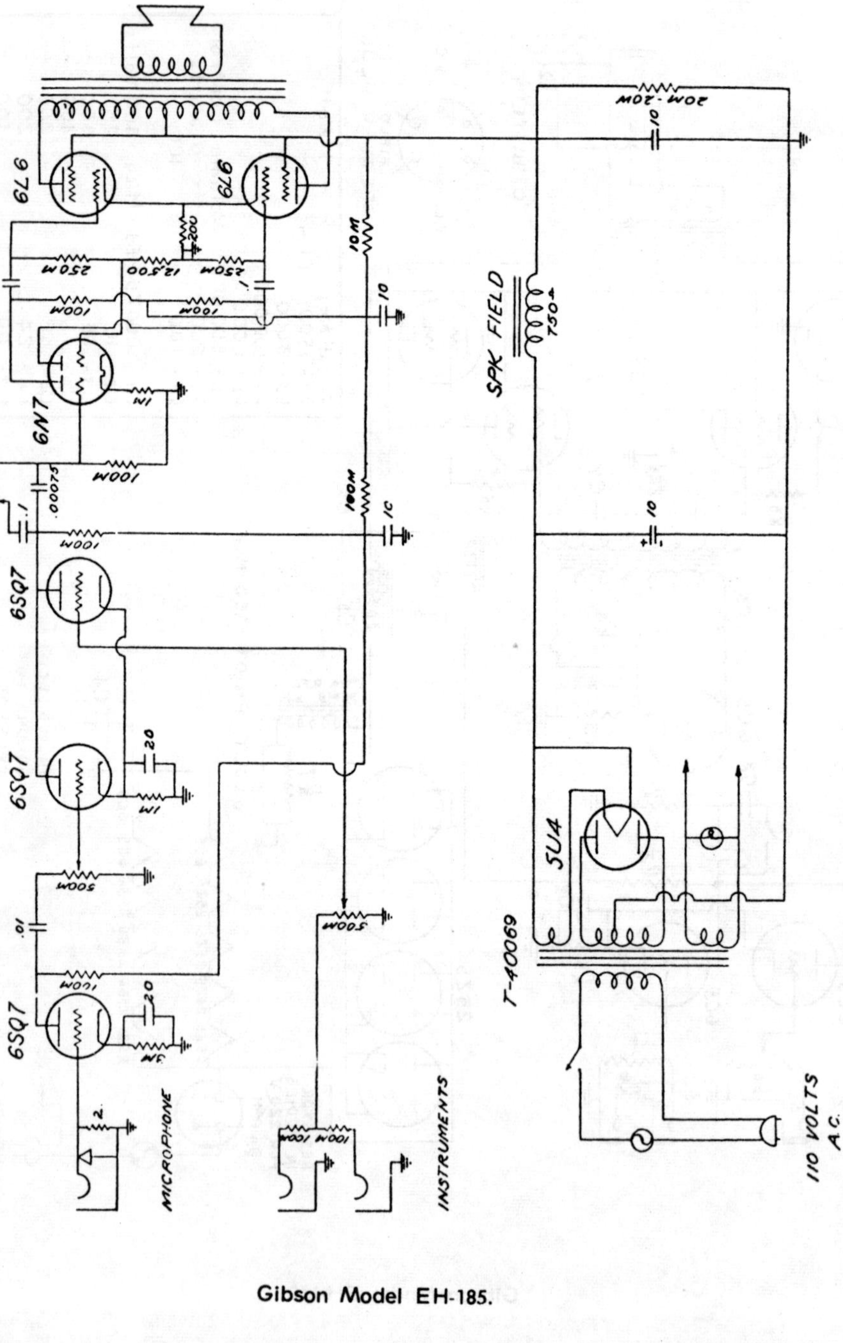

Gibson Model EH-185.

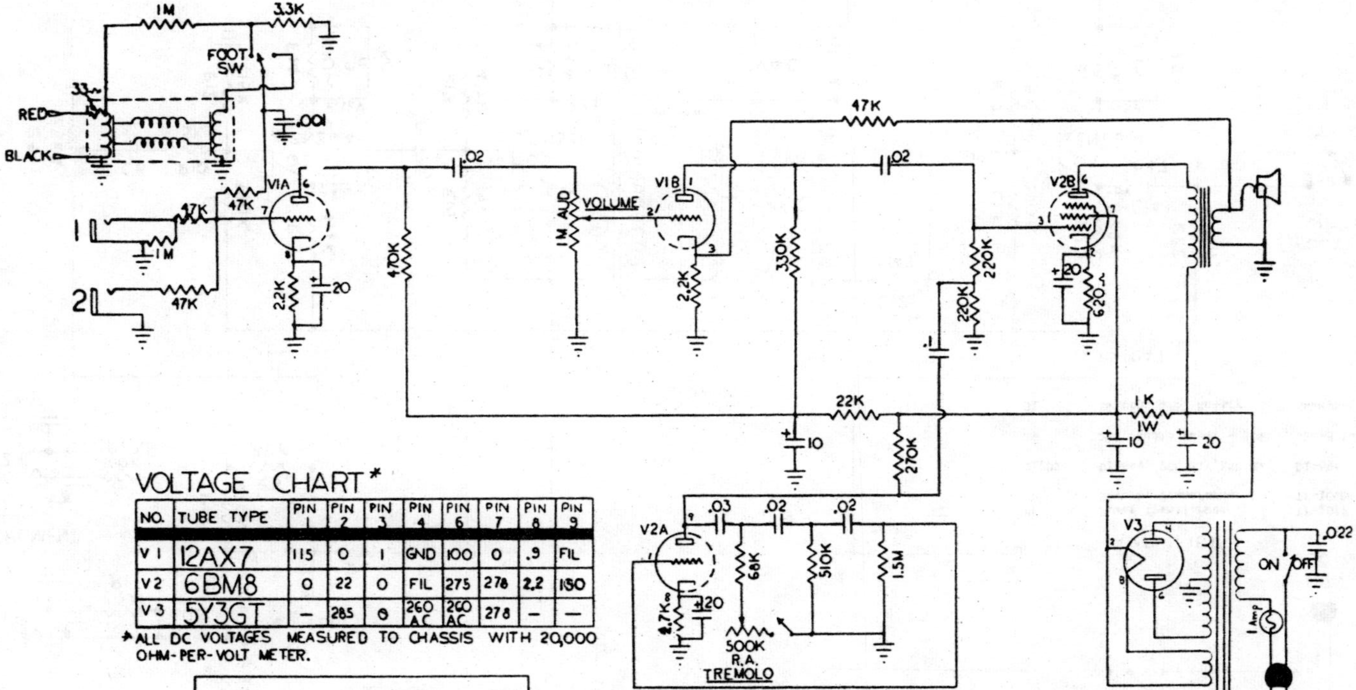

VOLTAGE CHART*

NO.	TUBE TYPE	PIN 1	PIN 2	PIN 3	PIN 4	PIN 6	PIN 7	PIN 8	PIN 9
V 1	12AX7	115	0	1	GND	100	0	.9	FIL
V 2	6BM8	0	22	0	FIL	275	278	2.2	160
V 3	5Y3GT	—	285	0	260 AC	260 AC	278	—	—

*ALL DC VOLTAGES MEASURED TO CHASSIS WITH 20,000 OHM-PER-VOLT METER.

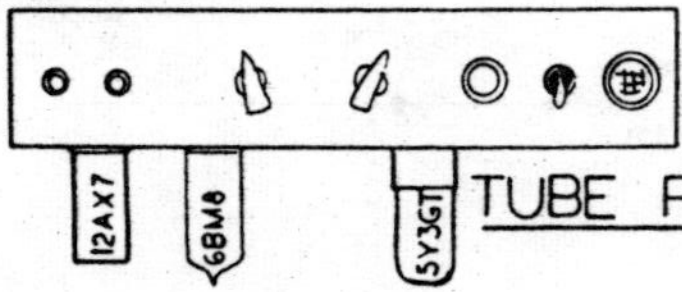

TUBE PLACEMENT

Gibson Model GA-1RT-1.

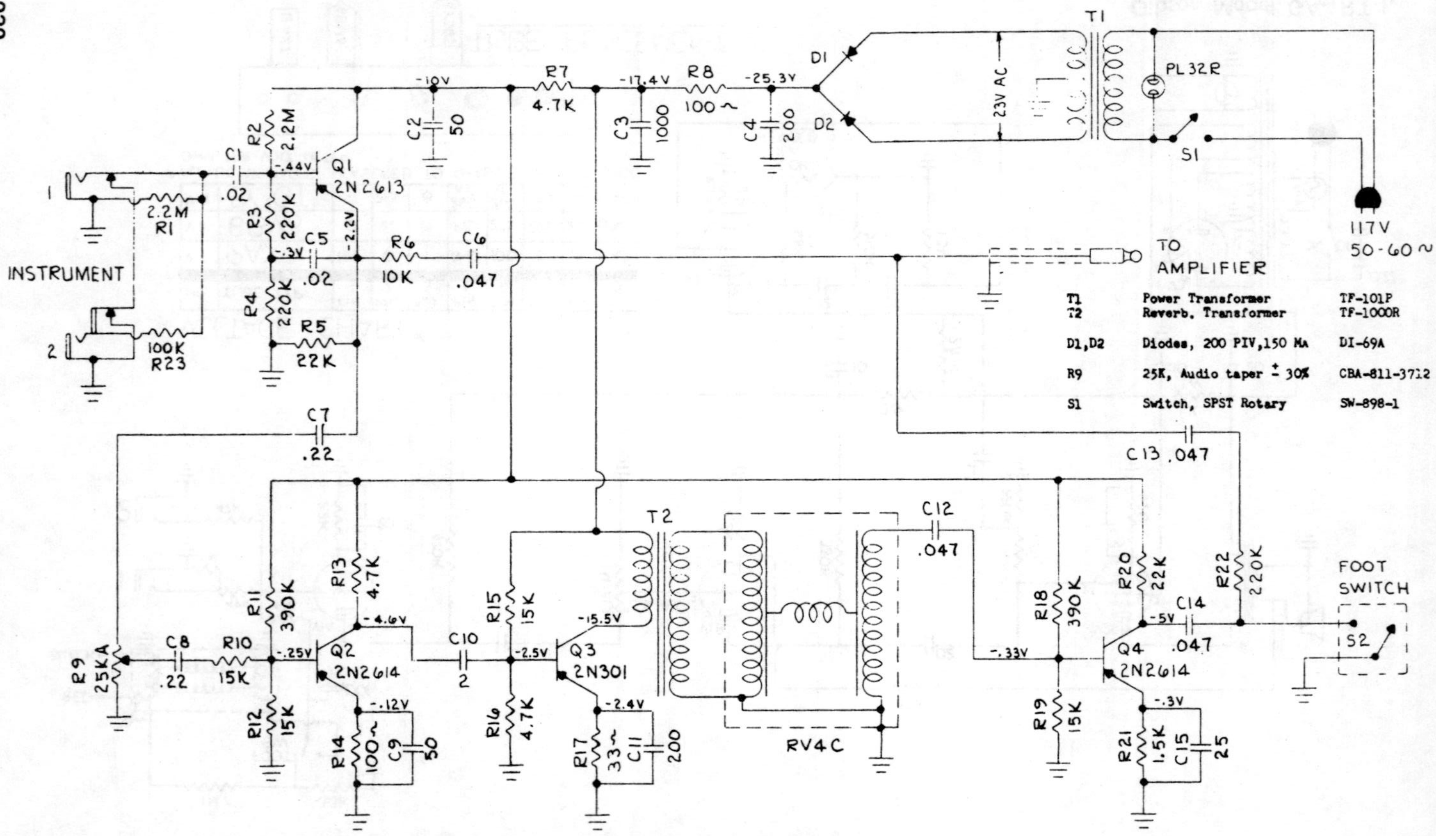

T1	Power Transformer	TF-101P
T2	Reverb. Transformer	TF-1000R
D1,D2	Diodes, 200 PIV,150 MA	DI-69A
R9	25K, Audio taper ± 30%	CBA-811-3712
S1	Switch, SPST Rotary	SW-898-1

Gibson Model GA-3RV.

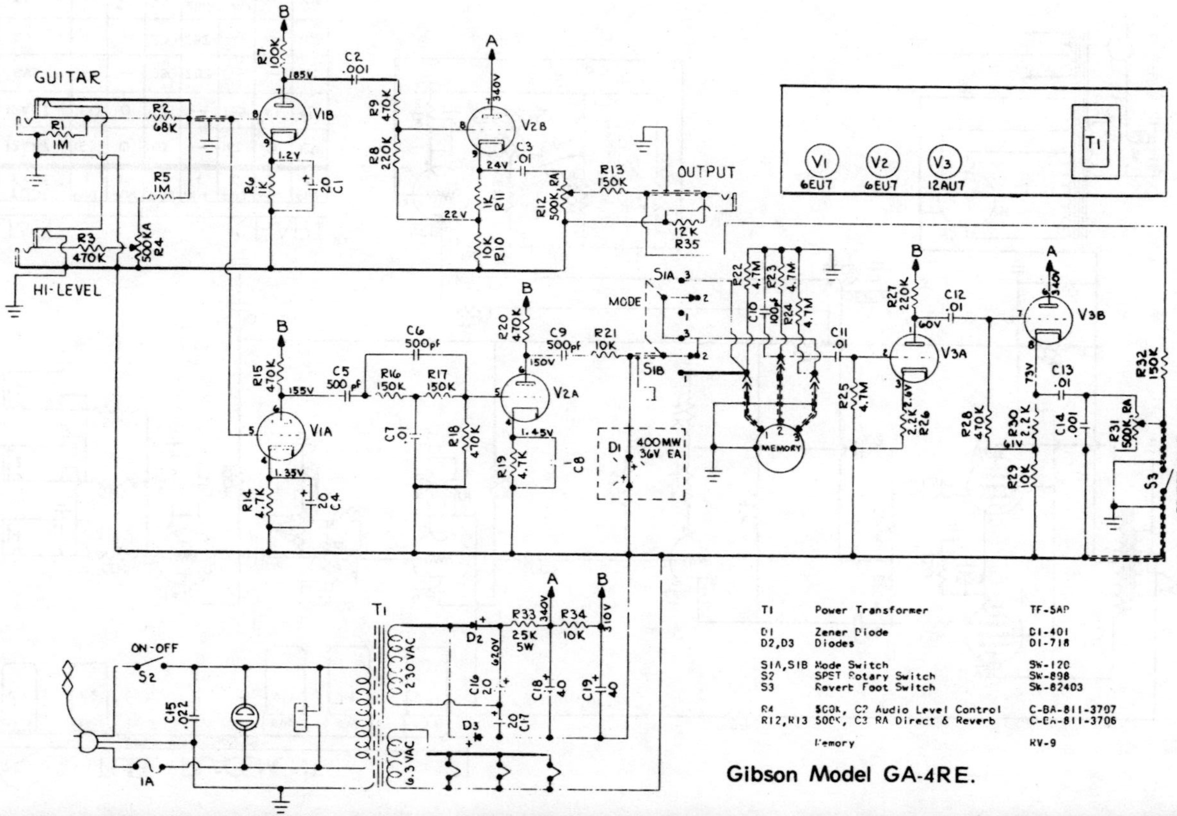

T1	Power Transformer	TF-5AP
D1	Zener Diode	DI-401
D2,D3	Diodes	DI-718
S1A,S1B	Mode Switch	SW-120
S2	SPST Rotary Switch	SW-898
S3	Revert Foot Switch	SW-82403
R4	500K, C2 Audio Level Control	C-BA-811-3707
R12,R13	500K, C3 RA Direct & Reverb	C-BA-811-3706
	Memory	RV-9

Gibson Model GA-4RE.

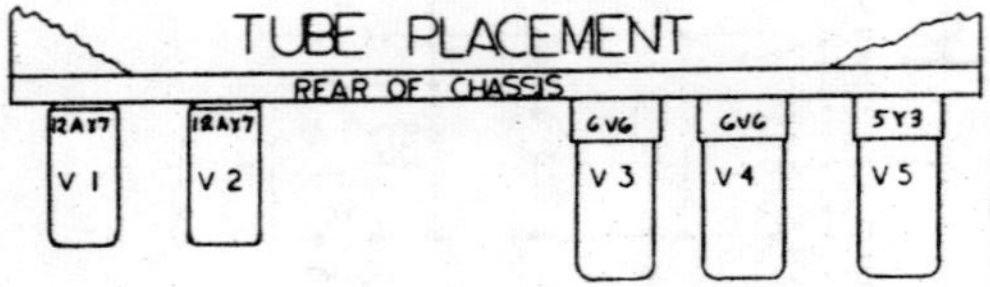

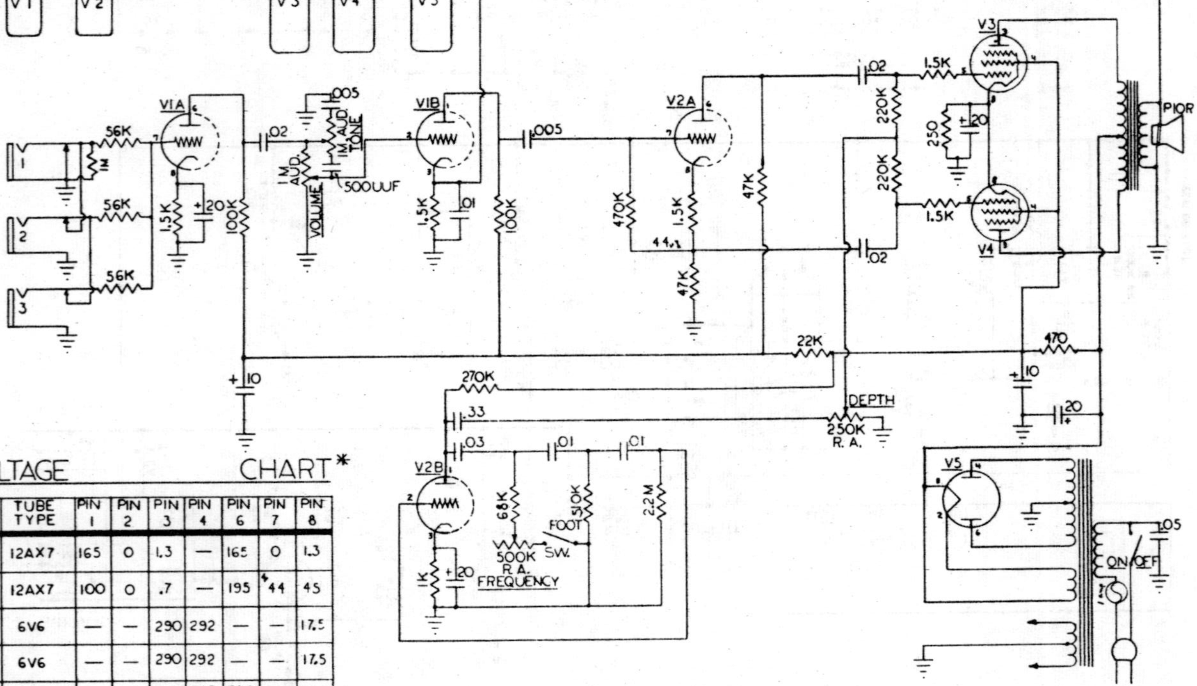

VOLTAGE CHART*

NO.	TUBE TYPE	PIN 1	PIN 2	PIN 3	PIN 4	PIN 6	PIN 7	PIN 8
V 1	12AX7	165	0	1.3	—	165	0	1.3
V 2	12AX7	100	0	.7	—	195	44	45
V 3	6V6	—	—	290	292	—	—	17.5
V 4	6V6	—	—	290	292	—	—	17.5
V 5	5Y3	—	5.2 AC	—	280 AC	280 AC	—	305

*ALL D.C. VOLTAGES MEASURED TO CHASSIS WITH 20,000 OHM/VOLT METER.

Gibson Model GA-16T.

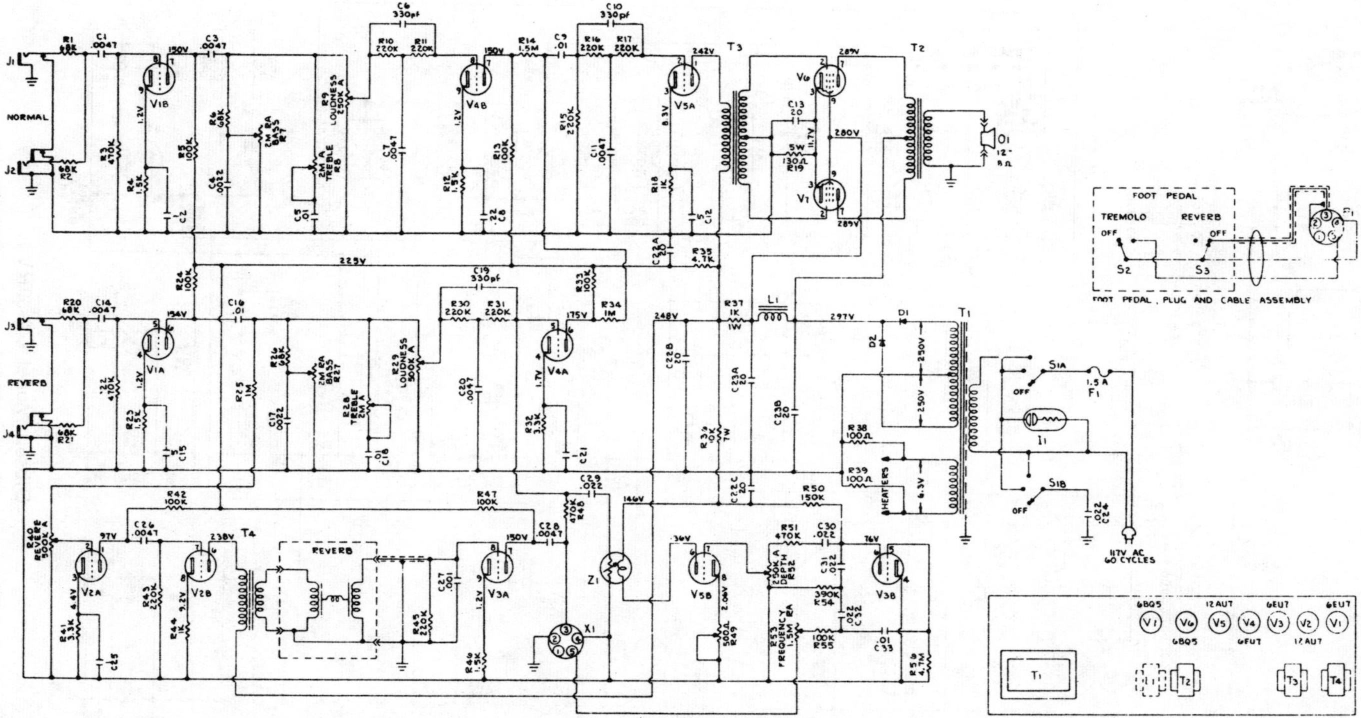

Gibson Model GA-20RVT.

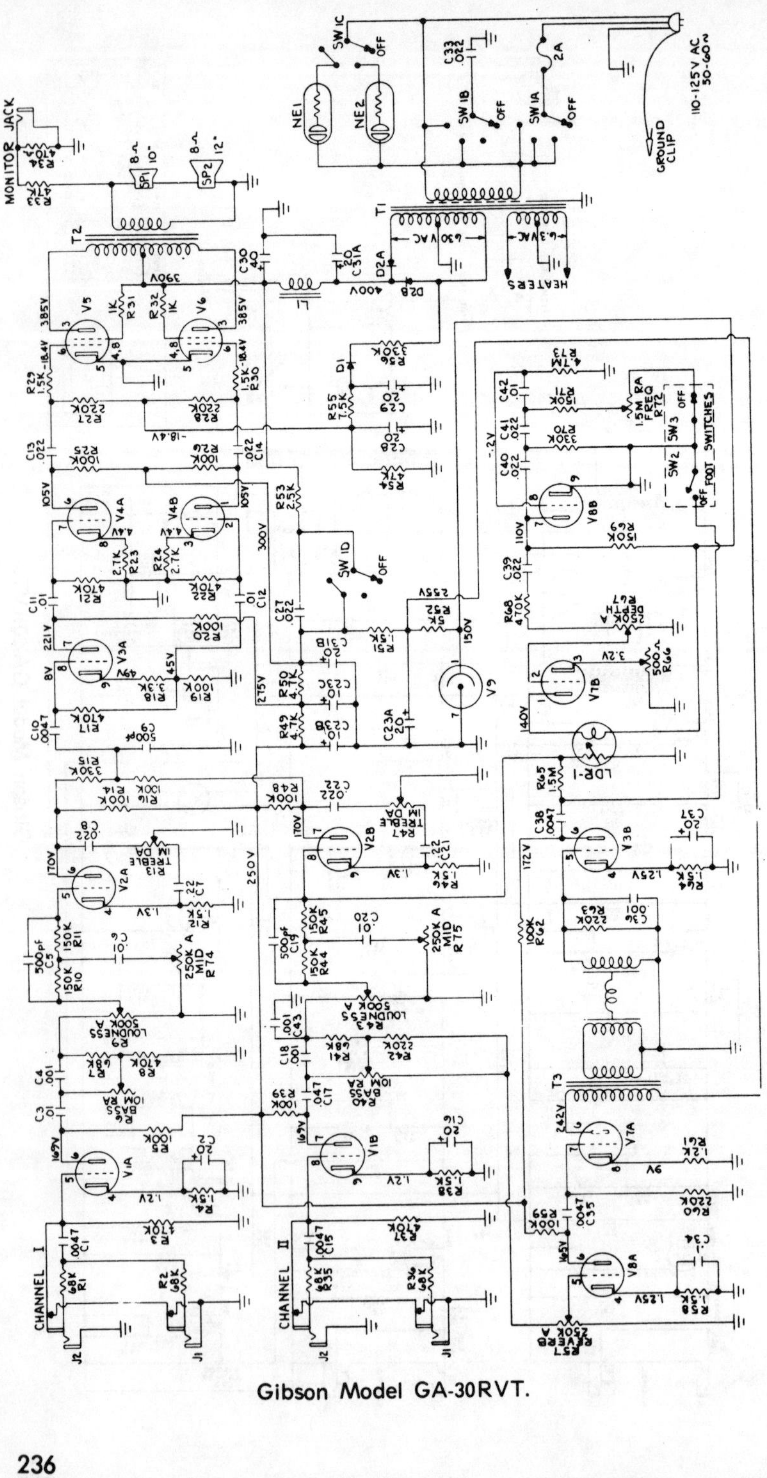

Gibson Model GA-30RVT.

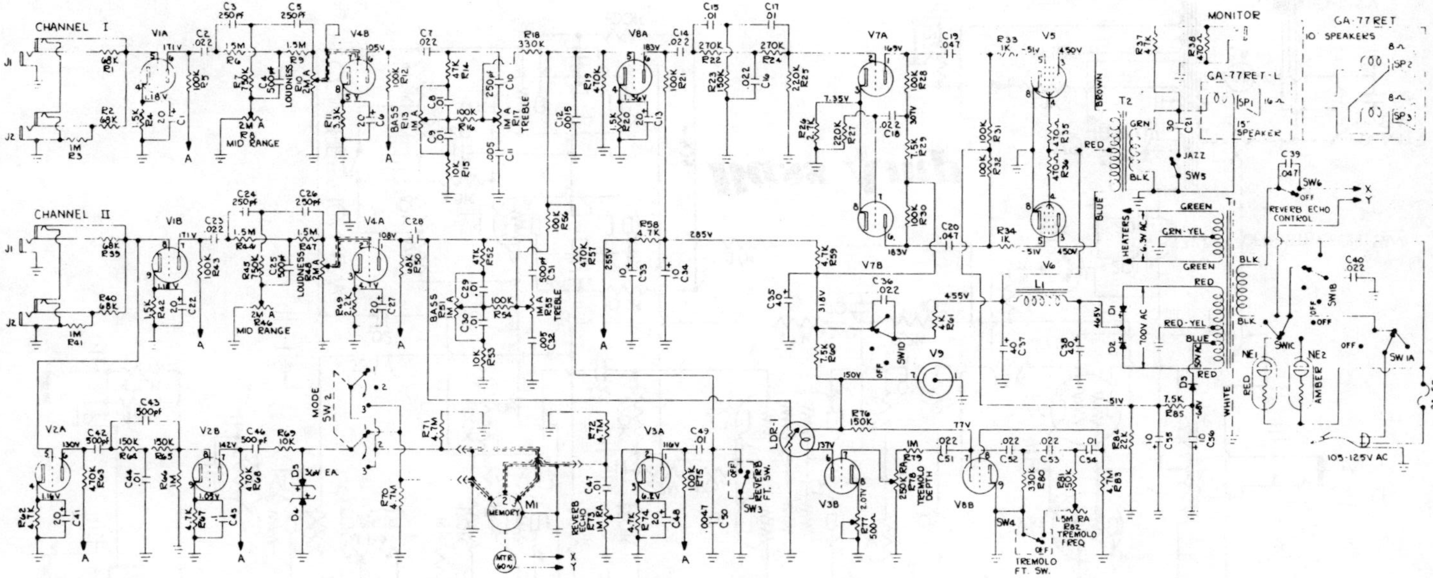

Note: Circuit ground located at input jacks.

Gibson Model GA-77RET.

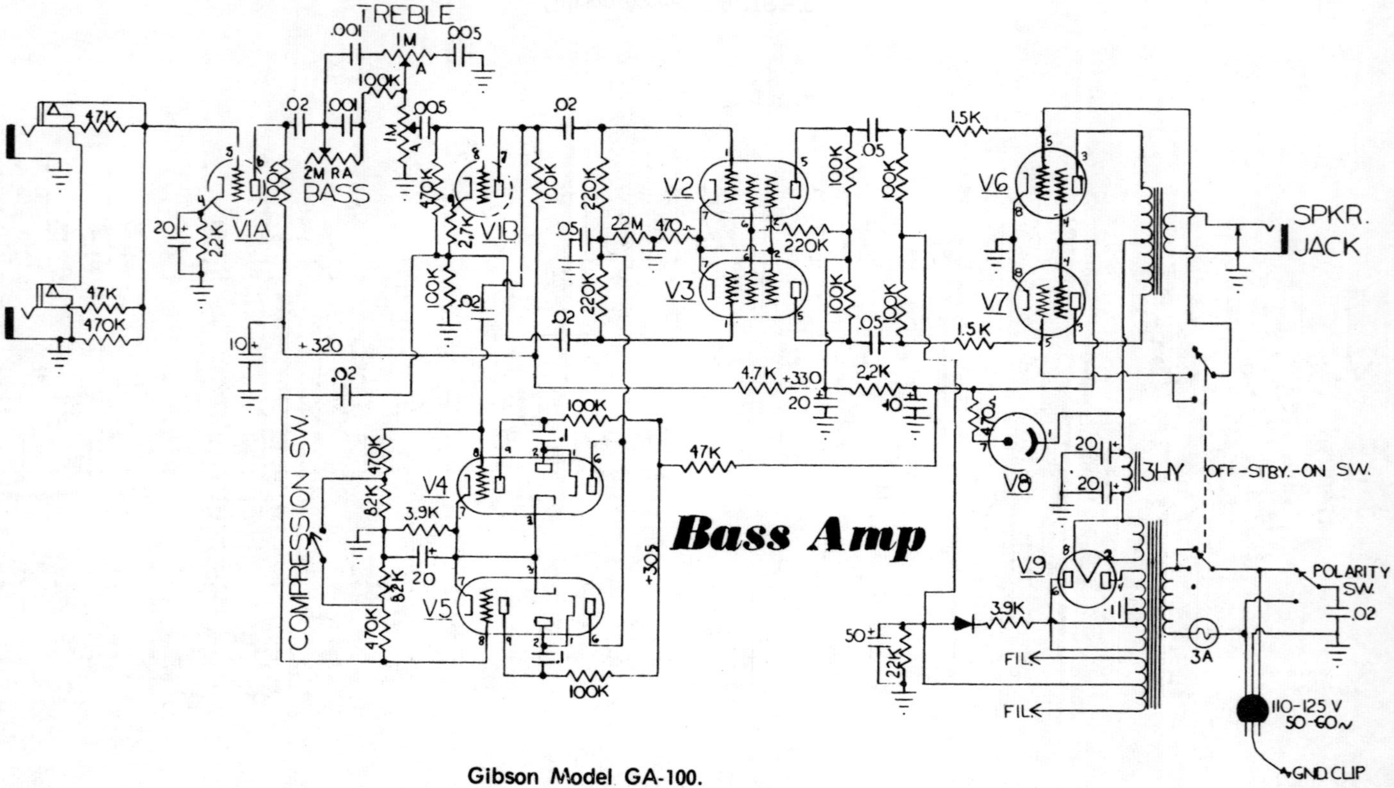

Gibson Model GA-100.

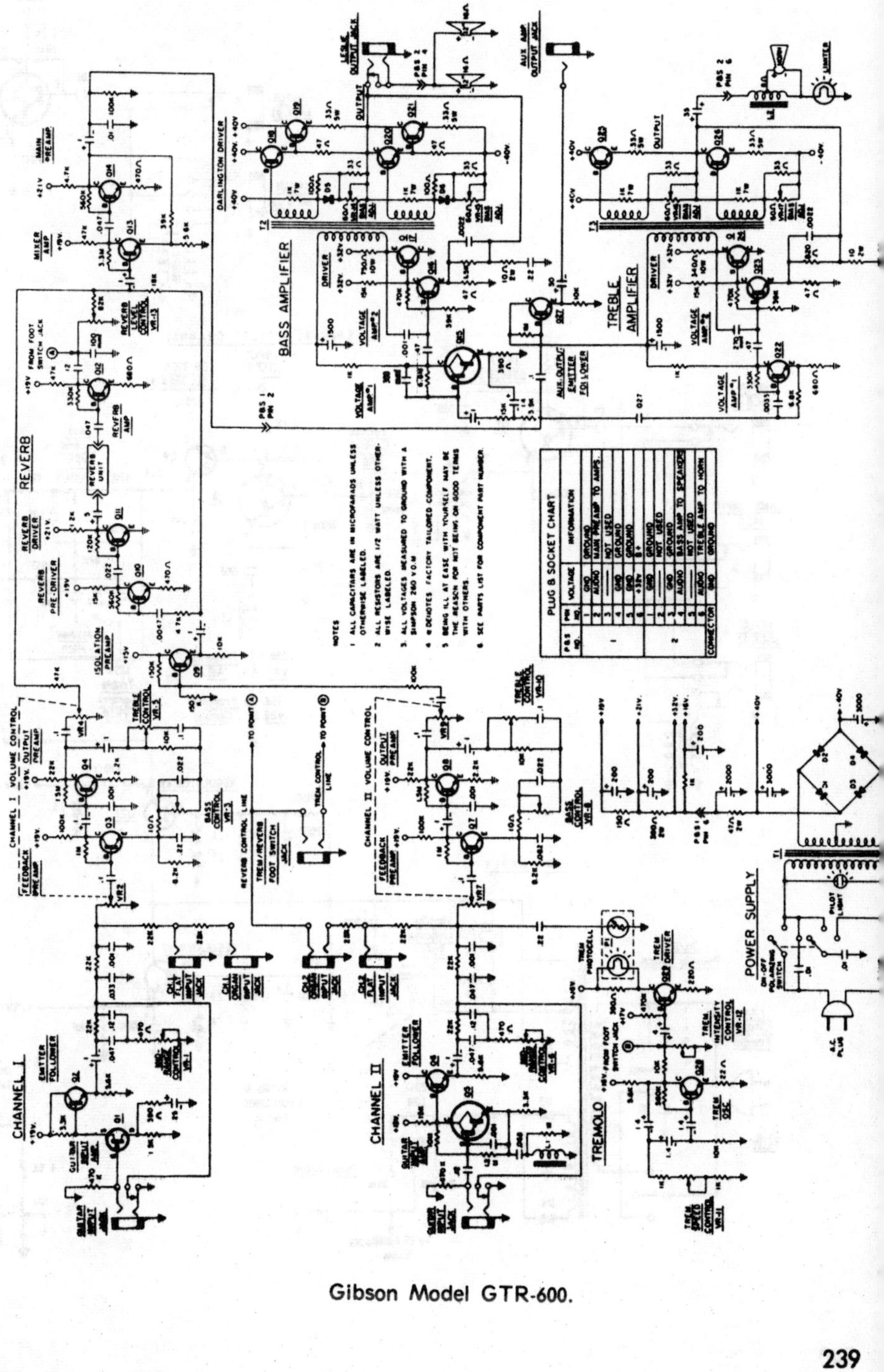

Gibson Model GTR-600.

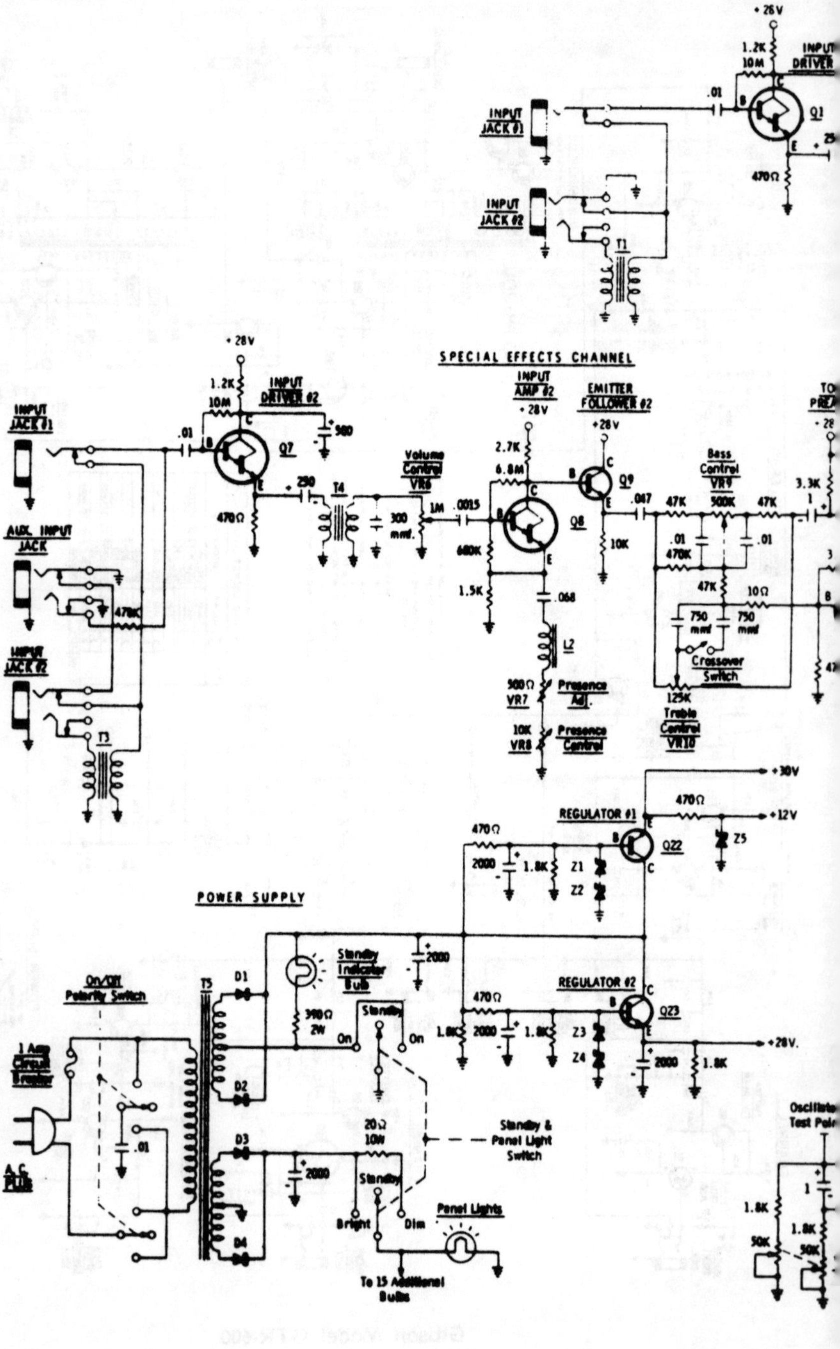
INPUT JACK #1
INPUT JACK #2
INPUT DRIVER
T1
Q1
SPECIAL EFFECTS CHANNEL
INPUT DRIVER #2
Q7
AUX. INPUT JACK
T3
T4
Volume Control VR6
INPUT AMP #2
Q8
EMITTER FOLLOWER #2
Q9
L2
Presence Adj.
Presence Control
Bass Control VR9
Crossover Switch
Treble Control VR10
REGULATOR #1
Q22
REGULATOR #2
Q23
POWER SUPPLY
On/Off Polarity Switch
1 Amp Circuit Breaker
A.C. Plug
T5
Standby Indicator Bulb
Standby & Panel Light Switch
Panel Lights
To 15 Additional Bulbs
Oscillator Test Point

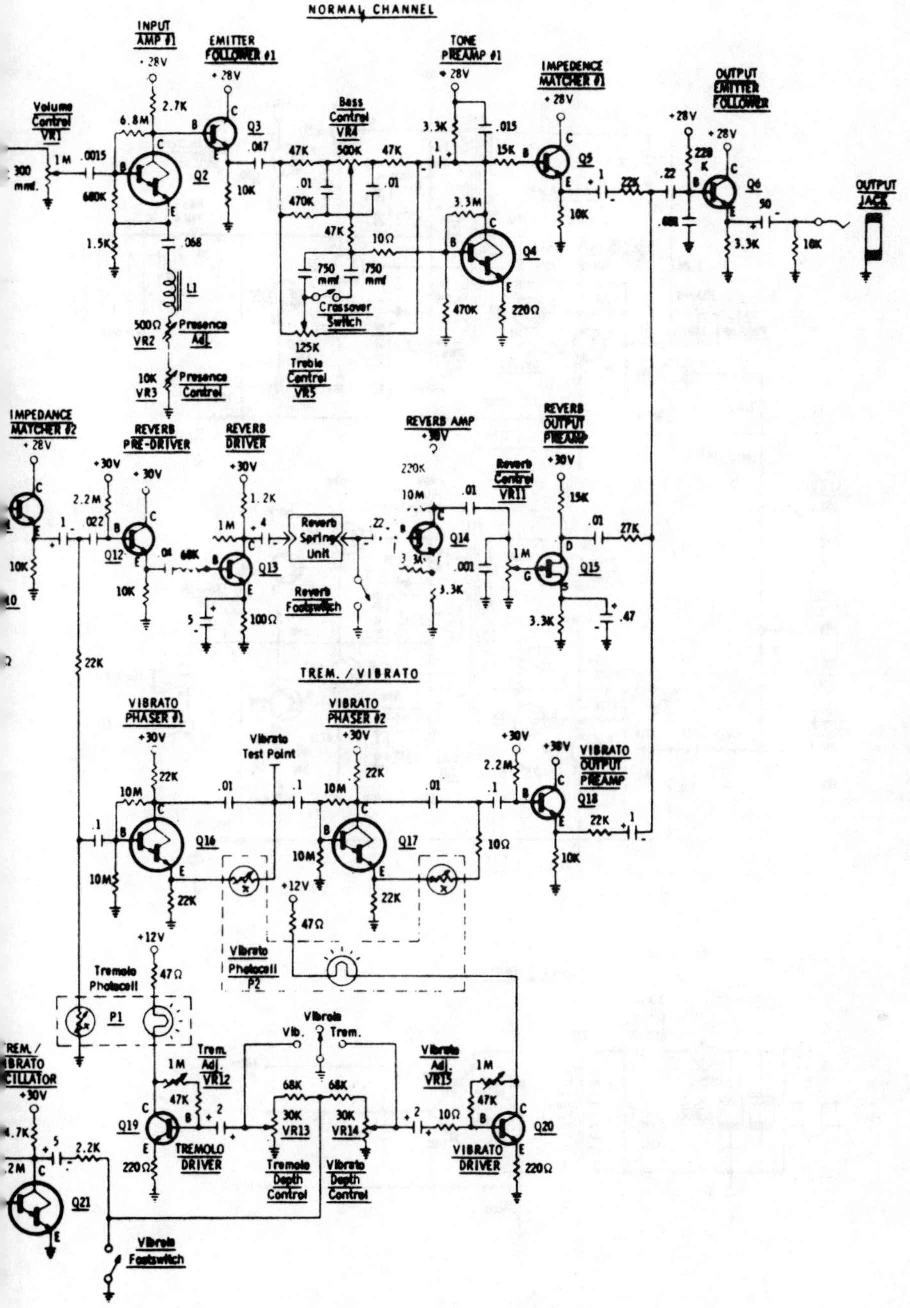

Gibson Model LP-1 preamp.

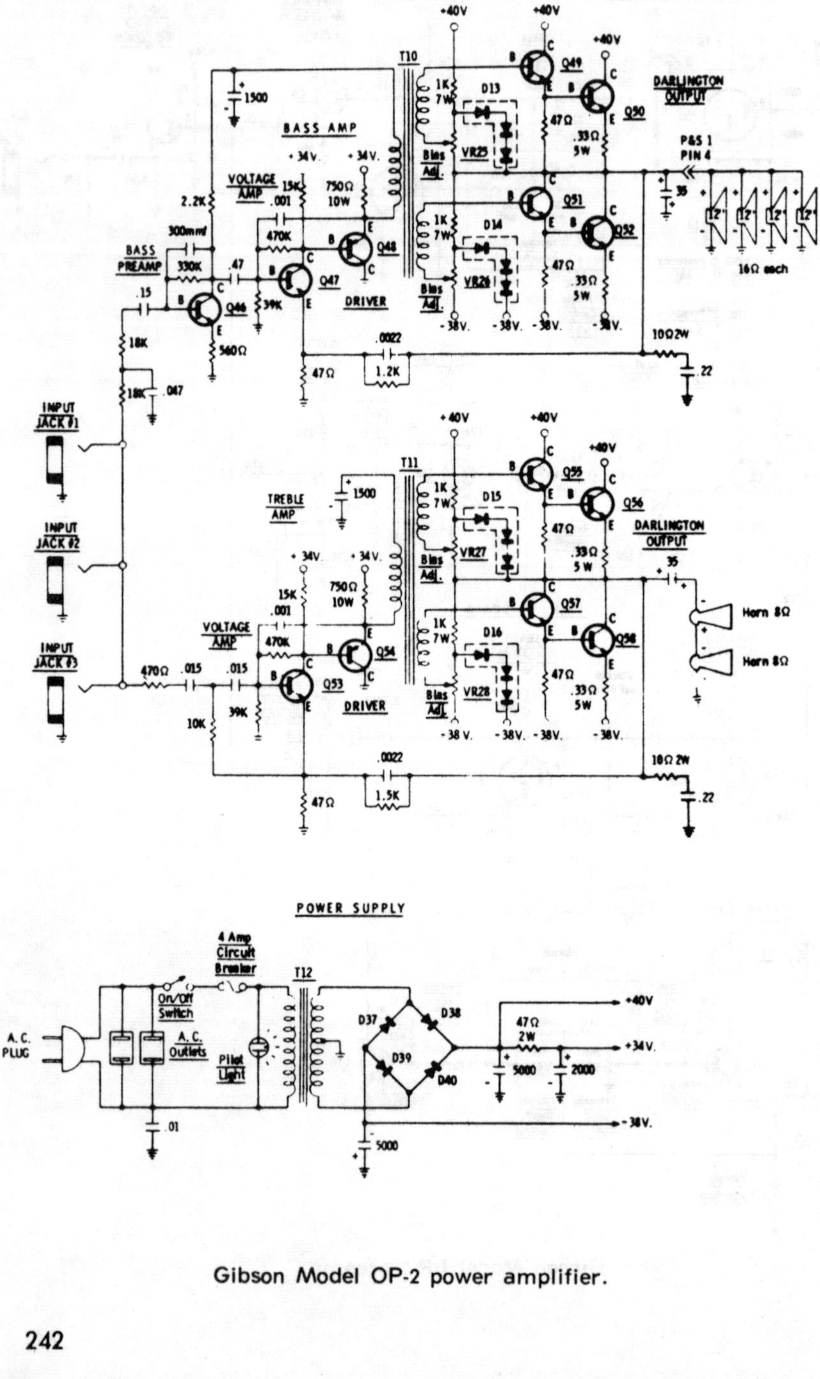

Gibson Model OP-2 power amplifier.

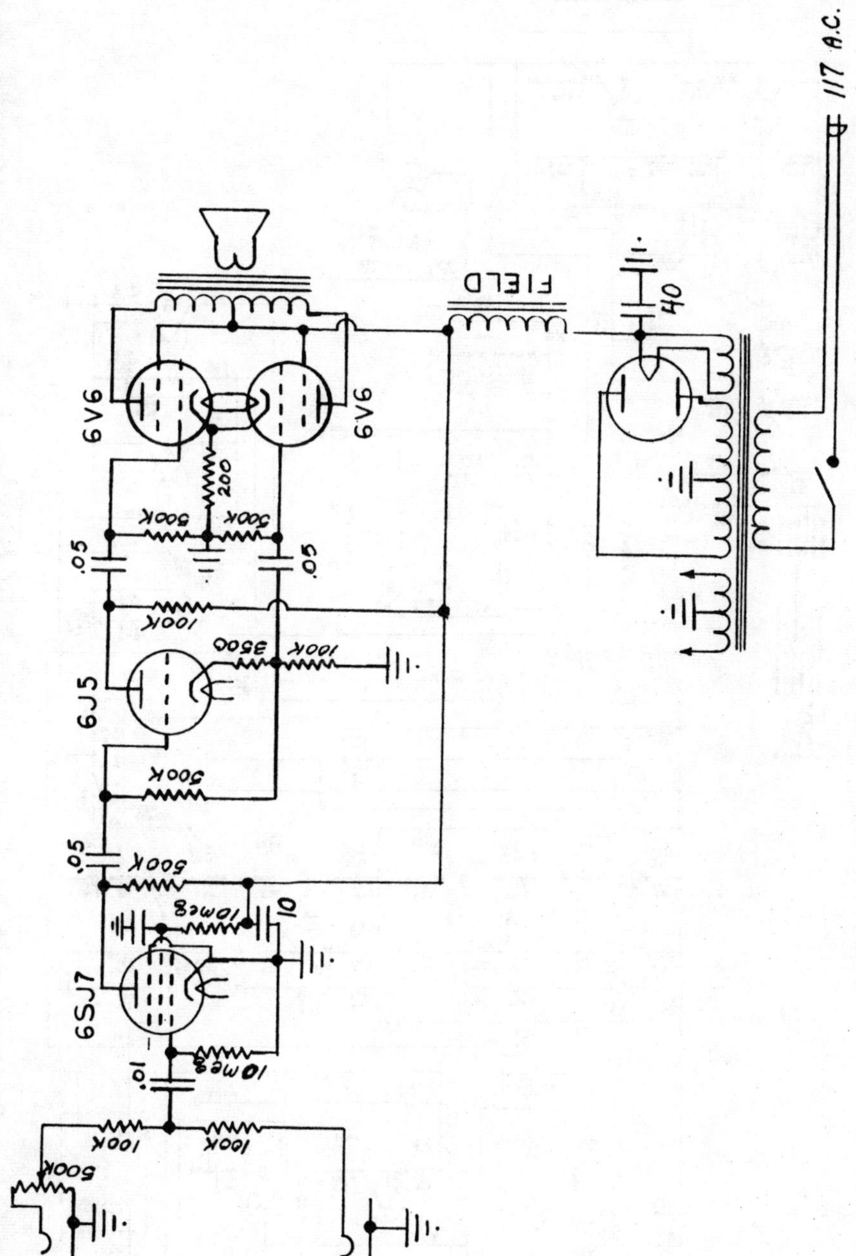

Gibson Model KEH.

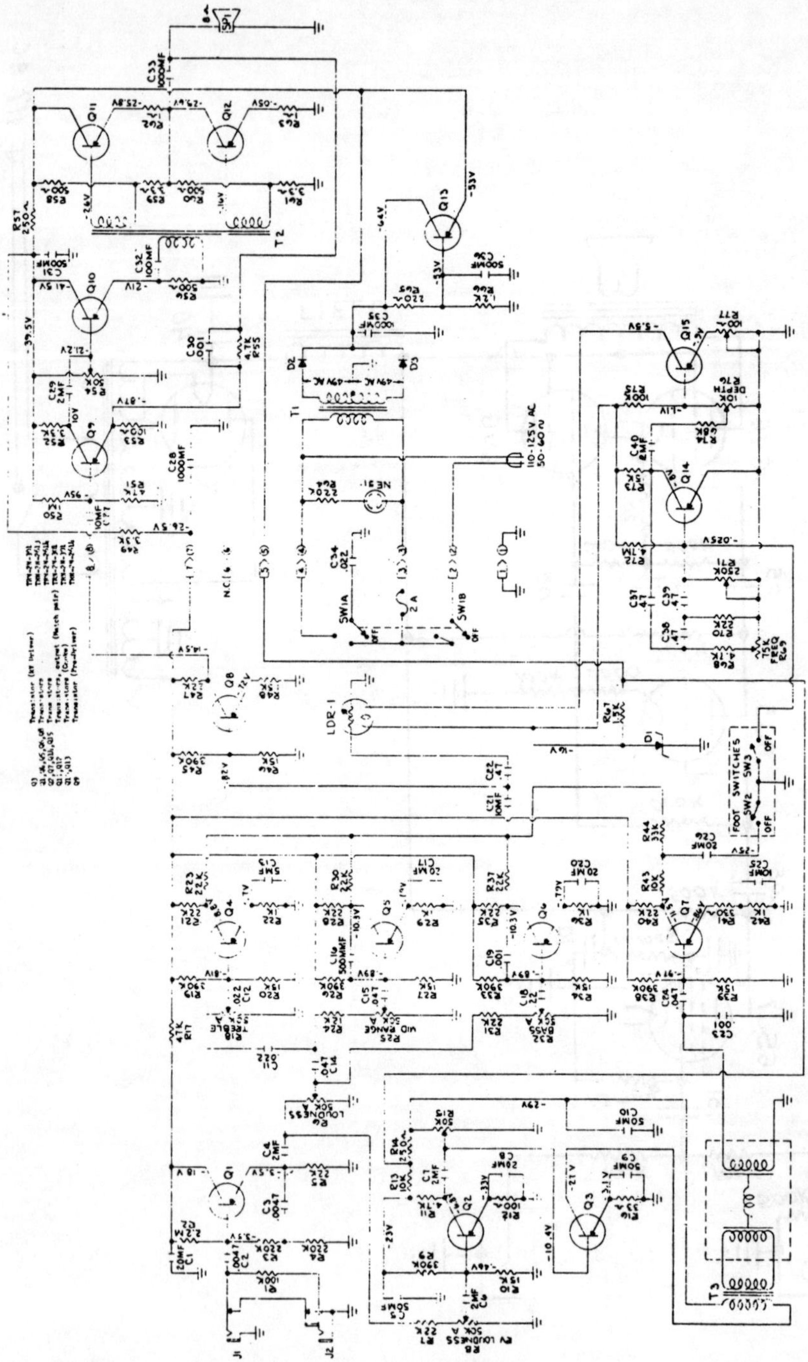

Gibson Model TR-1000 RVT.

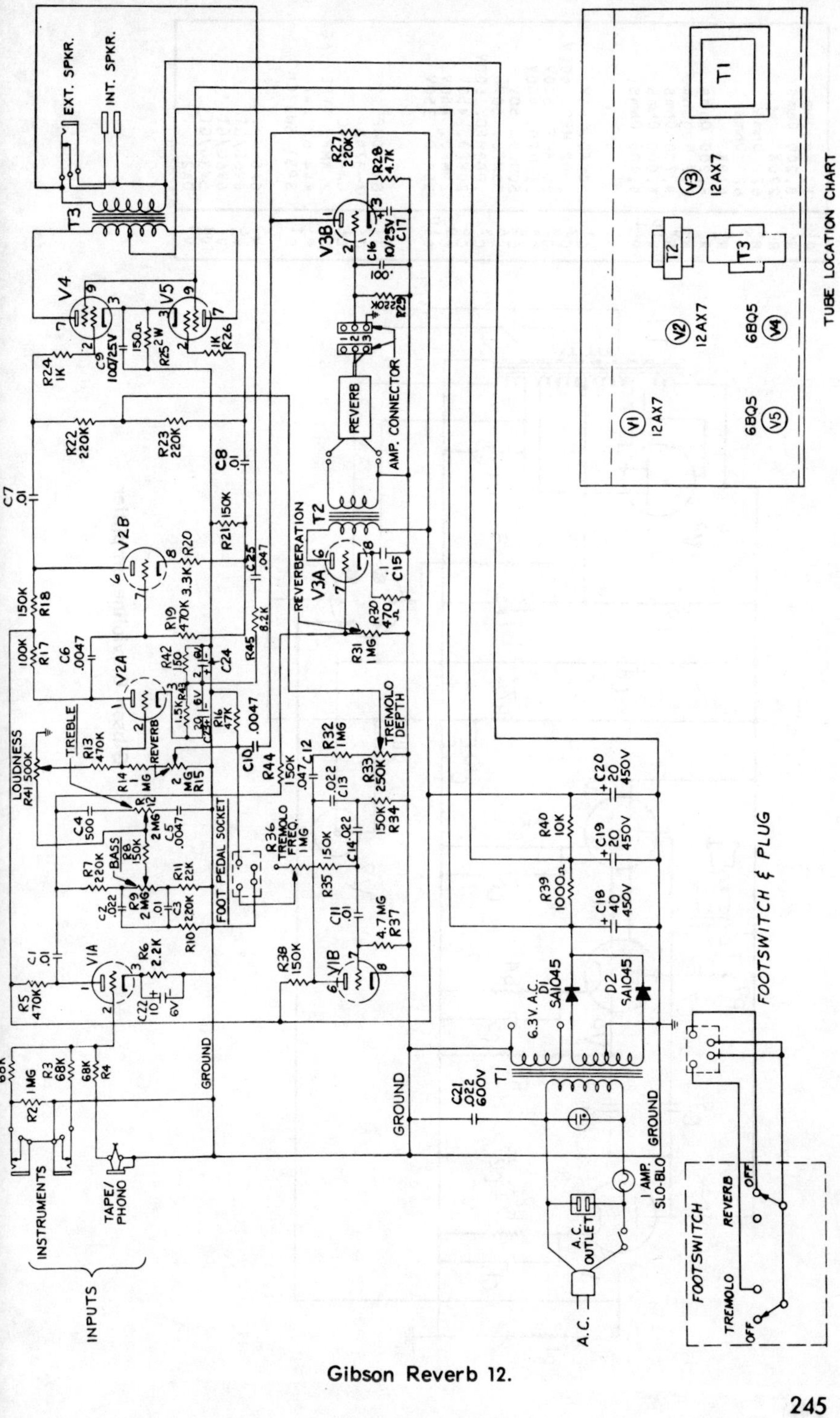

Gibson Reverb 12.

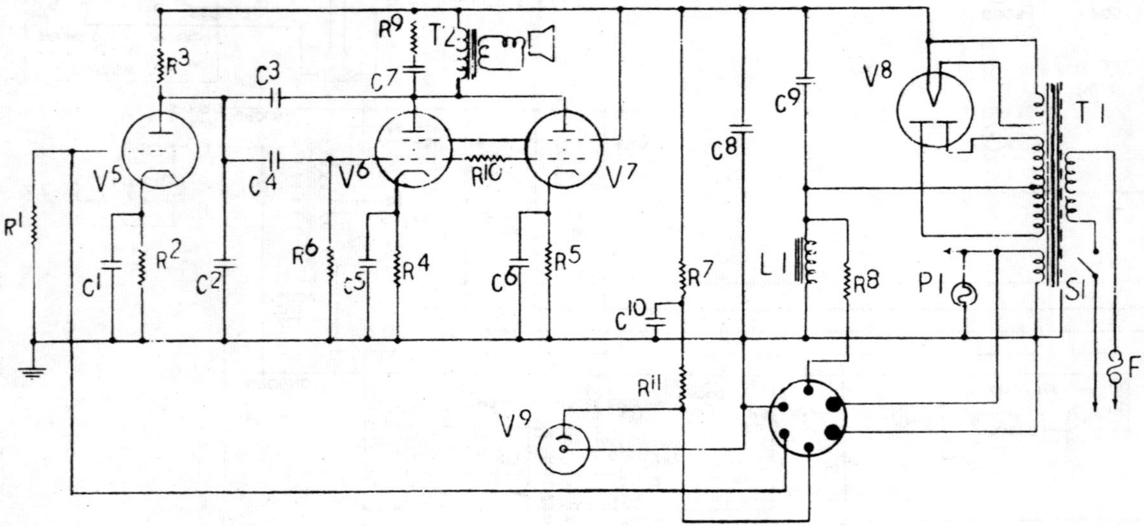

R1	1. Megohm
R2	8,200 Ohms
R3	270K
R4	620 Ohms
R5	620 Ohms
R6	470K
R7	8,200 Ohms
R8	2.2 Megohm
R9	4,700 Ohms
R10	1,000 Ohms
R11	4,700 Ohms
C1	20MFD. 25V
C2	.002 MFD. 600V
C3	50 MMF. 500V
C4	.1 MFD. 400V
C5	50MFD. 50V
C6	50MFD. 50V
C7	.003MFD. 600V
C8	20MFD. 450V
C9	20MFD. 450V
C10	35MFD. 350V
T1	GA-40-P
T2	X-3740
L1	GA-10-C
F1	2 AMP. TYPE 3AG
P1	#44 or #47
S1	SPST SWITCH
V5	6J5
V6	6V6G/GT
V7	6V6G/GT
V8	5V3G/GT
V9	OA2

Gibson Clavioline amplifier.

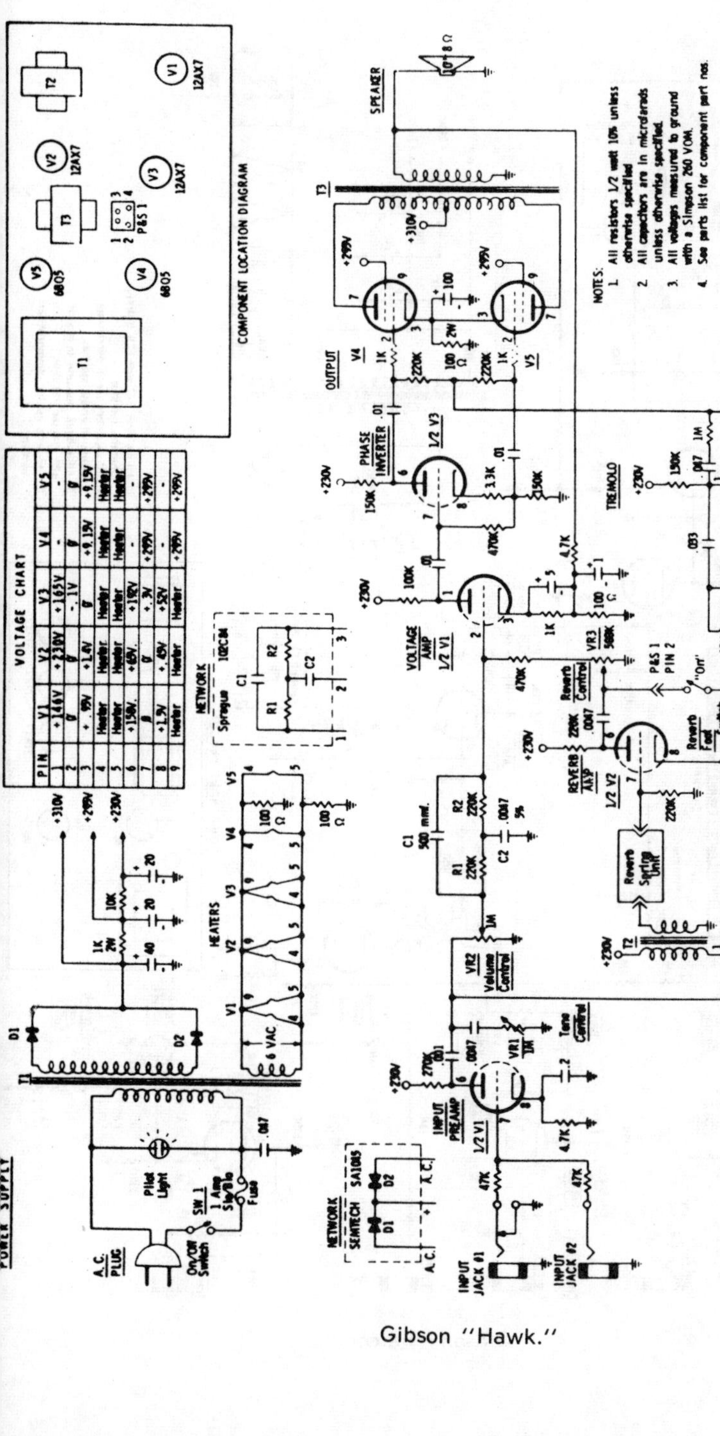

VOLTAGE CHART

PIN	V1	V2	V3	V4	V5
1	+146V	+230V	+165V	-	-
2	0	0	-.1V	0	0
3	+.95V	+1.4V	0	+9.15V	+9.15V
4	Heater	Heater	Heater	Heater	Heater
5	Heater	Heater	Heater	Heater	Heater
6	+158V.	+65V.	+192V	-	-
7	0	0	+.3V	+295V	+295V
8	+1.9V	+.45V	+52V	-	-
9	Heater	Heater	Heater	+295V	+295V

Gibson "Hawk."

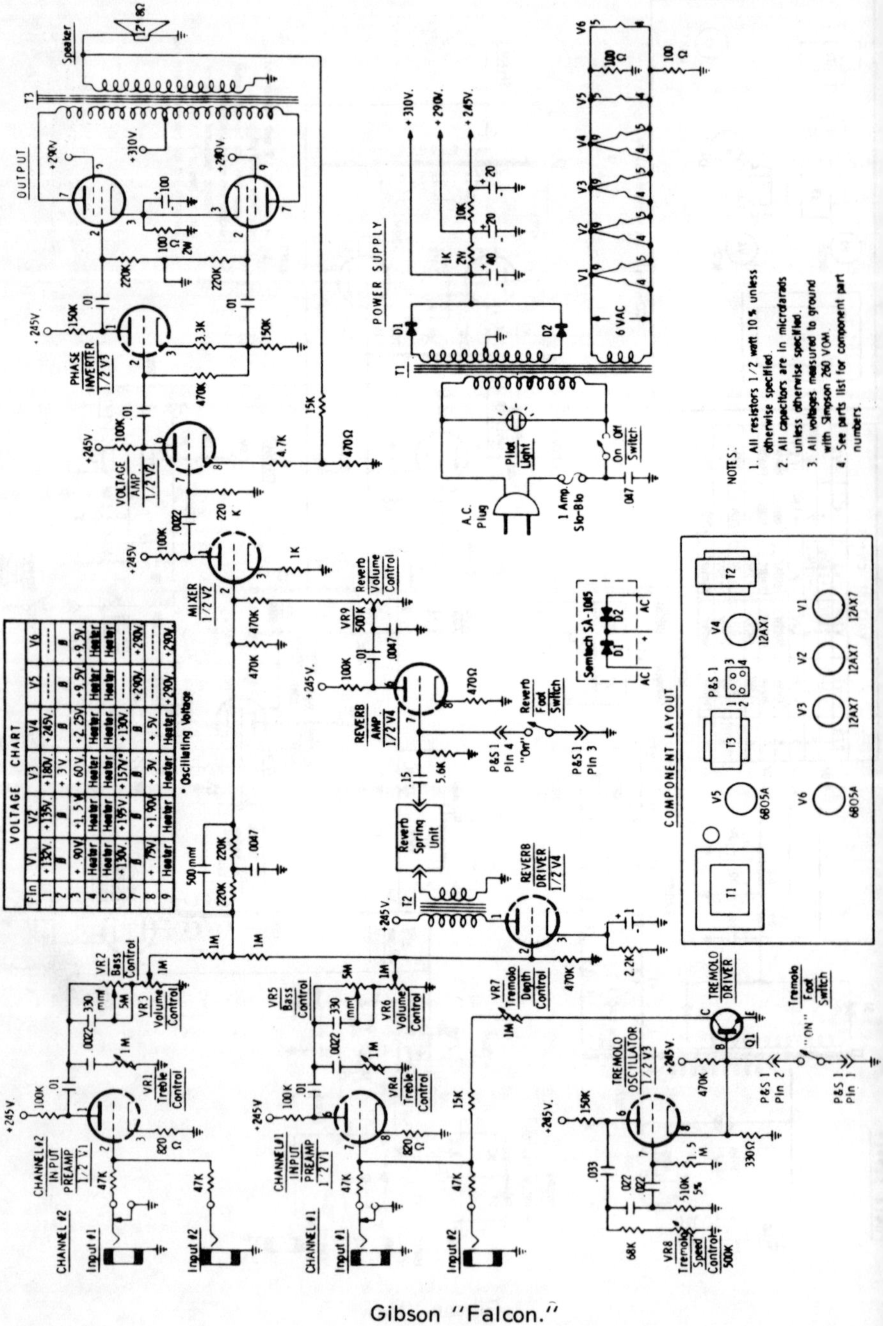

VOLTAGE CHART

Pin	V1	V2	V3	V4	V5	V6
1	+132V.	+135V.	+180V.	+245V.	-----	-----
2	Ø	Ø	+.3V.	Ø	Ø	Ø
3	+.90V.	+1.5V.	+60V.	+2.25V.	+9.5V.	+9.5V.
4	Heater	Heater	Heater	Heater	Heater	Heater
5	Heater	Heater	Heater	Heater	Heater	Heater
6	+130V.	+195V.	+157V.*	+130V.	-----	-----
7	Ø	Ø	Ø	Ø	+290V.	+290V.
8	+.75V.	+1.90V.	+.3V.	+.5V.	-----	-----
9	Heater	Heater	Heater	Heater	+290V.	+290V.

* Oscillating Voltage

NOTES:

1. All resistors 1/2 watt 10% unless otherwise specified.
2. All capacitors are in microfarads unless otherwise specified.
3. All voltages measured to ground with Simpson 260 VOM.
4. See parts list for component part numbers.

Gibson "Falcon."

Non-Electronic Repairs

8

When a job comes in for repair, there are ways that you can pyramid or build on the actual repair work and restore its appearance. It usually takes only a little bit of thought, and when you find a way to solve a problem at a reasonable cost, the customer can't help but say yes, and appreciate your interest in his equipment.

RESTORATION

This type of work falls into two separate categories, and we sincerely hope that when you get a job in, you do begin by cleaning up the inside of the unit, even though it doesn't show from the outside. Dust can form a nice, protective blanket over tubes, and when they get sufficiently coated, they stop breathing, don't cool off, and their life is sharply curtailed.

But the customer is most apt to see the outside first, and anything you can do to restore the outside to its original like-new appearance is going to win you a friend, or at least a client who can see that more was done than a quick and dirty repair job. In general terms, unless the customer specifically asks to have a blemish or a mar removed, we like to surprise them with an all-over clean-up job and not charge them any extra for it.

You rarely see wooden amplifier cabinets any more with the wood exposed. You're more apt to see leather-grained vinyls over wood, or other plastic surfaces. We have found that a spray can of vinyl cleaner and finish (try your local automotive supply store for this stuff—they use it for cleaning interior vinyl upholstery) can work wonders for you. Spray the cleaner on liberally, following the directions on the can, and then buff it off with a soft cloth.

Some of the metalwork trim on a cabinet can be enhanced just by cleaning it up. A bit of mild abrasive or a metal cleaner can help "doll" the unit up.

Many amplifiers are covered with a perforated steel cover, to protect the delicate components and still allow the unit to get some air. Remove the cover, if it looks beat up, and you will find that a ball-peen hammer used with care can knock some of the dents out of it. Finish the job up with a can of spray enamel, and it will look as good as new. These little touches take hardly any time, and provide you with additional impact when you return the client's unit to him.

Most musicians are prone to leave glasses or cigarette butts on the top of the amplifier, and when they look again, there's a mar. You can't really do an awful lot with these, but there are some tricks that will save you from having to recover the entire cabinet.

You will find minor damages, such as burns, or even places where alcoholic drinks have softened and marked the plastic cover. If the cover has not been burned through, obtain a solvent-type cement used for fusing vinyls. Apply this sparingly, and when the vinyl has softened sufficiently, you will find that you can sort of move it around like a sticky puddle. Use a finger to spread some of the softened vinyl from a good area to a bad one. Do this carefully, for if you are too heavy-handed, you may find yourself creating more damage than the unit originally came in with!

Where the damage is extensive, or where the covering has been damaged to the point where the wood shows through from underneath, more drastic measures are called for. Start by obtaining a matching piece of vinyl. Often, you can locate exactly what you need inside the amplifier cabinet by clipping off a piece of the excess that doesn't show. Apply some of the cement over the damaged area, and put some additional cement over the patch that you have made. Allow both to become slightly tacky, then press the patch directly over the damage. To make the bond firm and strong, roll it over with a wooden roller, such as is used in applying wallpaper. Apply plenty of pressure, and roll it over all the surfaces, concentrating on the edges. Should any of the cement ooze out, wipe it away at once with a clean, soft cloth or a tissue. When the patch has dried thoroughly, you can complete the job by applying some of the vinyl spray.

How Far To Go?

This depends on a number of factors. If you're getting a one-dollar fee for changing a fuse, it hardly pays to spend eight hours cleaning up and dressing up the amplifier. At the same time, if you quote a minimum fee of, say, $5.00, and all you have to do is change a fuse, the cleanup is a heck of a good way to justify the added customer cost.

There's another thing that you must consider also. Very often, a customer will bring in a unit that needs such extensive work that it really doesn't pay to do it. The factors that affect the final go no-go decision will include the following:

Original cost of unit.

Length of time in service.

Cost to purchase a new unit of similar quality.

Value of old unit as a trade-in.

We mention this only to point out that if a guy originally paid $100 for an amplifier, and you want $50 to repair it, but will allow him $25 on the purchase of a new one, he's going to have to be pretty hard-pressed to say, "go ahead and fix it." If you make a part of your income by selling new amplifiers, you'd be well advised, when a marginally-priced job such as this comes into the shop, to up the price sufficiently. There's more overall money to be made in selling a new amplifier than in repairing an old one. And if you can accept a trade on the old unit and then repair it at your leisure, you may be able to resell it later on as a used unit. When you sell such a new unit, you may also find that the client is ready to upgrade, and you might suggest to him that he could walk out with a far better amplifier than the old one ever was. He comes out ahead of the game, and so do you.

On the other hand, if you do not sell amplifiers, then watch your pricing carefully when you quote on a repair. You may find that you are pricing yourself right out of the job, and the customer walks out to the nearest shop where he can get a trade-in allowance on the old amplifier on the purchase of a new one. So set your prices very carefully, if you want to make out in this business.

Metal Cabinets

Metal cabinets are usually as scarce as wood cabinets, but they do crop up now and again. We've found the perfect way to eliminate unsightly scratches that go through the paint and into the raw metal. In fact, you might even try this on your car the next time it gets a scratch, since it works equally well on any painted surface.

Start with a box of children's assorted coloring crayons. Get the largest color assortment that you can, and then select the one crayon that most closely matches the color of the cabinet (or any surface) you are repairing. With the painted surface as clean as you can get it, carefully rub the crayon cross-ways over the scratch, using a fast, vigorous motion. The cabinet should be at room temperature for this operation. The heat generated by the rubbing, as well as the abrasive action of the scratch, will soon fill the entire scratched area with the colored wax. When you have completely filled the scratched area, let it stand for awhile, and then, using a clean soft cloth which you rotate often, buff across the scratch until the wax has been rubbed level with the rest of the paint.

The wax fills in the surface of the metal so it will not oxidize, and, properly buffed, the coloring blends right in. Pay very careful attention while you do this and especially when you get near completion. If you happen to glance aside during this work, you may not be able to locate the scratched area again!

LOUDSPEAKER ENCLOSURES

It may strike you, after awhile, that some of these guys are playing in some pretty weird places, judging from the condition of the equipment they bring in for servicing. You'll see speaker boxes that have warped so badly that they're little more than held together by their fabric covering. And you'll see boxes that have the covering ripped, torn and all but destroyed.

About all you can do in a case like this is to evaluate the extent of the repair against the cost of a replacement. In many cases you are well-advised to recommend replacement rather than repair. Where glue joints in the wood have separated, or have begun to separate, you must first clear away the old glue. Start by boiling some water, and then brush the water over the glue to remove the dried excess. The glue usually used in these boxes is called hide glue, and it responds to this hot water treatment. Allow the wood at least a day to dry out once again.

Melt some fresh hide glue and apply it to the surfaces to be joined. Then clamp them until the glue sets and dries. Small, corrugated nails can be driven into both parts being joined to strengthen the joint. Additional support can be obtained by steel L brackets as well.

Sometimes, due to a fault in manufacturing, a trapped air bubble under the plastic or fabric covering over the enclosure will lift away. The resulting effect isn't pretty, and you may be asked to do something about it. The cure for this is relatively simple.

Start with a very sharp razor blade and make a small cut, right at the bubble's center. Using an injector-type glue gun, fill the bubble with glue, and work it around with the fingers so it spreads to all areas where the fabric has risen. Carefully press the fabric back down on the wood, trying to squeeze all of the excess cement out through the razor cut. Make certain that no excess remains under the fabric. As you press it down, working from the edges toward the center, you are also re-seating the fabric. When you get to the razor cut, one last press will complete the job, and the razor cut seems to vanish as well. Place a heavy, flat weight over the repaired area to make sure that it stays in place until the cement sets properly. To make sure that no excess cement will adhere to your weight, a sheet of double-waxed paper should be placed between the weight and the cabinet.

Where a covering has become frayed, there are two possibilities open to you. You can try touching this up with a bit of paint. Or, if the frayed area is extensive, all you can do is completely recover the box. To recover, you must first remove all of the contents, including amplifiers, speakers, connecting cords, etc.

Remove the grille cloth. This may be held in place with a tension loop that keeps the grille cloth flush with the speaker face. If a tensioning loop is used, save it for reuse when you put the unit back together again. Finally, strip away all of the covering that is now in place on the cabinet, taking particular care to remove all covering and excess cement from the loudspeaker opening and from places where control shafts pass through the cabinet.

We have had excellent success in recovering cabinets with Naugahyde(TM), or similar materials, but do not compromise on the gauge; the thinner materials not only won't wear as well, they are much harder to work with and are prone to wrinkle.

You will notice that this fabric has a "grain" in that it stretches farther in one direction than in the other. Place it face down on a flat, clean surface, so the maximum stretch is across the longest face of the object to be covered. Liberally paint the entire front surface of the cabinet with a good, slow-drying contact adhesive, then lay the box face down on the fabric. At this point, you've got to start working fast, before the cement starts to set up.

Apply another good coat of cement to the top of the cabinet and yet another to the bottom. Pull the excess fabric around the top to the inside of the cabinet and staple it to the inside, about one inch in from the edge of the box.

Now invert the box, so the front face is toward you. Using a rubber roller, such as the type used by photographers to dry prints, roll the excess cement from the stapled edge toward the front of the box. Continue this rolling over the face of the box toward the bottom (unstapled) edge. Be careful **not** to roll over the area where the speaker opening occurs. You don't want to put weight on any unsupported area of the fabric. Fold the remaining fabric up over the bottom of the box, roll it to remove any excess cement. Then pull the fabric hard to stretch it tautly and staple it inside the box, just as you did at the top.

Now cut four "darts" or straight cuts from each corner of the box to the edge of the fabric. This will enable you to fold the sides up neatly. The cuts should be made parallel to the top and bottom of the box. Apply cement to the sides and fold the excess material from the top and bottom around the sides. Pull this taut, and place a couple of flush staples into this to keep it in place. Observe that the top and bottom of the box is now complete and should be smooth and clean.

Apply additional cement to the sides to cover the fabric that was just stapled down. Fold the sides up along the sides of the box, roll out the excess cement, and pull tightly. Staple to the inside of the cabinet as well. Because we made the dart cuts parallel with the top and bottom of the box, there should be no surplus material, and the box should be covered with a smooth, continuous covering of the fabric.

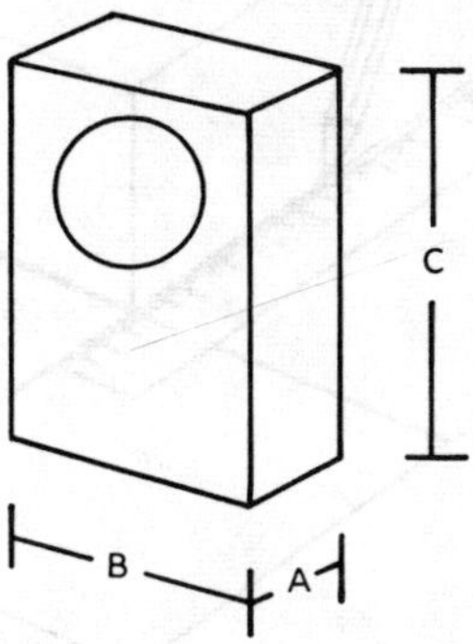

Measure the cabinet. The vinyl should be "B" + 2 x "A" + 6" BY "C" + 2 x "A" + 6".

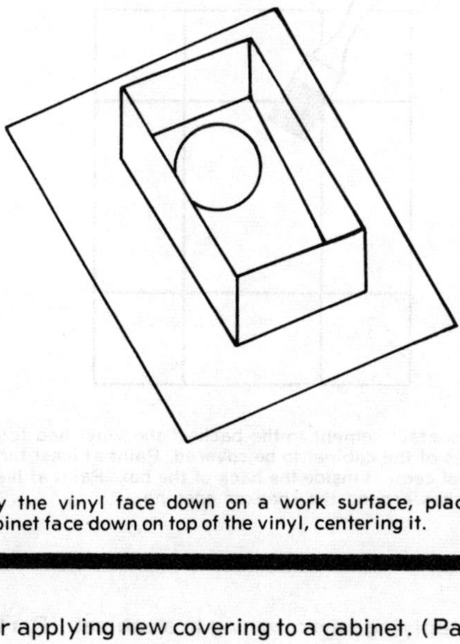

Lay the vinyl face down on a work surface, place the cabinet face down on top of the vinyl, centering it.

Procedure for applying new covering to a cabinet. (Part 1 of 5 parts.)

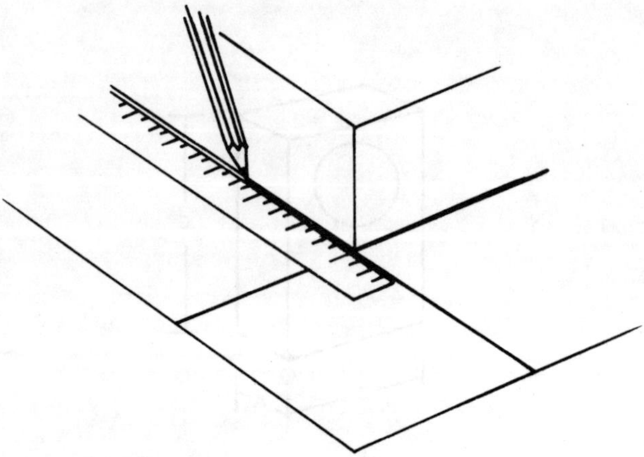

Place a ruler along the edges. Pencil mark the outline of the cabinet to all edges of the vinyl.

Apply contact cement to the back of the vinyl and to all surfaces of the cabinet to be covered. Paint at least three inches of cement inside the back of the box. Paint at least two inches around the speaker opening.

Procedure for applying new covering to a cabinet. (Part 2 of 5 parts.)

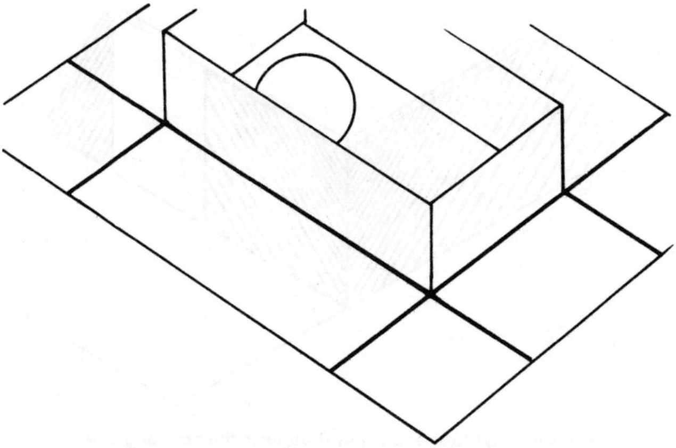

Carefully position the cabinet over the vinyl so it is centered on the pencil marks. The vinyl cannot be moved after the cabinet is in place, so work carefully.

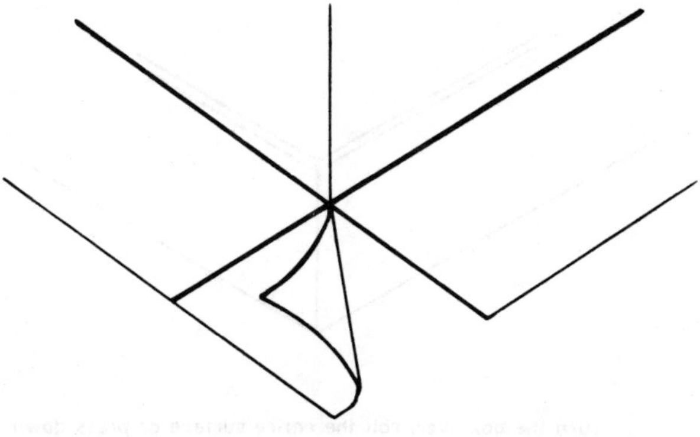

Make a straight cut on the four corners, following the pencil lines.

Procedure for applying new covering to a cabinet. (Part 3 of 5 parts.)

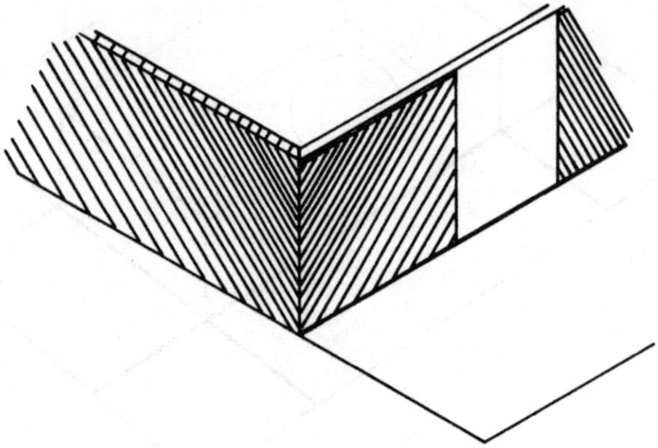

Pull the vinyl taut and press it against the two long sides. Fold it over the top edge and down along the inside as far as it will go. Press it down tightly. The excess edge is now placed over the top and bottom. If one is available, go over the surface with a rubber photographic print roller. Don't worry about small entrapped air bubbles at this time.

Now apply additional contact cement to the top and bottom of the cabinet, so the vinyl surfaces at the top and bottom are also coated. Bring the bottom and top vinyl into position as shown.

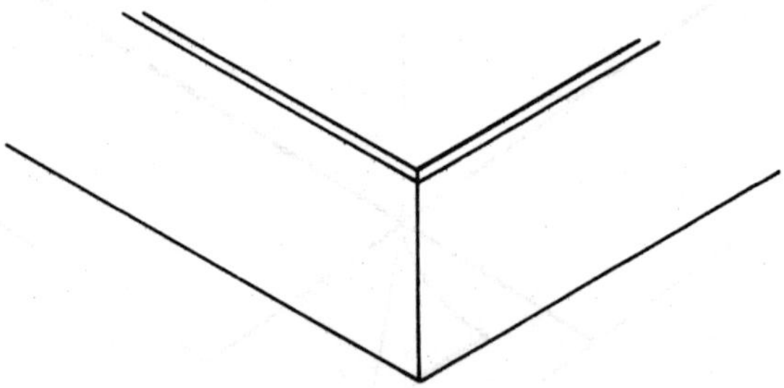

Turn the box over, roll the entire surface or press down with your hand. Use a small straight pin to puncture any air bubbles trapped under the vinyl. With the fingers, squeeze the air out and press the vinyl down.

Procedure for applying new covering to a cabinet. (Part 4 of 5 parts.)

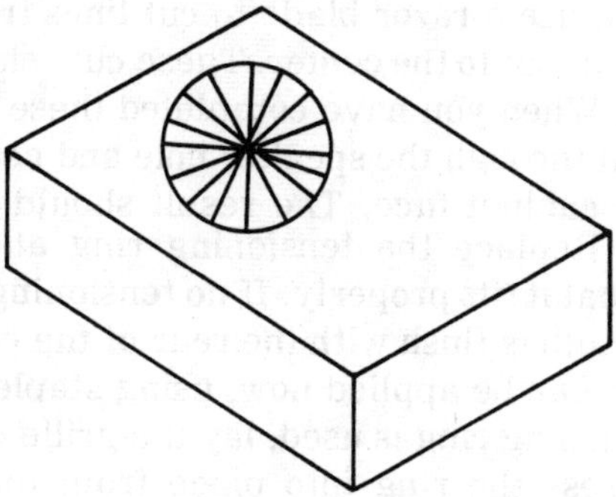

Using a sharp razor blade, cut gores in the vinyl over the loudspeaker opening. The smaller these gores are, the neater the final job will be.

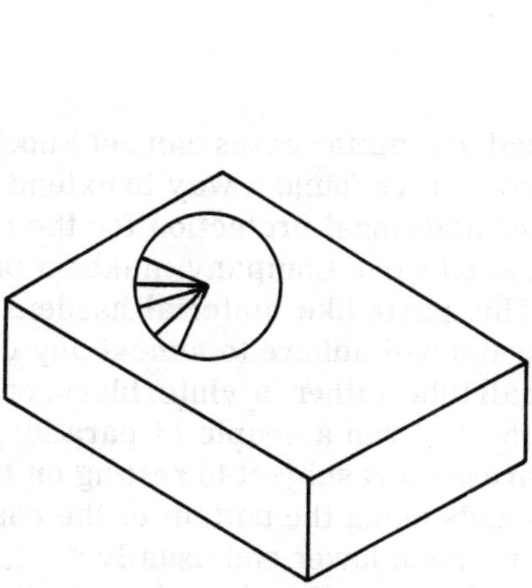

Press the gores down through the speaker opening and against the inside of the box. Continue until the speaker opening is round. Roll the edge to make it conform to the cut-out.

Procedure for applying new covering to a cabinet. (Part 5 of 5 parts.)

When the cement has thoroughly dried, place the box face up on a work surface. Then, starting at the center of the speaker cut-out, use a razor blade to cut lines from the edges of the speaker cut-out to the center. These cuts should be about one inch apart. When you have completed these cuts, fold the excess material through the speaker hole and cement them to the rear of the cabinet face. The result should be a smooth, round cut-out. Replace the tensioning ring at this time, to make certain that it fits properly. If no tensioning ring is used, and the grille cloth is flush with the rear of the cabinet's face, new grille cloth can be applied now, using staples to hold it in place. If a tensioning ring is used, lay the grille cloth on a flat surface and press the ring into place from the rear of the cabinet until the cloth is flush with the front surface.

Complete the job by replacing all of the cabinet accessories and contents, including cords, speakers, controls and amplifier. Wipe away any excess cement, and after everything has properly dried and set, apply a bit of plastic-care spray to add a like-new sheen.

Guitar Cases

We've noticed that guitar cases can get knocked around a good bit. However, we've found a way to extend the case life, and thereby offer additional protection for the instrument as well. The General Electric Company makes a product called RTV Silicone. This paste-like material hardens to a rubber-like consistency and will adhere to almost any clean surface. It comes in a small tube, either in white, black, or clear.

Open the tube and run a couple of parallel beads of this stuff along the areas most subject to resting on the floor. Two or three small beads along the bottom of the case, and a few more along the rounded lower end usually do it, but you may want a few more along the edge directly opposite the carrying handle. When this stuff sets up, it adds years of wear to the case and absorbs some of the mechanical shock that might otherwise be passed along to the guitar.

LOUDSPEAKERS

Loudspeakers and loudspeaker systems are subject to any of a number of common faults. Some of these can easily be handled by a local repair shop, while others require the services of a professional loudspeaker repairman. In most cases, and outside of a few isolated instances, repairs on loudspeakers are strictly limited to removing and replacing the loudspeaker unit that is faulty. Any attempt to make a detailed repair, such as replacing a voice coil or a speaker cone, will not only result in additional long-range problems, but will be non-productive and most certainly not profitable when you weigh the time-cost factors.

As a first step to any speaker examination, determine positively that it is the speaker that is causing the problem, and then determine whether or not the problem is one that you can reasonably repair quickly and simply. You may well find that even sending it out for repair will cost more than the price of a replacement loudspeaker!

As a typical example of a repairable loudspeaker, one system produced a buzzing noise when a certain note was struck on an amplified guitar. Changing to another loudspeaker system off the shelf eliminated the problem, so obviously it was caused by the system's loudspeaker. The speaker cabinet was opened and everything appeared to be in good order. The loudspeaker was mounted to the cabinet front by six bolts and nuts. More out of curiosity than an effort to make a repair, the technician removed the nuts and the loudspeaker. Out poured a collection of assorted sand and dust. The musician suddenly remembered a beach job he had played some months previously. A quick clean-up corrected the problem.

What you'll find when you open the speaker up is anybody's guess. One technician found small perforations randomly located on the back of the loudspeaker. Shaking the speaker box, he heard small objects rolling around. It seems that this musician's younger brother had an air rifle, and found the speaker box a convenient back-stop and bullet trap.

This calls to mind an interesting problem that one musician brought into a shop. His complaint was a strange one—the amplifier was giving off a poison gas. He knew, because he has been in the army and they taught him about a poison gas that smelled of apples. When the amplifier warmed up, it gave off the smell of apples, and therefore, poison gas.

The technician nodded and turned on the amplifier. Before long, the shop was well-scented with the smell of apples. Not burning insulation, not transformers smoking, apples! He opened the unit up and immediately spotted the problem. There was a half-eaten, moldy apple-jelly covered bread slice lying atop the rectifier stack. When a kid thinks he's gonna get caught snacking between meals, he'll duck the evidence anyplace, and Dad's amplifier just happened to be nearby. It was a mess to clean up, but that youngster didn't sit for a week!

Another common loudspeaker problem is a brittle cone, and there's really not too much that can be done to correct this, because as a speaker cone ages, it dries out. There is an aerosol spray available that can be applied to the speaker cone to revitalize it, but this is surface treatment at best, and short of reconing, there's not too much that you can or should try to do to a speaker cone.

MECHANICAL PROBLEMS

Sometimes a speaker cone is moved mechanically so that the voice coil is thrown out of alignment and rubs on the spindle or magnet. Since the usual answer to such a problem is to replace the entire speaker, you have nothing to lose in attempting a repair yourself. Grasp the cone firmly, using large cardboard strips to spread the finger pressure over as much of the cone surface as possible, and press hard. If you get the cone properly seated once again, you've saved a replacement job. It's a cure-or-kill process, but the patient is as good as dead anyway so you have nothing to lose.

If a speaker has shifted in its mountings, you might try loosening the mounting screws and repositioning it, after which you can try to tighten the screws once again. You may find a loose mounting screw and this can create some problems, since the screws are generally placed in from the front and you have to mar the wood covering to get at them. There's a better and easier way. If the screws are sufficiently long, slip a flat washer, then a lockwasher and a hex nut over the screw and turn it down as far as you can with your fingers, holding the threads of the screw to keep it from turning. Now screw two more hex nuts over the top of the screw, keeping them near the top. When the upper one is flush with the screw, turn the lower one tightly against it as a locknut. With a pair of pliers, the upper nuts should serve to hold the screw threads while you firmly tighten the lower nut to hold the loose screw tightly. Now add an additional flat washer, lockwasher and nut to the other mounting screws to keep the speaker frame straight, and you can replace the speaker properly.

9 Customer Relations

When you take your car to a mechanic, or go for a visit to a doctor, you expect to see some scientific mumbo-jumbo that will convince you that the mechanic or the doctor has some special knowledge that you do not possess yourself.

How would you feel, for example, if you went into a mechanic and told him "My freebis seems to be acting up. I've got a banging sound every time I step on the brake." Suppose the mechanic just yawned, looked at the car's taillight, and said "uh-huh." Then suppose he tapped it with one finger and the banging vanished. You'd feel cheated if he charged you more than half a buck for that tap!

Suppose you went to a doctor and complained of a pain in your right knee. If he looked at your knee, said "uh-huh," tapped you on the elbow, and made the pain disappear, how would you feel when he asked you for a ten-dollar fee?

We've got the same sort of problem in electronics. We try to educate the customer to show him how clever we are. But if you tell the customer that "all you needed was a 25 cent capacitor," how are you going to justify a $10 charge? You can't.

They tell the story about the huge factory that had a problem. The janitor told the foreman that the boiler was leaking. The foreman reported this fact to the manager, who reported it to the vice president. The veep went into the president's office. "I've heard," he said, "that the boiler is leaking."

"Get a plumber," the president said. That's why he was the president—he could really make decisions!

The vice president went back to the manager and told him, "Get a plumber." The manager told the foreman, "Get a plumber." The foreman told the janitor, "Get a plumber, stupid!"

The plumber came over, knocked a plug into the boiler and submitted a bill for $10.10. The bill finally worked its way to the president's desk and he blew his top. He called the plumber in and asked him to explain the bill.

"The plug," said the plumber, "is only 10 cents. The $10 is for knowing what to do with it."

You know what to do with an amplifier that isn't working. But you don't have to tell the customer what an easy job it was. He isn't the least bit concerned with how hard you worked, except as it relates to the charge you make for the repair.

BE IMPRESSIVE

Some of the tools available to you, and tools that you may not use, could include an oscilloscope, a signal generator in the audio range, and an assortment of meters.

Now imagine your next customer coming in with an amplifier that isn't working. You connect the scope leads to the speaker terminals, feed a signal in from the audio generator, and the client will see the signal on the scope when you bring it back to where signal can be picked up.

He has no idea whatever about what you are doing, but that dancing green line certainly looks impressive. You explain that this is just a preliminary examination, and when he gets the bill, he'll at least feel that you've done something.

Is this ethical? Is it warranted? You bet your sweet life it is! More than one technician has suffered at the hands of a customer who didn't realize that integrity was the technician's middle name.

A young newcomer to our ranks had this problem. He was quite competent, but didn't know how to price his work. When an amplifier came into the shop, he located a shorted bypass capacitor, replaced it, did a thorough cleanup job on the unit, and then charged three dollars plus the cost of the capacitor. The customer was delighted; he was pleased with the sound of the amplifier, and payed up promptly, taking the unit with him. Two weeks later, the amplifier had troubles once again. This time, a tube had quit. The customer took the amplifier to another repairman; he blamed the second failure on the "cheap repair job" he got the first time!

THE LOCAL EXPERT

What you really want to do is establish yourself as the guy to see in your area when an amplifier needs repair. Get the word out to the people who play amplified instruments that you can do a good job on repairs, and that your prices are reasonable.

How do you get to be an expert? You'd be surprised at some of the things you can do to establish yourself in this area. Naturally, you will want to advertise the fact, and a good place to start is with a large poster in your shop window. Run an advertisement in the yellow pages of your telephone directory also.

If you want to really take the bull by the horns, contact the local musician's union and place some flyers announcing your service in their meeting hall or on their bulletin board. Make yourself known to the local schools also. Many schools have music departments and will refer repair work locally. If you have the money and the inclination, you might even offer to sponsor a rock group at the next high school dance and just pay their cost.

Offer yourself as a guest speaker at no charge. There are many civic groups in your area who will be happy to have you talk about music or instrumentation, and you can build a very nice lecture around the guitar, or amplified instruments, complete with demonstrations. One chap in the Midwest does an excellent job of speaking on the history of the guitar. He recruits youngsters from the local high school to assist him, beginning with the earliest of stringed instruments, the Lyre. He has a youngster dressed in the costume of the period who comes on stage as he is completing that phase of his talk. The lights dim, a spotlight surrounds the young performer as he sings "Greensleeves," accompanying himself on the instrument. He features other stringed instruments, including the Russian balalaika, the Greek bazoukia, and others, all demonstrated by youngsters with the proper ethnic background and the ability with the instrument. Your local schools will yield many similar kids. The talk, naturally, goes on through the swing era. He has the Hawaiian guitar demonstrated, then into such jazz instruments as the banjo, and finally, gets really up-to-date with some hard acid rock and bass guitars.

How does he capitalize on these talks? For one thing, he charges a small admission fee, but the real money comes from the customers that are generated when he runs his free newspaper notices announcing his upcoming talks. He follows these with additional press copy, when the newspaper's reviewers (who get free tickets, incidentally) report on his offering. Naturally, the name of his shop is always mentioned, and so is the fact that he is an "expert" on guitars and other musical instruments. Establishing yourself as an expert requires a lot of time and diligent effort on your part, but it always seems to pay off.

DON'T LEARN THE JARGON

It's only natural to think that the youngsters are the ones that will bring you the most business, and you are probably right. A lot of the kids are the ones with the amplifiers these days. But don't get the idea that you have to meet them on their own level in order to communicate with them. They have their own friends. They want you to be a super technician and nothing more. The technician, however well-meaning, who tries to "talk their language" can only hope to make a botch of it. Chances are that he will use words that are currently declasse, and will be laughed at. Take a listen to the following conversation at a repair counter:

"Hey man, the amplifier pulled a bummer."
"I dig you daddy-o."
"Daddy-o? Like what's that?"
"Ooh-oo bobba-dee, how are things in birdland?"
"Birdland? Man, are you ---"
"Twenty-three skiddoo, kiddo."

At this point, the kids are either rolling on the floor with laughter, or they figure this is the world's biggest put-down and are out the door, amplifier in hand, in a huff.

If the kids seem to have a language all their own, remember that they are truly bilingual. They all have parents who don't understand them any more than you do, so they do have to speak at least some basic English. Don't try to talk to them in their own language. They'll communicate in yours and respect you for it.

YOU'VE GOT TO SELL!

What you have to sell is service. But because service is an after-the-fact thing, it is difficult to sell, unless you use all of your "smarts." Nobody is going to come in with an amplifier that has nothing wrong with it. And the truth of the matter is that almost every amplifier has something wrong with it. Maybe it's something that the musician has learned to live with, maybe it's a minor thing that doesn't really stop the musician from using the unit, but there's always something you can find wrong, if you look hard enough.

One technician in a large city advertised a "special." For a fee of five dollars, he'd clean up the amplifier, check it out thoroughly, and give the musician a complete report on its status. It's like the school dentist offering a free checkup to all the kids. He finds cavities, and, as a result of his donation of time, he drums up a lot of business too.

Our friend with the $5 checkup advises a careful program of preventive maintenance. The price is low enough to bring people into the shop, and he has his checkout procedure worked out to an exact science now. When the amplifier comes in, he opens it up, cleans the inside, checks all the tubes, and inspects for visible problems such as torn loudspeaker cones, or dried-out cones.

When the customer comes back to pick up the instrument, he gets a complete report on work that ought to be done before it gets worse. The technician is always—at the very least—able to peddle a few new tubes over and above the $5 fee!

When a customer balks at a repair job, his objection is nothing more than a request for additional information. To handle an objection and get the job, start by re-stating the objection so that the client knows that you understand it. Then prepare him for your reply, make the reply, and finish up with a good, related open-ended question. Let's try this "objection cycle," as salesmen call it, for size:

"But I think the price is too high!"

"Yes sir, I know money is tight, and it may seem like a high price for the job. However, our prices have had to go up because our costs are mounting. Would you like the unit back tomorrow, or can we take until Friday morning?"

When possible, offer the client a minor choice. You're selling a new amplifier, right? Don't offer the client a closed choice, but an open, minor choice. You'll get far better results with, "Would you prefer the 10-inch or 12-inch speaker?" than you get with "Wanna buy it?"

Selling is truly an art, and, while there are such things as "natural" salesmen, the skills can be learned with practice. You may have gone into repair work simply because you don't like sales, or feel that you aren't sufficiently adept at it. The truth of the matter is that you do sell, even if what you are selling is your repair service!

The good salesman is one who receives a sensitive feedback from his customer, who recognizes a potential sale coming up, and who anticipates any objections and answers them even before they are voiced. As we said, these are skills that you can learn.

You may feel that when a client comes into the shop with an amplifier that needs repair, you've got him ten ways against the middle. After all, he did come in voluntarily, he did ask for a repair, so what do you have to sell? You have to sell your service and yourself. And that client can just as easily turn right around and walk out of the shop, too.

One thing you've got to be attuned to is what salesmen call the "hot button." You catch this just by listening. Here's an important fact: Most people can speak at the rate of 125 words per minute, maximum. However, we can listen at the rate of 600 words per minute. This means that while you are talking, your client has ample opportunity to allow other thoughts to creep into his mind. And when he's talking, you might be thinking ahead to what you are going to say, and you just might miss the hot button. Nature, which gave us two ears and one mouth, must have been trying to tell us something, and that something is **listen**!

But back to the hot button we just spoke of. Very often, a customer will not directly voice a need, or a desire. However, he will, if you allow him to, tell you about it just as plainly as if he did voice it.

"It will cost fifteen dollars to repair? How much would a new amplifier cost?"

"While you've got it in for repair, can you do something to increase the power?"

"Can I get two additional inputs added?"

"Can you equip it for fuzz?"

These clients are asking perfectly simple questions, but they are also expressing hot buttons if you trouble to read between the lines. In each case, the client is looking for something he doesn't have at present. The first guy, asking the price of a new amplifier, is really saying to you that he wants the repair bill high enough, and the new amplifier cost low enough so that he can justify the purchase of the new one. Offer him a new one and a good trade on the old one, and you've converted the sale!

The guy who wants added power, additional inputs or fuzz is also fishing for a new amplifier. Proof? How many times has a client asked for additional inputs, or additional accessories such as fuzz or tremolo, and when you quoted what was a perfectly fair price, he balked? He wasn't looking for something to be added to his present amplifier! He wanted a new one, and could justify it with the need for facilities he doesn't have at present.

Naturally, there is always the exception. You can qualify these hot buttons by testing them. Offer the new amplifier, or at least open a discussion in that direction. If the customer balks at the idea of a new unit, you can always quote the requested price for the requested work.

REPAIR APPRAISALS

When a musician walks into the shop with a bum amplifier, his first question is, "Can you fix it?" You say that you can, and he follows this with, "What will it cost?" Now you have to frame an appraisal. How much does it cost to repair an amplifier that isn't working? It depends, of course, on what's wrong with it to begin with, and how much it's going to cost you, both in time and components that need replacing. But how can you, without making a single test on the unit—without opening it up or even touching it—even guess at what it's going to cost? You can't. But the customer isn't going to leave that unit with you for a minute until he knows what it's going to cost him to fix it and until the price is agreeable with him.

This means that you have to be able to quote a realistic figure before you really know what's wrong with the unit. How can you do this? Well, some technicians, rather than lose a job, will quote on the basis of time plus costs. This won't really satisfy the customer, for he will want to know, in dollars and cents, what this means. Another way out is to quote the top possible cost, and chances are that if you do this, the customer will take the job elsewhere. You won't satisfy him by saying, "Certainly, no more than..."

However, there's a realistic way to solve the problem to everybody's satisfaction, more or less. You explain to the customer that you really can't tell him how much it will cost to fix it until you get into it. That getting into it, you might just as well make the repair. So you offer instead to give him a quote on the work, after examining the unit; but you must first settle on a price for the quote itself, which will be applied toward the repair should he wish to have it done. In this way, he is charged a minimum fee, and you at least get something before you start turning the screws. After an examination, you can make a reasonable quote, and then, should the customer decide to have the work done, you get the added costs you quoted.

Analyzing For A Quote

There's a strong temptation to really do a repair when you're preparing a quote, for in making up the quote, you must really find out what's wrong with the unit. Don't do it! If you quickly find the trouble, by all means make a note of what has to be done, so you won't have to analyze the job all over again. But don't actually make the repair at this time.

Suppose you do not find the trouble at once? How far should you go in seeking the cause of the problem before you make a guess at the time and charges to repair the unit? Let's face facts; this is a good way to guarantee that you won't take a shellacking on the job, so it pays to be a little thorough.

It's a fairly simple matter to run a check for the presence of proper levels of B+, and lacking this, to check for correct AC voltages at the transformer leads. You can, with the power off, run a resistance check between B+ and ground to see if there's a short or a leaky capacitor some place.

After a cursory examination, you ought to be able to pretty well pin the trouble down, or at least have a ball-park guess at what the problem is and, if not what the problem is, where you're going to have to go to look for it. With this information, you can take a fair guess at how much it will cost to make the repair, and when the customer comes back for his appraisal, you can quote him a realistic price.

However, do not work at all on the unit until you are paid to do so. Don't even try to clean it up. After your examination, button it up the way it was and prepare to return it to the customer, assuming that his answer will be to pay you the front money and say no.

The secret of making an appraisal is to always assume that the very worst thing that can happen has happened, and that the most expensive components in any given circuit have failed. In this way, when the customer says, "Go ahead and fix it," you can't get hurt.

Quite frankly, having been both routes myself, I can tell you that you are always better off to have the customer walk out with his amplifier tucked under his arm because a price quoted was too high than to have to quote low and try to bring in a tough-dog at a too-low price. The alternative that you must be thinking of at this point—tell him later that it's going to cost more than you quoted—will bring his wrath and ire down about your head, and if he's sufficiently wrathful and indignant, he'll call the Better Business Bureau, Chamber of Commerce, the mayor's office, and everyone else he can think of. No, I'd rather quote on the high side and lose the customer.

What if You Were, er, uh, Wrong?

It happens. Let's face it. Sometimes, you quote very high, suspecting the very worst. Then the customer says, "Go ahead and fix it." And you dig into the job and find that the trouble—the only trouble—is a lousy blown fuse? You can replace that fuse for pennies, and there you sit with a high estimate waiting for the customer. Consider for just a moment, what the ramifications are.

If you charge him only for replacing the fuse, he's liable to be happy about the much lower cost, isn't he? But then, he's also liable to think that you are a real clunk about knowing your business, or why else did you come up with such a ridiculous figure to start with?

On the other hand, suppose you don't tell him about the fuse. Suppose you simply say it was a tough job, and had to undergo major surgery. You hand him a brown paper bag full of old parts, including a few capacitors, some worn-out resistors, and a few other things that were lying around. You tell him that actually, you underbid on the job, and are taking such a loss that you face bankruptcy proceedings all because of his job. But after all, you are an honest man, and you did make a bid, so you'll stick with it and face the consequences. And you collect the full amount.

Well, between you and me, you'd probably get away with that latter tack, but for my own part, I'd rather take the first route. Tell the customer he was lucky, it was just a fuse, and that the cost will be negligible. Not only that, you can even refund him a part of the fee he paid just for the evaluation, too. Maybe it's bad business, and maybe he won't be all that impressed, but I like to think this will result in a new friend and a permanent client who will keep coming back to the "only honest repairman" he knows! Besides, you do have to live with yourself, right?

Upgrading at the Same Time

Once in awhile, you get a customer that makes a lot of sense. He knows that his amplifier isn't the best in the world, and as long as you've got it in for repairs, can you do something to improve it while it's all apart? When you get the amplifier open, there are certain things that you can do to improve its performance, and do within reasonable cost to you, reasonable cost to the client, and profit to yourself.

One of the things you might do is take a quick look at the baffle board that holds the speaker. Many manufacturers use adapter rings so that if they're mounting, say, an 8-inch speaker instead of a 12-inch job, they can use the adapter and put in the smaller unit. If this is the case, it's an easy matter for you to pull out the baffle and the small speaker and put in the larger one. You might even find pre-formed cutouts for tweeters that you can add also.

You can check and clean all of the controls, making certain that there are no rough spots that mean a control should be replaced. You also can run a burnishing abrasive over all the contacts in the various inputs jacks so they're bright and shiny. Sometimes, by putting a small capacitor across the tone control, you can add a little more bass boost to the amplifier than the guy had when he brought it in; this is usually considered as an advantage by most musicians.

THE DISSATISFIED CUSTOMER

Sometimes you complete a repair, get the unit working properly, and the customer doesn't care at all for what you've done.

"It doesn't sound at all like it used to." He eyes you suspiciously, and may even intimate that you switched speakers on him.

About 30 years ago, a major publication carried an article entitled "THE RADIO MAN WILL CHEAT YOU IF YOU DON'T WATCH OUT." They allegedly ran a survey which was said to have proved that technicians take advantage—sometimes. We've been suffering ever since. But it's a two-way street.

Al was a TV technician who got a call to a very wealthy neighborhood to do a repair job on a TV set. He looked at the set admiringly, for it was an old Stromberg-Carlson set in a classy Chippendale cabinet. He pulled the back (no, the back wasn't pressed board, but a sheet of solid mahogony held in place by some fancy-headed wood screws) and started checking the suspect tubes. He found the "bummer," and replaced it. The set worked.

The lady of the house looked at the picture and said, "Yes, you've got it working, but I want it like when it was **new**." Al checked all the tubes, replacing all the weak ones. He cleaned up the picture tube face, cleaned the inside of the front glass, cleaned up all the controls and also the tuner. Then he called the lady in again.

"Oh yes, I can see the difference. It's fine, but not as good as when it was____" Al got back to work. He went down to the truck for some test equipment, did a complete alignment, and, when he explained to the lady that the only thing left to do was replace the antenna, lead-in and picture tube, he did that, too.

He called her in once again. She had said that price was no object, and boy, did she rack up a price. He turned the set on, and even impressed himself with the sharp, brilliant performance of this set.

"Yes, that's really a better picture, but it **still** isn't as good a picture as when the set was new."

"Don't go away," Al said. He reached behind the set and started the picture slowly flipping by rotating the vertical hold. "Now," he said, "tell me when you see a picture you like, and I'll lock that one into place."

"That one."

He smiled, set the vertical hold, collected a fat fee, and was on his way.

Sometimes you do a repair job and the customer isn't happy. The tone could be off, the level requires more or less setting. Lots of things can upset the client. And you can't always determine what he's talking about, because he may not be sure himself. Ask for specifics when you get a complaint like that, because oftentimes the so-called "difference" is really an improvement.

If a customer is being unreasonable, and if you've done the job to the best of your ability, offer to send it back to the factory (at his expense) to have the set checked against specifications. It's a bet that few customers will take.

Try whenever possible to stay away from the two types of do-it-yourselfers, for all you can get is trouble. The first guy to watch out for is the one who repairs his own equipment or invites his so-called knowledgeable friend to do the repairs. The other is the guy who builds his own or has it built. These jobs will always cost you more than they're worth.

On the other hand, there was an interesting case reported by a friend of ours. Jerry finally got even. The commercial rig was brought in with a blown capacitor, and it was replaced. The tubes were checked, the set cleaned up and returned to the owner with a suitable bill. Not a big bill or a small bill, just a proper bill for the work. The guy even gave the kids back the burned-out capacitor with advice to junk it. They showed up a few days later, with Jerry in tow.

"Jerry sez" they said, "You charged too much."

GUARANTEES AND WARRANTIES

Just what are your obligations on your work? If you do a repair job, are you obligated to make all additional repairs free of charge for the next 30, 60 or 90 days? Of course not! But let's start at the beginning.

When you sell a new amplifier, it comes with a manufacturer's guarantee on parts and workmanship. If it should fail for any reason during the honored period, the client returns the unit to the manufacturer (perhaps through you) and gets full service and/or replacement.

To ensure that no tampering takes place, many manufacturers use a paper seal or a dab of enamel over a mounting screw. If the seal is broken, the warranty is void. If you do a repair and are asked about guarantees, you can specify that should the component that you've installed fail within a given time period that you will replace it at no charge. But don't ever make any unconditional guarantees, because you'll surely get burned. Electronic components are just not that stable. You can replace a two-dollar tube today, offer an unconditional guaranty, and have the patient walk in tomorrow with a melted power transformer. Result? Debits on the bottom line.

No, we like to guarantee our workmanship and the components that we use. But we aren't idiotic about it, either. We give the customer a detailed bill, explaining all of our work. We list our time charges, list all components replaced, and then the bill is totaled. We keep a copy of each bill in our files, and the customer gets a copy, too. Because all parts and work are detailed on the bill, our guaranty is protected against future breakdowns that occur elsewhere in the circuit.

One thing you can depend on, and that's Murphy's Law which says that if anything can go wrong, it will. Chances are that when you offer a really tight guarantee on parts and workmanship, you'll be hard-pressed to convince your customer that the second thing that went wrong wasn't directly related to the first thing.

Look at it from his point of view. He brings the amplifier in for a repair job, because it isn't working. You repair it, and while he's paying you, he casually asks what was wrong with it. You tell him that the frammis blew out and you had to replace it. He nods and leaves. Two weeks later, the amplifier isn't working again, and he brings it back, thoroughly convinced that it's the frammis again. You check the unit thoroughly, and find that the widgit has gone.

From the customer's point of view, he doesn't know beans about framisses and widgits. All he knows is that it didn't work, you fixed it, you guaranteed it, and now it doesn't work again, and your classy guarantee isn't worth a hoot.

In setting up a guarantee policy, consider how the automotive repairmen work. Your work runs a close parallel in the area of guarantees, and they have the same problems. Perhaps you feel that if the customer isn't satisfied with your work or your guarantee, you'll lose the customer. You know how you feel about such matters. You'd pay the bill and never go back to that shop again, right?

Does this mean that you should give in on all counts simply because you want to protect your reputation? Not by any means! That can put you out of business even more rapidly. Do what you know to be the honorable thing: Offer to have the unit checked out against your last bill by any shop in the city, and then just relax. Some customers, let's face it, are difficult to convince.

SYSTEM CONSULTATION

You are going to be called on as a consultant when you merchandise an amplifier or system. Your customer is going to ask, "Exactly how much amplification do I need?" Your answer will depend on a number of variable factors. As a general rule, the customer's pocket book is a major factor. He doesn't need more amplification than he can afford to buy, and, also as a general rule, the more amplification he buys, the more it's going to cost him. Many times, it's Pop who foots the bill, and he will appreciate your going easy on the advice, too. Not just for reasons of money, but for his own sanity and peace of mind.

Ask Some Questions

The level of amplification needed is a function of the size of the room in which the musician is to play. It's a function of the amount of business the room does. Fill it up with people, and you've got a need for more sound to overcome the damping effect of all those bodies. And the same exact system will need a lot less in the way of sound when the same room is empty.

In general terms, you can always reduce the sound level with the volume control, but there are top limits that you can't exceed even with the gain cranked all the way open. What's more, if you operate with full volume, chances are that you will get more than your share of distortion. The best advice, therefore, from the performer's point of view, is to buy the most amplifier that he can afford and make his first expense his last expense.

In the early days of musical instrument amplification, the very novelty of an electric guitar was that, by remoting the loudspeakers, you could have the instrument played at one location and the sound appear at another. As a result, many a dance band sat the guitarist at one side and his loudspeaker at the other side, and felt they were getting the benefit of two guitars for the price of one. In many of the popular dance halls, the only amplified instrument was the guitar, and it used switch-connected loudspeakers that allowed the musician to play from any corner of the room!

Today we're a bit more sophisticated. We don't simply depend on the novelty in choosing amplification. We want the instrument to blend, not dominate, the sound. We don't want the instrument to overpower other instruments or voices in the ensemble. This is done by carefully setting volume levels not only of the one instrument, but of all of them. If you have separate amplifier-speaker systems for each instrument, you have to set the levels of all of them very carefully in order to maintain a proper balance of volume values for the whole.

In the early days of radio, it was the custom to have an "acoustics engineer" check the studio before going on the air. These guys had a real boondoggle going for them, and the story is still told about the acoustics engineer who walked into a studio during a rehearsal of an orchestra. He walked slowly around the entire studio, with one hand cupped behind his ear, snapping his finger with the other hand. His activities were so interesting, that the orchestra leader stopped the rehearsal so all could watch.

Studiously, this man walked through the audience section, listening and snapping. He spent half an hour doing this, always with a pained, troubled expression on his face. Finally, he made his way to the bandstand, and moved in and around the musicians. After another ten minutes of this, he ran over to the first violinist, slammed his plush-lined violin case shut with an angry glare at the musician. He snapped three more times in fast succession, and then, satisfied, he strode out of the room!

Sound can play strange tricks on you, and if you are called on as a consultant in audio work, there are some things you should know to keep these tricks at a minimum.

Room Design

Your biggest enemy is going to be reverberation that is not controlled. In the average room, you can control reverberation by having all facing surfaces covered. Got two walls opposite each another? Put drapes on one of them. Got a bare floor and a bare ceiling? Put carpeting on the floor. In this way, you can reduce the amount of bounced sound. Of course, people are very good dampers, too. Fill a room with people and your entire acoustics picture changes.

Where you have an angled room off the main hall, you can't really expect a faithful reproduction of the sound in both places, but in this area, you are getting more into public address than amplification of instruments, and you might have to offer an even different solution to this sort of problem.

The point is that today's modern instrumentalist wants his instrument to be a part of the whole, and not just a single, strident solo voice. Sure, it's been said that a "quartet is a group of four musicians, each of whom thinks the other three are lousy." But if you are consulting to a group, you'd better make it clear that "combo" is a short term for combination, and this means a blending of sounds each in support of the others.

Generally, when you sell an amplifier, it's to an individual instrumentalist who has ultimate aspirations to working with a group and as a result, you generally find that a combo or group consists of several musicians, each with his own amplifier. Properly set up, this presents no problem. However, you frequently run into grandstanding, where a guy cranks his level up to take a solo, and then "forgets" to put it down again later. A recent trend, believe it or not, is to get away from the loud and raucous sound of hard rock, and go after a more quiet type of sound.

Lots of the youngsters are turning off on the hard sound; instead, they are looking to folk music, which they sing with unamplified instruments, and sing **sotto voce** or almost in a whisper. Guitars are "touched" or caressed instead of beaten to death to get more volume. If they use any amplification at all these youngsters use a single mike that serves both voice and guitar, and the volume is deliberately left low.

What happens in clubs where such music is played is that the audience quiets and pays closer attention. There's less talking, less noise, and the music must be almost strained to be heard, instead of having to strain over the music to hear a neighbor's words.

With this return to what used to be, the amplifier becomes the property of the club rather than the property of the individual instrumentalist, and as a result, while there may be fewer high-powered amplifiers in individual's hands, what happens is that the individuals own smaller amplifiers, and the various nighteries own the big ones. This means that instead of waiting for clients to come tapping at your door, you ought to go out and see what you can line up in the way of some bigger and better outside business.

Service Contracts

Service contracts can work for you or against you. If you price them right, they can be your biggest ally and can lead you into a lot of excellent business. Pay a few visits to your own local restaurants that offer entertainment and volunteer to assume full responsibility for the amplifying equipment at a price, of course. You'll find that you pick up some nice extra business this way, too. People won't pay you to fix things that aren't working as readily as they will pay you to fix things so they don't have to worry about their not working. That's what service contracts are all about.

It's got to be spelled out in writing, and in exchange for a fee that covers all service calls, you have to be available to make emergency repairs. If you're smart, you'll show up a few times a month to "check the system" and at least appear to be earning your fee. Never make such calls during the business hours, but rather, in the mornings between 10 and 11 for places that serve lunch, and between two and three for those who cater to an evening crowd.

But let's get back, for just a moment, to sound re-enforcement. In this form of amplification, we try to achieve unity gain. That is to say, we have the same sound level coming out of the speakers as we have going into the microphones. You might well ask just what is the advantage of such a system. What results is the original, unamplified voice, and this is supported by the amplified portion so what you get is re-enforcement. The original, soft sound, plus a small amount of electronic gain, so that the final outcome sounds very like the human voice, souped up ever so slightly with electronics.

CUSTOMER SENSITIVITY

If you think you've seen suffering in the past, just wait until a musician brings in his pet instrument for a repair. You see, they can become pretty attached to these things, and though an instrument is truly an inanimate object until a capable musician brings it to life, it still has many attachments to the people that own them.

We got our first real taste of this when a kid came in with what absolutely had to be the saddest looking guitar we'd ever seen. It was scratched, nicked, gouged, and was really in terrible condition. We were about to suggest a new instrument when he asked if we could perform some major surgery. The kid really seemed agitated, too. We asked what was wrong, as if we couldn't see what was wrong.

"It's my girl friend" he said. "She gave me this beautiful hand-made leather neck strap..."

We looked at the "beautiful hand-made leather neck strap." This girl had tried to hand-tool and paint a man's leather belt, using enamel paints that had already started to flake and chip. Her old man must have been hunting high and low for that belt, too. Still had the holes in it.

"So," we asked "What?"

"So," he said, "My guitar doesn't have a peg for a neck strap, and I want one installed. Can do?"

Big deal. Install a peg. If he had asked to have a peg simply "put in" it would have been a lot less expensive. We can do a job of "putting in" a lot cheaper than we "install." So I pulled a spare peg out of the box, picked up the electric drill, and up-ended the guitar.

"Eeeeyikes!" yiked the kid. "You mean you're gonna do it now, right here, in FRONT of me?"

"Maybe you'd like me to gown up and scrub like Dr. Kildare before I make a hole?"

"No," the kid said, "But right now, Right here?"

I took the instrument out back and listened to him scream as he heard the drill start. "Interesting," I thought, "this kid screaming and the drill whining—makes a nice augmented chord." I just happen to have absolute pitch myself.

We brought the guitar back with the new neck strap attached to the new peg and handed the thing to the kid, who was near tears.

"Did he hurt you?"

"Naw," I offered. "Used Novocaine. Guitar didn't feel a thing."

The kid left, cradling the guitar in his arms. Nuts? heck no! You may see a guitar, but this could be the kid's first guitar, or the amplifier his girl friend got for him, or, gosh only knows what. If a musician seems to be personifying his equipment, handle it with the same reverence that he shows, and always say something "nice" about it. Even if it's only "Boy! That must have been some swell instrument in its day!"

Index

A

B

C

D

E

F

G

H

I

J

K

L

M

N

O

P

Q

R

U

V

W

Y

X